Performance
ETHNOGRAPHY

Performance ETHNOGRAPHY
Critical Pedagogy and the Politics of Culture

Norman K. Denzin
University of Illinois at Urbana-Champaign

SAGE Publications
International Educational and Professional Publisher
Thousand Oaks ▪ London ▪ New Delhi

For information:

 Sage Publications, Inc.
2455 Teller Road
Thousand Oaks, California 91320
E-mail: order@sagepub.com

SAGE Publications Ltd
1 Oliver's Yard
55 City Road
London EC1Y 1SP

SAGE Publications India Pvt Ltd
B-42, Panchsheel Enclave
Post Box 4109
New Delhi 110 017

Printed in the United States of America

Library of Congress Cataloging-in-Publication Data

Denzin, Norman K.
Performance ethnography : critical pedagogy and the politics of culture / by Norman K. Denzin.
    p. cm.
Includes bibliographical references and index.
ISBN 0-7619-1038-7 — ISBN 0-7619-1039-5 (paper)
    1. Social sciences-Research-United States. 2. Performance art-United States. 3. Democracy-United States. 4. Racism-United States. I. Title.
H62.5.D396 2003
306.4'7—dc21

2003002136

Printed on acid-free paper

03 04 05 06 07 08 09 10 9 8 7 6 5 4 3 2 1

Acquiring Editor:	Margaret H. Seawell
Editorial Assistant:	Alicia Carter
Production Editor:	Claudia A. Hoffman
Copy Editor:	Judy Selhorst
Typesetter:	C&M Digitals (P) Ltd.
Indexer:	Molly Hall

Contents

Preface

Performance is everywhere these days. Perhaps I should celebrate.

—D. Soyini Madison, "Performing Theory/
Embodied Writing," 1999

The good news is that in recent decades there has been a remarkable constellation of thinking around performance.

—Dwight Conquergood, "Beyond the Text:
Toward a Performative Cultural Politics," 1998

Ethnography is the eye of the needle through which the threads of the imagination must pass.

—Paul Willis, *The Ethnographic
Imagination*, 2000

This book is a performance text about the performance turn in the human disciplines.[1] For at least a decade, interpretive ethnographers have been staging reflexive ethnographic performances, using their field notes and autoethnographic observations to shape performance narratives, an anthropology and sociology of performance (Bochner and Ellis 1996a, 1996b, 2002; McCall 2000:423; Ellis and Bochner 2000; Turner 1986a). We are in the seventh moment of qualitative inquiry, a postexperimental phase, performing culture as we write it.[2] It is time to take stock; it is time to review how far reflexive performance and (auto)ethnography have come, and to imagine where we may go next.[3]

This book is about rethinking performance (auto)ethnography, about the formation of a critical performative cultural politics, about what happens when everything, as Du Bois (1926:134) observes, is already performative, when the dividing line between performativity and performance disappears (Conquergood 1998:25; Schechner 1998:361; Butler 1997:6; Pollock 1998a, 1998b, 1999; Madison 1993, 1998, 1999; Diamond 1996:5–6; Dimitriadis and McCarthy 2001:194; Dimitriadis 2001:125; Garoian 1999:8; Coffey 1999; James, Hockey, and Dawson 1997; Spencer 2001; Wellin 1996; Wolcott 2002:133; Saldana 2002).[4] This book reflects my desire to contribute to a critical discourse that addresses central issues confronting democracy and racism in postmodern America (Denzin 1991, 1995a, 2001b, 2001e). Building on this desire, in the chapters that follow I attempt to chart a performance-based social science, modeled in part after the arguments of Della Pollock (1998a, 1998b, 1999), D. Soyini Madison (1998, 1999), Victor Turner (1986a), and Dwight Conquergood (1992, 1998), as well as the arguments of indigenous scholars who seek to decolonize various Western methodologies (see Bishop 1998; Brayboy 2000; Lopez 1998; Smith 1999; Tillman 1998). Several chapters draw on my ongoing auto-ethnography of a small Montana town. I seek a performance rhetoric that turns notes from the field into texts that are performed.

A single yet complex thesis organizes my argument: We inhabit a performance-based, dramaturgical culture. The dividing line between performer and audience blurs, and culture itself becomes a dramatic performance. Performance ethnography enters a gendered culture in which nearly invisible boundaries separate everyday theatrical performances from formal theater, dance, music, MTV, video, and film (Birringer 1993:182; Denzin 1997:93). Performance texts are situated in complex systems of discourse, where traditional, everyday, and avant-garde meanings of theater, film, video, ethnography, cinema, performance, text, and audience all circulate and inform one another. As Collins (1990:210) has argued, the meanings of lived experience are inscribed and made visible in these performances.

Performance ethnography simultaneously creates and enacts moral texts that move from the personal to the political, from the local to the historical and the cultural. As Conquergood (1985) observes, these dialogic works create spaces for give-and-take, doing more than turning the other into the object of a voyeuristic, fetishistic, custodial, or paternalistic gaze.

A performance-based social science is a minimalist social science. It uses few concepts. It is dramaturgical (Goffman 1959; Lemert 1997:xxiv; Branaman 1997:xlix) and performative (Turner 1986a,

1986b). It attempts to stay close to how people experience everyday life. A performative discourse simultaneously writes and criticizes performances. In showing how people enact cultural meanings in their daily lives, such a discourse focuses on how these meanings and performances shape experiences of injustice, prejudice, and stereotyping.

Shaped by the critical sociological imagination (Mills 1959), this version of doing social science attempts to do more than just show how biography, history, gender, race, ethnicity, family, and history interact and shape one another in concrete social situations. The desire is to show how the histories and the performances that persons live are shaped by forces that exist behind their backs (Marx [1888] 1983).

A critical sociological imagination responds in three ways to the successive crises of democracy and capitalism that shape daily life. It criticizes those formations by showing how they repressively enter into and shape the stories and performances persons share with one another. At the same time, it shows how people bring dignity and meaning to their lives through these same performances. In so doing, it also offers kernels of utopian hope, suggestions for how things might be different, and better.

❖ THE PERFORMANCE TURN

The narrative and performance turn in the human disciplines poses three closely interrelated problems for my project—namely, how to *construct, perform,* and *critically analyze* performance texts (see Stern and Henderson 1993). In this book I examine all three problems, but I privilege coperformance (audience-performer) texts and narratives. A coperformance story brings the audience back into the text, creating a field of shared emotional experience. The phenomenon being described is created through the acts of representation and presentation. A resistance model of textual performance and interpretation is foregrounded. A good performance text must be more than cathartic—it must be political, moving people to action, reflection, or both.

The current attention to performance among scholars is interdisciplinary; sociologists (Mienczakowski 2001; McCall 2000; Richardson 1997), anthropologists (Kirshenblatt-Gimblett 1998; Turner 1986a), and communication and education theorists (Conquergood 1998; Lather 2001) are calling for texts that move beyond the purely representational and toward the presentational. At the same time, action researchers

(Stringer 1999), communitarian researchers (Christians 2000), feminist researchers (Olesen 2000), constructivist researchers (Lincoln 1995), cooperative inquiry researchers (Reason 1994), and participant researchers are exploring nontraditional presentational formats that will enable them and their research participants in participatory inquiry settings to co-construct meaning through action research (Stringer 1999). This call merges with a feminist, communitarian ethic and with a moral ethnography that presumes a researcher who builds collaborative, reciprocal, trusting, and friendly relations with the persons he or she studies.

❖ THIS BOOK

In the chapters that follow, I read, write, and perform performance (auto)ethnography. As Richardson (2002a) has noted, "Writing is never innocent" (p. 879). Writing creates the worlds we inhabit. In this book, I create several worlds. The worlds of pedagogy, ethnography, performance, and theory are privileged in the five chapters in Part I. In particular, in these chapters I navigate the discourses surrounding critical pedagogy, reflexive ethnography, and performance autoethnography. These chapters lay the foundation for a performative social science. In them, I create the spaces for a radical cultural politics that I hope will help us to imagine a more humane, pluralistic, and just racial order.

In Chapter 1, I outline the key terms and arguments in my framework. In Chapter 2, I offer a vocabulary of performance terms and discuss the history of that vocabulary. In Chapter 3, I locate performances within the cultural apparatuses of the cinematic society, giving explicit attention to the reflexive interview. In Chapter 4, I draw on the work of Anna Deavere Smith to apply the performative model to performance interviewing and to performance writing. In Chapter 5, I struggle with issues concerning the reading and writing of performance texts—specifically, the need for criteria on which to base our interpretation and assessment of such texts.

The seven short chapters that make up Part II focus on a different set of landscapes: the worlds of family, nature, praxis, and action. Each of these chapters is part memoir, part essay, part short story, part literary autoethnography. The chapters move back and forth between personal history and biography, addressing issues of race and racial performances in the New West and in the Midwest. In the two chapters in Part III, I return to themes in Chapter 1 concerning the ethics and practical politics of performance autoethnography. I anchor these chapters in the post-9/11 discourse in the United States, drawing many of my arguments from Paulo Freire (1998, [1992] 1999, 2001) and from First and Fourth World activist scholars who are concerned with an indigenous research ethic (Smith 1999; Bishop 1998; Grande 2000; Rains, Archibald, and Deyhle 2000). In Chapter 14, I offer a performance ethic, following a critique of the biomedical ethical model that shapes much of social inquiry today.

A Critical Performative Pedagogy

Like my earlier work *Reading Race* (Denzin 2002d), this project reflects two concerns. For nearly four decades, I have been working with undergraduate and graduate students at the University of Illinois, experimenting with new ways of reading, writing, and performing culture. We have learned how to write and coperform texts based on epiphanies surrounding race, gender, and the politics of identity. I owe these students a great debt, as together we have worked through many of the themes and issues addressed in these pages; this book is partial payment on that debt.

Second, I continue to believe that the members of the current generation of college students in North America have the opportunity to make a difference in the arena of race relations. It is possible to imagine and perform a multiracial society, a society where differences are honored. If the students of this generation are to make a difference, that difference will be defined, in part, in terms of opposition or resistance to acceptance of the representations and interpretations of the racial order and the color line that circulate in the mass media and the majority of social science writings. This resistance, in turn, will be shaped by how we read, write, perform, and critique culture.

In this book, I advance a critical performative pedagogy that turns the ethnographic into the performative and the performative into the political. It is my hope that this pedagogy will allow us to dream our way into a militant democratic utopian space, a space where the color line disappears and justice for all is more than a dream.

—Norman K. Denzin

Acknowledgments

I would like to thank Mitch Allen, Peter Labella, David Silverman, Art Bochner, and Carolyn Ellis for their quick and early support of this project, which started out as a book on performance narrative and somewhere along the way turned into a book on performance (auto)ethnography. I thank Margaret Seawell for helping to see the changed project through to conclusion. My interactions with individuals in the Unit for Criticism and Interpretive Theory and in the Program in Cultural Studies and Interpretive Research at the University of Illinois as well as conversations with Katherine Ryan, Nate Summers, Yvonna Lincoln, Cliff Christians, Patricia Clough, Michal McCall, Barbara Heyl, Anahid Kassabian, Laurel Richardson, Andy Fontana, Art Frank, Kathy Charmaz, Henry Giroux, Peter McLaren, Joe Kincheloe, Bryant Alexander, Dwight Conquergood, Jack Bratich, David Silverman, Joe Schneider, Jay Gubrium, Jim Holstein, Sara Delamont, Paul Atkinson, Ed Bruner, Susan Davis, and Walt Harrington helped to clarify my arguments. I wish to thank Claudia Hoffman for her careful assistance during production, Judy Selhorst for copyediting and for patience and assistance throughout, Grant Kien, David Monje, and James Salvo for meticulous reading of the page proofs, and Molly Hall for production of the index. I also thank the students at the University of Illinois who patiently sat through formal and informal seminars and listened to earlier versions of my arguments about performance ethnography, cultural studies, politics, and pedagogy. I especially thank Kathy Charmaz, editor of *Symbolic Interaction*, who published early versions of several of the more experimental chapters that appear in revised form in this book. Finally, I gratefully acknowledge the moral, intellectual, and financial support provided for this project by Dean Kim Rotzoll of the College of Communication and Paula Treichler, director of the Institute of Communications Research, my now not so new home at the University of Illinois.

Portions of the material in Chapter 1 appeared in my article "The Call to Performance," *Symbolic Interaction*, vol. 25 (2002:327-46). Portions of the material in Chapter 3 appeared in my chapter "The Cinematic Society and the Reflexive Interview," in *Handbook of Interview Research: Context and Method*, edited by Jaber F. Gubrium and James A. Holstein (Sage, 2002). Portions of the material in Chapter 4 appeared in my article "The Reflexive Interview and a Performative Social Science," *Qualitative Research*, vol. 1 (2001:23–46). Portions of the material in Chapter 5 appeared in my article "Aesthetics and the Practices of Qualitative Inquiry," *Qualitative Inquiry*, vol. 6 (2000:256–65). Portions of the material in Chapter 6 appeared in my article "Two-Stepping in the '90s," *Qualitative Inquiry*, vol. 5 (1999:568–72). Portions of the material in Chapter 8 appeared in my chapter "Performing Montana," in *Qualitative Sociology as Everyday Life*, edited by Barry Glassner and Rosanna Hertz (Sage, 1999). Portions of the material in Chapter 9 appeared in my article "Rock Creek History," *Symbolic Interaction*, vol. 23 (2000:71–81). Portions of the material in Chapter 10 appeared in my article "Cowboys and Indians," *Symbolic Interaction*, vol. 25 (2002:251–61). Portions of the material in Chapter 11 will appear in my forthcoming article "Redskins Everywhere," *Cultural Studies↔Critical Methodologies*. Portions of the material in Chapter 12 appeared in my article "Searching for Yellowstone," *Symbolic Interaction*, vol. 26 (2003:181–93).

Publisher's Credits

Chapter 1

Parts of this chapter © 2003 by the Society for the Study of Symbolic Interaction. Reprinted from *Symbolic Interaction, 26*:1, by permission of the University of California Press.

Excerpt from "This Evolution Will Not Be Televised" by Mary Weems from *I Speak from the Wound that is My Mouth* (2002). Reprinted with permission of Peter Lang Publishing, Inc.

Excerpt from "Visiting Mario" by Stephen Hartnett from *Democracy Is Difficult* (1998). Copyright © by the National Communication Association, 1998. Reproduced by permission of the publisher.

Excerpt from "The Way We Were, Are, and Might Be: Torch Singing as Autoethnography," by S. Holman Jones in *Ethnographically Speaking*, 2002, edited by A. P. Bochner & C. Ellis. Reprinted with permission from Alta Mira Press.

Excerpt from "Poem from September 11" by Laurel Richardson from "Small World" in *Cultural Studies 2*, 1:23-25 (2002). Reprinted by permission of Sage.

Chapter 2

Excerpt from "The People of Illinois Welcome You" by Mary Weems from *I Speak from the Wound that is My Mouth* (2002). Reprinted with permission of Peter Lang Publishing, Inc.

Excerpt from "Democracy is Difficult" by Stephen Hartnett in S. Dailey's "The Future of Performance Studies." Copyright © by the National Communication Association. Reproduced by permission of the publisher.

Excerpt from "In the Name of Tradition" by H. Campuzano. Used by permission.

Excerpt from "Remembering Me" by T. A. LaRaviere (2001). Used by permission.

Excerpt from "Grandma's Stories" by R. Bai (2001). Used by permission.

Excerpt from M. Fine's "The Mourning After" (2002) reprinted by permission from *Qualitative Inquiry, 8*. Copyright © Sage.

Excerpt from L. Richardson's "Poem from September 11" from "Small World" (2002) reprinted by permission from *Cultural Studies–Critical Methodologies, 2,* 1:23-25. Copyright © Sage.

Chapter 3

Chapter 4

Chapter 5

Chapter 6

Chapter 8

Chapter 9

Chapter 10

Chapter 12

Excerpt from *Big Rock Candy Mountain* by Wallace Stegner, copyright © 1938, 1940, 1942, 1943 by Wallace Stegner. Used by permission of Doubleday, a division of Random House, Inc.

Chapter 13

Excerpt from M. Dowd's "Texas on the Tigris" (2002) Copyright © 2002 by the *New York Times Co.* Reprinted with permission.

PART I

Performance Ethnography

1

The Call to Performance

Educated hope... registers politics as a pedagogical and performative act.

—Henry A. Giroux, *Public Spaces, Private Lives: Beyond the Culture of Cynicism,* 2001

I n this chapter, which takes the form of a manifesto, I invite social scientists and ethnographers to think through the practical, progressive politics of a performative cultural studies.[5] Such an emancipatory discourse connects critical pedagogy with new ways of writing and performing culture (Kincheloe and McLaren 2000:285).[6] I believe that performance-based human disciplines can contribute to radical social change, to economic justice, to a cultural politics that extends critical race theory and "the principles of a radical democracy to all aspects of society" (Giroux 2000a:x, 25), and to change that "envisions a democracy founded in a social justice that is 'not yet'" (Weems 2002:3). I believe that interpretive ethnographers should be part of this project (see Denzin 1992, 1995a, 1997, 2001b, 2001d, 2001e).[7]

Shaped by the critical sociological imagination (Mills 1959) and building on the work of Perinbanayagam (1985:59, 1991:113, 171,

2000:3–5) and George Herbert Mead's (1938:460) discursive, performative model of the act (see also Dunn 1998:184), this way of doing ethnography imagines and explores the multiple ways in which we can understand performance, including as imitation, or *mimesis;* as construction, or *poiesis;* and as motion or movement, or *kinesis* (Conquergood 1998:31). The ethnographer moves from a view of performance as imitation, or dramaturgical staging (Goffman 1959), to an emphasis on performance as liminality and construction (Turner 1986a), then to a view of performance as struggle, as intervention, as breaking and remaking, as kinesis, as a sociopolitical act (Conquergood 1998:32). Viewed as struggles and interventions, performances and performance events become transgressive achievements, political accomplishments that break through "sedimented meanings and normative traditions" (Conquergood 1998:32).

My argument in this chapter unfolds in several parts. I begin by addressing race and the call to performance. I then define several terms, including *performance* and *performativity.* I next present a discussion of a performative cultural politics that includes consideration of the relationships among performance, pedagogy, politics, and the turn to performance in ethnography. I then address performance art and a politics of resistance. I conclude with a discussion of cultural politics and the pedagogical as performative.

In the spirit of Dewey, Mead, Blumer, hooks, and West, I intend to create a dialogue within the community of ethnographers, and thus move our discourse more fully into the spaces of a progressive pragmatism. I want to extend those political impulses within the pragmatist tradition that imagine a radical democratic philosophy (Lyman and Vidich 1988:xi). Following Du Bois and West, I want to show how these impulses constantly interrogate the relevance of pragmatism and critical theory for race relations and inequality in the capitalist democratic state (Reynolds 2000:12).

❖ RACE AND THE CALL TO PERFORMANCE

Many ethnographers are in the seventh moment of qualitative inquiry, performing culture as they write it, understanding that the dividing line between performativity (doing) and performance (done) has disappeared (Conquergood 1998:25). But even as this disappearance occurs, matters of racial injustice remain. On this subject, W. E. B. Du Bois ([1901] 1978) reminds us that "the problem of the twenty-first century will be the problem of the color line" (p. 281) and that "modern democracy cannot succeed unless peoples of different races and religions are also integrated into the democratic whole" (p. 288). Du Bois addressed race from a performance standpoint. As Elam (2001) notes, Du Bois understood that "from the arrival of the first African slaves on American soil . . . the definitions and meanings of blackness, have been intricately linked to issues of theatre and performance" (p. 4).[8]

In his manifesto for an all-black theater, Du Bois (1926) imagined a site for pedagogical performances that articulate positive black "social and cultural agency" (Elam 2001:6). His radical theater (Du Bois 1926:134), like the radical theater of Amiri Baraka (1979), Anna Deavere Smith (1993, 1994, 2000), and August Wilson (1996), is a political theater about blacks, written by blacks, for blacks, performed by blacks on local stages. Radical theater is a weapon for fighting racism and white privilege.

Other authors, such as bell hooks, have elaborated the need for a black political performance aesthetic. Writing about her childhood, hooks (1990) has described how she and her sisters learned about race in America by watching

> the Ed Sullivan show on Sunday nights. . . . seeing on that show the great Louis Armstrong, Daddy, who was usually silent, would talk about the music, the way Armstrong was being treated, and the political implications of his appearance. . . . responding to televised cultural production, black people could express rage about racism. . . . unfortunately . . . black folks were not engaged in writing a body of critical cultural analysis. (Pp. 3–4)

I fold my project into Du Bois's, and hooks's, by asking how a radical performative social science can confront and transcend the problems surrounding the color line in the 21st century. Such a project will write and perform culture in new ways. It will connect reflexive autoethnography with critical pedagogy and critical race theory (see Ladson-Billings 2000). It will necessarily treat political acts as pedagogical and performative, as acts that open new spaces for social citizenship and democratic dialogue, as acts that create critical race consciousness (Giroux 2001a:9). A performative, pedagogical politics of hope imagines a radically free democratic society, a society where ideals of the feminist, queer, environmental, green, civil rights, and labor movements are realized (McChesney 1999:290; Giroux 2001a:9).[9]

In their utopian forms, these movements offer "alternative models of radical democratic culture rooted in social relations that take seriously the democratic ideals of freedom, liberty, and the pursuit of happiness" (Giroux 2001a:9). The following excerpt from Mary Weems's (2002:4) poem "This Evolution Will Not Be Televised" clarifies my project. Weems, like hooks, shows how the media and white culture shape African American experience:

Our image, our braids, our music, our mistakes,

our asses, our rhythms are played on TV

like a long 78 album in commercial after commercial

The Colonel in plantation-dress raps and moonwalks

selling a black woman's stolen fried chicken, black kids

snap their fingers, think that's so cool, bug their mamas

for extra-crispy

This is a never-ending story, that won't be televised . . .

❖ INDIGENOUS VOICES AND
     ANTICOLONIALIST DISCOURSE

Lopez (1998) observes that "there is a large-scale social movement of anticolonialist discourse" (p. 226), and this movement is evident in the emergence of Africa American, Chicano, Native American, and Maori standpoint theories. These theories question the epistemologies of Western science that are used to validate knowledge about indigenous peoples. Maori scholar Russell Bishop (1998) presents a participatory and participant perspective (Tillman 1998:221) that values an embodied and moral commitment on the part of the researcher to the members of the community with whom he or she is working. This kind of research is characterized by the absence of the researcher's need to be in control (Bishop 1998:203; Heshusius 1994). Such a commitment reflects the researcher's desire to be connected to and to be a part of moral community. The researcher's goal is compassionate understanding (Heshusius 1994).

The researcher is forced to develop new story lines that reflect this understanding. The researcher wants nothing more than to participate in a collaborative, altruistic relationship, where nothing "is desired for the self" (Bishop 1998:207). Participant-driven criteria are used to evaluate such research. Bishop (1998) describes the cultural values and practices that circulate in Maori culture, for example, including metaphors that stress self-determination, the sacredness of relationships, embodied understanding, and the priority of community. These participant-driven criteria function as resources for researchers who want to resist positivist and neoconservative desires to "establish and maintain control of the criteria for evaluating Maori experience" (p. 212).

Native American indigenous scholars thicken the argument by articulating a spoken indigenous epistemology "developed over *thousands* of years of *sustained* living on this Land" (Rains, Archibald, and Deyhle 2000:337). Grande (2000) describes an American Indian "red pedagogy" that criticizes simplistic readings of race, ethnicity, and identity. This red pedagogy privileges personal-identity performance narratives—that is, stories and poetry that emphasize self-determination and indigenous theory (Brayboy 2000). For Grande, this red pedagogy has four characteristics: (a) politically, it maintains "a quest for sovereignty, and the dismantling of global capitalism"; (b) epistemologically, it privileges indigenous knowledge; (c) it views the Earth as its "spiritual center"; and (d) socioculturally, it is grounded in "tribal and traditional ways of ways of life" (p. 355). The performance of these rituals validates traditional ways of life. The performance embodies the ritual. It is the ritual. In this sense, the performance becomes a form of public pedagogy. It uses the aesthetic to foreground cultural meanings and to teach these meanings to performers and audience members alike.

❖ PERFORMANCE, PEDAGOGY, AND POLITICS

The current historical moment requires morally informed performance and arts-based disciplines that will help people recover meaning in the face of senseless, brutal violence, violence that produces voiceless screams of terror and insanity (see Finley forthcoming; Mullins forthcoming).[10] Cynicism and despair reign (Giroux 2000a:110). Never have we had a greater need for a militant utopianism to help us imagine a world free of conflict, terror, and death. We need an oppositional performative social science, performance disciplines that will enable us to create oppositional utopian spaces, discourses, and experiences within our public institutions. In these spaces and places, in neighborhoods, in experimental community theaters, in independent coffee shops and bookstores, in local and national parks, on playing fields, in wilderness areas, in experiences with nature, critical democratic culture is nurtured (see Giroux 2001b:125; Stegner 1980a:146; Mullins forthcoming; Finley forthcoming).

Conquergood (1998:26) and Diawara (1996) are correct in their assertion that we must find a space for a cultural studies that moves from textual ethnography to performative autoethnography.[11] "Performance-sensitive ways of knowing" (Conquergood 1998:26) contribute to an epistemological and political pluralism that challenges existing ways of knowing and representing the world. Such formations are more inclusionary and better suited than existing ways for thinking about postcolonial or "subaltern" cultural practices (Conquergood 1998:26). Performance approaches to knowing insist on immediacy and involvement. They consist of partial, plural, incomplete, and contingent understandings, not analytic distance or detachment, the hallmarks of the textual and positivist paradigms (Conquergood 1998:26; Pelias 1999:ix, xi).

Building on the work of Diawara (1996:304), this performative approach will create a multiracial cultural studies. Consistent with the pragmatic, interactionist tradition, performance ethnography is concerned with the ways in which people, "through communicative action, create and continue to create themselves within the American experience" (p. 304). This performative approach puts culture into motion. It examines, narrates, and performs the complex ways in which persons experience themselves within the shifting ethnoscapes of today's global world economy (McCall 2001:50).

Performance and Performativity

I want to examine the following terms in greater detail: *performance, performances, performance text, performer, performing, performativity, originals,* and *imitations.* A *performance* is an interpretive event involving actors, purposes, scripts, stories, stages, and interactions (Burke 1969). Cultural *performances* are encapsulated contingent events that are embedded in the flow of everyday life (Kirshenblatt-Gimblett 1998:64, 75). By *performances,* in the plural, I mean, following Kirshenblatt-Gimblett, "'events' that are usefully understood as performances" (quoted in Franklin 2001:217). These are pedagogical events that involve the politics of culture.

I mean *performance,* in the singular, again following Kirshenblatt-Gimblett, to be used "as an organizing concept for examining phenomena that may or may not be a performance in the conventional sense of the word . . . [including] museum exhibitions, tourist environments and the aesthetics of everyday life" (quoted in Franklin 2001:218). The act of performing "intervenes between experience and the story told" (Langellier 1999:128). Performance texts can take several forms: They can be dramatic texts, such as poems or plays; natural texts (transcriptions of everyday conversations); ethnodramas (see Mienczakowski 2001); or dramatic staged or improvised readings.

Performance is an act of intervention, a method of resistance, a form of criticism, a way of revealing agency (Alexander forthcoming). Performance becomes public pedagogy when it uses the aesthetic, the performative, to foreground the intersection of politics, institutional sites, and embodied experience (Alexander forthcoming). In this way performance is a form of agency, a way of bringing culture and the person into play.

Performances are embedded in language. That is, certain words do or accomplish things, and what they do, performatively, refers back to meanings embedded in language and culture (Austin 1962; Derrida 1973, 1988; Butler 1993a, 1993b, 1997).[12] For Kirshenblatt-Gimblett, performativity "gets at agency—what performance and display do" (quoted in Franklin 2001:218). For Butler (1993a), performativity is the "power of discourse to reproduce the phenomenon that it regulates and constrains" (p. 2). Hence in performative utterances, the speaking subject is already spoken for, by and in language (Pollock 1998b:39).

Schechner (1998) contends that we inhabit a world where cultures, texts, and performances collide. Such collisions require a distinction between "'as' and 'is'" (p. 361). As fluid, ongoing events, performances "mark and bend identities, remake time and adorn and reshape the body, tell stories and allow people to play with behavior that is restored, or 'twice-behaved'" (p. 361). The way a performance is enacted describes performative behavior, "how people play gender, heightening their constructed identity, performing slightly or radically different selves in different situations" (p. 361).[13] This view of the performative makes it "increasingly difficult to sustain any distinction between appearances and facts, surfaces and depths, illusions and substances. Appearances are actualities" (p. 362).

Performance and performativity intersect in a speaking subject, a subject with a gendered and racialized body. Performativity "situates performance narrative within the forces of discourse" (Langellier 1999:129), for example, the discourses of race and gender. In transgressive performances, performing bodies contest gendered identities, creating spaces for a queer politics of resistance (Butler 1993a:12; Pollock 1998b:42; see also Garoian 1999:5).

Butler (1993a) reminds us that there are no original performances, or identities, no "preexisting identity by which an act or attribute might be measured" (p. 141). Every performance is an imitation, a form of mimesis, Butler (1993b) states: "If heterosexuality is an impossible imitation of itself, an imitation that performatively constitutes itself as the original, then the imitative parody of 'heterosexuality' . . . is always and only an imitation, a copy of a copy, for which there is no original" (p. 644). Every performance is an original and an imitation.

If there is no original, then the concept of performance as mimesis is challenged. But Taussig (1993) and Haraway (1991) show that imitation can be subversive, like the Coyote, "witty actor and agent, the coding trickster with whom we must learn to converse" (Haraway 1991:201; see also Taussig 1993:255). So even the imitation is an original, a transgression. Further, every performance becomes a form of kinesis, of motion, a decentering of agency and person through movement, disruption, action, a way of questioning the status quo (Denzin 2001b:20).

If performances are actualities that matter, then gender reality, Butler (1993a) asserts, "as in other ritual social dramas . . . is only sustained through social performances" (pp. 140–41), through performances that are repeated. And here, as Schechner (1985) argues, performance is best seen as "'restored' or 'twice-behaved behavior'" (p. 35). As cultural practices, performances reaffirm, resist, transgress, "re-inscribe or passionately reinvent" (Diamond 1996:2) repressive understandings that circulate in daily life.

Clearly, performativity and performance exist in tension with one another, in a tension between *doing*, or performing, and the *done*, the text, the performance. Performance is sensuous and contingent. As Pollock (1998b) notes, performativity "becomes the everyday practice of *doing* what's *done*" (p. 43). Performativity is "*what happens* when history/textuality sees itself in the mirror—and suddenly sees double; it is the disorienting, [the] disruptive" (p. 43). Performativity derives its power and prerogative in the breaking and remaking of the very textual frameworks that give it meaning in the first place (p. 44). An improvisatory politics of resistance is anchored in the spaces where the doing and the done collide.

Read aloud the following lines from Stephen Hartnett's (2001:25, 37) investigative poem "Visiting Mario." Performing and performativity interact in these lines:

"Somewhere Near Salinas, Lord" Kristofferson/Joplin

ten-thousand sprinklers spin slowly

in overlapping circles . . .

drinking water from plastic jugs

hats propped on knees leathery

hands scarred from lifetimes

of harvesting glory

of California

for five dollars a day . . .

choking the old Mexican woman sobs

her boy is cuffed and taken back to hell

the Vietnamese couple whispers to their son

who looks over their hunched shoulders. . . .

A performative politics of resistance is written across every word in Hartnett's poetry, an investigative poetry that critiques the very formations it describes.

❖ TOWARD A PERFORMATIVE CULTURAL POLITICS

With terms in place, I turn to a discussion of five questions raised by the call to performance within the ethnographic and arts-based communities.[14] Each of these questions pairs *performance* with another term (Conquergood 1991:190, 1998; Schechner 1998:360), and each pair is predicated on the proposition that if the world is a performance, not a text, then today we need a model of social science that is performative.

This means that we must rethink the relationships between the elements in each of the following pairs (Conquergood 1991:190):

❖ Performance and cultural process
❖ Performance and ethnographic praxis
❖ Performance and hermeneutics
❖ Performance and the act of scholarly representation
❖ Performance and the politics of culture

All pragmatists and ethnographers who have studied Dewey would agree on the relationship between the first pair; *culture* is a verb, a process, an ongoing performance, not a noun, a product or a static thing. Performances and their representations reside in the center of lived experience. We cannot study experience directly. We study it through and in its performative representations. Culture, so conceived, turns performance into a site where memory, emotion, fantasy, and desire interact with one another (Madison 1998:277). Every performance is political, a site where the performance of possibilities occurs (Madison 1998:277).

The second pair brings performance and ethnographic praxis into play, highlighting the methodological implications of thinking about fieldwork as a collaborative process, or a coperformance (Conquergood 1991:190). The observer and the observed are coperformers in a performance event. Autoethnographer-performers insert their experiences into the cultural performances that they study.

Stacey Holman Jones (2002) writes of herself, and of her love of unrequited love. Speaking of love, she finds herself crying as she watches the final scene of *The Way We Were:*

> I am crying. I cry each time I see the final scene between Katie and Hubbell in *The Way We Were.* I have to see only that last scene, hear only those last sounds, "Memories . . ." I cry for Katie and Hubbell, for the way they tried, but just couldn't make their relationship work. (P. 45)

Consider now this poem by Jones (2002:49), in which she expresses her relationship to torch singers such as Billie Holiday. Jones begins by first referencing Peggy Phelan (1993), who states, "All seeing is hooded by loss . . . in looking at the other . . . the subject seeks to see" herself (p. 16). Jones writes:

I feel the slipping away, welcome it.

Turn over the memory of a long, lost

other. . . . Your eyes, green like mine, on me,

Steadily

watching myself reflected in your gaze. Look

at you seeing me . . .

I want to live the torch song I think, write, dream about.

The third pair connects performance to hermeneutics and privileges performed experience as a way of knowing, as a method of critical inquiry, and as a mode of understanding. For example, reading Jones's poem aloud allows me to hear her voice and, through my voice, connect to Holiday, through Peggy Phelan. In these sounds and feelings I feel closer to her desire to live the torch song. Similarly, reading the lines from Hartnett's poem takes me back to Janis Joplin, to "Me and Bobby McGee," to Kris Kristofferson, to Mexican laborers in the Salinas Valley, tangled-up memories, California prisons, violence, injustice, and the Vietnam War.

Hermeneutics is the work of interpretation and understanding. *Knowing* refers to those embodied, sensuous experiences that create the conditions for understanding (Denzin 1984:282). Through performance, I experience Jones's feelings, which are present in her performance text. Thus performed experiences are the sites where felt emotion, memory, desire, and understanding come together.

The fourth and fifth pairs question the unbreakable links connecting hermeneutics, politics, pedagogy, ethics, and scholarly representation. Conquergood (1991:190) remains firm on this point, arguing that we should treat performances as a complementary form of research publication, an alternative method or way of interpreting and presenting the results of an ethnographer's work. Performances deconstruct, or at least challenge, the scholarly article as the preferred form of presentation (and representation). A performance authorizes itself not through the citation of scholarly texts, but through its ability to evoke and invoke shared emotional experience and understanding between performer and audience.

Performance becomes a critical site of power, and politics, in the fifth pair. A radical pedagogy underlies this notion of performative cultural politics. Foucault (1980b) reminds us that power always elicits resistance. The performative becomes an act of doing, an act of resistance, a way of connecting the biographical, the pedagogical, and the political (Giroux 2000a:134–35).

The concepts of militant utopianism and educated hope are realized in the moment of resistance (Giroux, 2001b:109). This utopianism and vision of hope moves from private to public, from biographical to institutional, linking personal troubles with public issues. This utopianism tells and performs stories of resistance, compassion, justice, joy, community, and love (Hardt and Negri 2000:413).

As pedagogical practices, performances make sites of oppression visible. In the process, they affirm an oppositional politics that reasserts the value of self-determination and mutual solidarity. This pedagogy of hope rescues radical democracy from the conservative politics of neoliberalism (Giroux, 2001b:115). A militant utopianism offers a new language of resistance in the public and private spheres. Thus performance pedagogy energizes a radical participatory democratic vision for this new century.

❖   THE MOVE TO PERFORMANCE ETHNOGRAPHY

The move to performance has been accompanied by a shift in the meaning of ethnography and ethnographic writing. Richardson (2000b) observes that the narrative genres connected to ethnographic writing have "been blurred, enlarged, altered to include poetry [and] drama" (p. 929; see also Richardson 2002a). She uses the term *creative analytic practices* to describe these many different reflexive performance narrative forms, which include not only performance autoethnography but also short stories, conversations, fiction, creative nonfiction, photographic essays, personal essays, personal narratives of the self, writing-stories, self-stories, fragmented or layered texts, critical autobiography, memoirs, personal histories, cultural criticism, co-constructed performance narratives, and performance writing, which blurs the boundaries separating text, representation, and criticism (see also Mullins forthcoming).[15]

In each of these forms the writer-as-performer is self-consciously present, morally and politically self-aware. The writer uses his or her own experiences in a culture "reflexively to bend back on self and look more deeply at self-other interactions" (Ellis and Bochner 2000:740; see also Kincheloe and McLaren 2000:301; Alexander 1999:309). The task of autoethnography is now apparent: It helps the writer "make sense of the autobiographic past" (Alexander 1999:309). Autoethnography becomes a way of "recreating and re-writing the biographic past, a way of making the past a part of the biographic present" (Pinar 1994:22; see also Alexander 1999:309).

What Will the Children Be Told?

On September 11, 2001, hours after the terrorist attacks on the World Trade Center and the Pentagon, Laurel Richardson (2002b) wrote the following words:

September 11, 2001:

When I hear of the airplanes and the towers, my first thoughts are—the children. . . . What will the children be told? . . .

And then I see that the children are being told, as the adults are, through television cameras and media voices. The children are seeing the airplane and the second tower, and the airplane/tower, airplane/tower over and over until it's All Fall Down. And All Fall Down again and again.

I call my children. I call my stepchildren. I call my grand-children. . . . My heart breaks for the children whose lives are broken. . . . What can I say? What can anyone say? My email Listservs are repositories for quick fixes, ideological purity. . . . I can't join the discussion. I refuse to intellectualize, analyze, or academize. I don't have any answers. . . .

I call my grandson's mother to see how Akiva is doing. She tells me that he was afraid an airplane would hit his school. . . . On Rosh Hashanah the rabbi said "Choose Life." I meditate on our small world. I pray. I write this piece. (P. 25)

As a performance autoethnographer, Richardson anchors her narrative in an ongoing moral dialogue with members of her local community, including family members, neighbors, and colleagues. Troubling the usual distinctions between self and other, she folds her reflections into the stories of others. This is a performance event.

Ethnographic Textualism

As Conquergood (1998:26) and Pollock (1998a, 1998b:40) observe, performance is a tool for questioning an earlier generation's ethnographic textualism, a textualism that produced books with titles such as *Writing Culture* (Clifford and Marcus 1988; see Conquergood 1998:26). Using the methods of inscription and thick description, ethnographers in the past have employed textual models to turn culture into an ensemble of written words (Geertz 1973:23–24; Conquergood 1998:28). These ethnographers have read culture as if it were an open book (Conquergood 1998:29). Textualism privileges distance, detachment—the said and not the saying, the done and not the doing (Conquergood 1998:31).

In contrast, performance autoethnographers struggle to put culture into motion (Rosaldo 1989:91), to perform culture by putting "mobility, action, and agency back into play" (Conquergood 1998:31). The performance paradigm privileges an "experiential, participatory epistemology" (Conquergood 1998:27). It values intimacy and involvement as forms of understanding. This stance allows the self to be vulnerable to its own experiences as well as to the experiences of the other (Behar 1996:3).

In this interactionist epistemology, context replaces text, verbs replace nouns, structures become processes. The emphasis is on change, contingency, locality, motion, improvisation, struggle, situationally specific practices and articulations, the performance of con/texts (Pollock 1998b:38). By privileging struggle, performance ethnographers take a stand (Conquergood 1998:31; Kirshenblatt-Gimblett 1998:74–78). The dividing line between text and context falls away. Texts are inseparable from contexts and from the "processes by which they are made, understood and deployed" (Pollock 1998b:38). In turn, context cannot be separated from cultural practices, which are performances.

Performances are the sites where context, agency, praxis, history, and subjectivity intersect (Langellier 1999:127). An improvisatory politics of resistance is anchored in this space where the doing and the done collide.

A Politics of Resistance

Performance autoethnography's emphasis on the politics of resistance connects it to critical Marxist participatory action theories

(McLaren 2001). Participatory action theories have roots in liberation theology, neo-Marxist approaches to community development, and human rights activism in Asia and elsewhere (Kemmis and McTaggart 2000:568). These theories enable social criticism and sanction nonviolent forms of civil disobedience (Christians 2000:148).

Performance autoethnography now becomes a civic, participatory, collaborative project. It is a project centered on an ongoing moral dialogue involving the shared ownership of the performance project itself. Together, members of the community, as cultural workers, create the performance text and the performance event (McCall 2000:426). These community-based interpretations represent an emancipatory commitment to community action that performs social change, much as Du Bois's all-black theater did (Kemmis and McTaggart 2000:568, 598). To paraphrase Kemmis and McTaggart (2000:598), this form of performance inquiry helps people to recover and release themselves from the repressive constraints embedded in the racist structures of global technocapitalism.

In these performances of resistance, as Langellier (1998:210) argues, the personal becomes political. This happens precisely at that moment when the conditions of identity construction are made problematic and located in concrete history, as when Mary Weems, the poet-performer, says, "This evolution will not be televised." In this moment, performers claim a positive utopian space where a politics of hope is imagined.

This performance ethic asks that interpretive work provide the foundations for social criticism by subjecting specific programs and policies to concrete analysis. Performers show how specific policies and practices affect and effect their lives (Mienczakowski 2001); bell hooks (1990) does this when she critically reflects on the way Ed Sullivan treated Louis Armstrong in the 1950s on Sullivan's Sunday-night television show. In rereading the Sullivan show, hooks lays the foundations for a critical race consciousness.

The autoethnographer invites members of the community to become coperformers in a drama of social resistance and social critique. Acting from an informed ethical position, offering emotional support to one another, coperformers bear witness to the need for social change (Langellier 1998:210–11). As members of an involved social citizenship, they enact a "politics of possibility, a politics that mobilizes people's memories, fantasies, and desires" (Madison 1998:277). These are pedagogical performances that matter. They give a voice to the subaltern. They do something in the world. They move people to action. As Baraka ([1969] 1998:1502) says:

we want poems that wrestle cops into

alleys

and take their weapons . . .

Pedagogical performances have artistic, moral, political, and material consequences (Madison 1998:283–84). In a performance of possibilities, moral responsibility and artistic excellence combine to produce an "active intervention to . . . *break through* unfair closures and remake the possibility for new openings" (Madison 1998:284). A performance of possibilities gives a voice to those on the margin, moving them for the moment to the political center (Madison 1998:284).

A Politics of Possibility

Madison (1998) shows how this politics of possibility works by telling the story of two African American women, cafeteria workers, who in 1968 led a strike against their employer, the University of North Carolina. The women protested for back pay, overtime pay, and better working conditions. During the course of the strike, the National Guard was called in. The Chapel Hill police "circled the cafeteria with guns in hand, and classes were canceled. For the two Africa-American women who led the strike, it was a difficult time and an unforgettable ordeal. One woman was fired; the other still works in the University cafeteria" (p. 279).

In 1993, the University of North Carolina was celebrating its bicentennial, and, as Madison (1998) relates, some people "felt it was time to honor the leaders of the (in)famous 1968 cafeteria workers strike, as well as labor culture on campus. After some time, a performance based on the personal narratives of the two leaders and other service workers was finally scheduled" (p. 279). On the opening night of what would be a series of performances, the strike leaders and their partners, children, grandchildren, and friends, as well as university cafeteria workers, housekeepers, brick masons, yard keepers, and mail carriers, "were the honored guests with reserved seats before an overflowing crowd" (p. 298). Madison observes that although the university never acknowledged the "strike leaders' struggle or their contribution to labor equity on campus, almost thirty years later, the leaders, Mrs. Smith and Mrs. Brooks, watched themselves and their story being performed in a crowded theatre" (p. 279).

At the end of the performance, Mrs. Smith and Mrs. Brooks were introduced, and "the audience gave them a thunderous and lengthy standing ovation" (p. 280). Mrs. Smith said that a night like this "made her struggle worthwhile" (p. 280). Her grandchildren reported that they "now understood their grandmother's life better after seeing the performance" (p. 280). The next day, the press reported that "the production told a true and previously untold tale" (p. 280). Madison reports that years later, workers still stop her on campus and "remember and want to talk, with pride and satisfaction, about that night four years ago when their stories were honored in performance" (p. 280).

The performance of the story of the cafeteria strike helped these workers tell their own stories, empowering them "before strangers and kin" (p. 280). The performance became an epiphany, a liminal event that marked a crisis in the university's history. The performance redressed this historical breach and brought dignity and stature to those who had been dishonored by the past actions of the university. The performance allowed these women and their families to bear witness to this suppressed history. This performance did not create a revolution, but it was "revolutionary in enlightening citizens to the possibilities that grate against injustice" (p. 280).

This kind of political theater moves in three directions at the same time, shaping subjects, audiences, and performers. In honoring subjects who have been mistreated, such performances contribute to a more "enlightened and involved citizenship" (p. 281). These performances interrogate and evaluate specific social, educational, economic, and political processes. This form of praxis can shape a cultural politics of change. It can help create a progressive and involved citizenship. The performance becomes the vehicle for moving persons, subjects, performers, and audience members into new, critical, political spaces. The performance gives the audience, and the performers, "equipment for [this] journey: empathy and intellect, passion and critique" (p. 282).

Such performances enact a performance-centered evaluation pedagogy. Thus fusion of critical pedagogy and performance praxis uses performance as a mode of inquiry, as a method of doing evaluation ethnography, as a path to understanding, as a tool for engaging collaboratively the meanings of experience, as a means to mobilize persons to take action in the world. This form of critical, collaborative performance pedagogy privileges experience, the concept of voice, and the importance of turning evaluation sites into democratic public spheres (see Worley 1998). Critical performance pedagogy informs practice, which in turn supports the pedagogical conditions for an emancipatory politics (Worley 1998:139).

To extend an observation made by Toni Morrison (1994), the best performance autoethnographies, like the best art, are "unquestionably political and irrevocably beautiful at the same time" (p. 497; quoted in Madison 1998:281). This performance ethic seeks its external grounding in its commitment to a post-Marxism and communitarian feminism with hope but no guarantees. It seeks to understand how power and ideology operate through and across systems of discourse. It understands that moral and aesthetic criteria are always fitted to the contingencies of concrete circumstances, assessed in terms of local understandings that flow from a feminist moral ethic (Christians 2000). This ethic calls for dialogic inquiry rooted in the concepts of care and shared governance. We cannot predict how this ethic will work in any specific situation; such inquiry has not been done before.

Hence, for example, an Afrocentric feminist aesthetic (and epistemology) stresses the importance of truth, knowledge, beauty ("Black is beautiful"), and a notion of wisdom that is experiential and shared. Wisdom, so conceived, is derived from local, lived experience and expresses lore, folktale, and myth (Collins 1990:212–13). This aesthetic asks that art (and ethnography) be politically committed.

❖ PERFORMANCE ART

This black performance aesthetic—art by, for, and about the people— complements a new movement in the arts, a movement that has had a variety of names, including *performance art, activist art, community art,* and *new genre public art* (Lacy 1995:20; Miles 1997:164; Rice 1990:207; Radford-Hill 2000:25).[16] Artist Suzanne Lacy (1995) states that new genre public art is "an art whose public strategies of engagement are an important part of its aesthetic language. . . . Unlike much what of has heretofore been called public art, new genre public art . . . might include . . . installations, performances, conceptual art, mixed-media art. . . . Attacking boundaries, new genre public art draws on ideas from vanguard forms" (pp. 9–10).

Performance art is "predicated on a history of cultural resistance" (Garoian 1999:10). Earlier formations can be found in the performance art and avant-garde experimental theater movements of the 1970s and

1980s (McCall 2000:423; Garoian 1999:10). New genre public art is performative, political, feminist, and activist (Garoian 1999:8). According to Lacy (1995:20), four historical factors, embedded in the conservative backlash of the 1980s and 1990s, shaped this movement: increased racial discrimination; threats to women's rights; cultural censorship targeted at women artists, homosexual artists, and artists who are members of ethnic minority groups; and deepening health (HIV/AIDS) and ecological crises. As Giroux (2000a) puts it, quoting Pierre Bourdieu, this art understands that "there is no genuine democracy without genuine opposition" (p. 136).

Performance art does not subscribe to the tradition of High Culture. It is revolutionary art. It reclaims the radical political identity of the artist as social critic (McCall 2000:421). In the hands of cultural workers such as Suzanne Lacy, performance art dissolves the "differences between artists and participants . . . showing how art should be a force for information, dialogue, and social change" (Giroux 2000a:136).[17] Rebecca Rice, black theater artist and educator, provides another example. Rice seeks a theater for social change, and her performances illuminate the beauty and dignity of black women who have been victims of violence, abuse, and addiction (see Rice 1990:212). The work of Anna Deavere Smith (1993, 1994) also illustrates the nature of performance art. Over the past decade, Smith has created a series of one-woman performance pieces about race and racism in America. She calls her series "On the Road: A Search for American Character."

To paraphrase Miles (1997:164), the value of new genre activist art such as critical performance ethnography lies in its ability to initiate a continuing process of social criticism in the public sphere. As Miles observes, this art engages "defined publics on issues from homelessness to the survival of the rain forests, domestic violence and AIDS" (p. 164). It transgresses "the confines of public and domestic domains" (p. 167) and shows how public laws and policies influence personal decisions. It shows how the limits of the public sphere shape changes in the private sphere (p. 169). Activist art challenges the relationship of art and the artist to the public domain.

❖ THE PEDAGOGICAL AS PERFORMATIVE

The new artistic formations described above move from the global to the local, from the political to the personal, from the pedagogical to the performative.[18] They make the "political visible through [performative] pedagogical practices that attempt to make a difference in the world rather than simply reflect it" (Giroux 2000a:137). Du Bois's radical black theater performs scenes of liberation for an oppressed people; bell hooks's black aesthetic and Rebecca Rice's black theater imagine and perform liberated subjectivities for African American women.

Six pedagogical strategies shape performance art, thereby troubling the relationships among ethnography, fieldwork, culture, language, ideology, race, the body, community, and technology (Garoian 1999:45). The first strategy is methodological. Performance art pedagogy redefines ethnography as reflexive, performative autoethnography (Garoian 1999:44). The second strategy focuses on the performance and use of language as a way of criticizing "the cultural metaphors that codify and stereotype the [racial] self and the body" (Garoian 1999:44). The third strategy uses performance art to generate spectacles of resistance that challenge the local power structures circulating in specific sites, such as schools or hospitals.

The fourth strategy performs community by empowering citizens to work collaboratively on "restoring ... civility in their neighborhoods" (Garoian 1999:44). Using the body as a site of intervention, the fifth and sixth strategies show how machine-body transactions scar and shape the material and lived body, its fantasies, desires, illnesses, and pains. At these levels, performance art pedagogy examines the aesthetic experiences that surround the embodied expression of a culture and its racial and gender codes (Garoian 1999:45).

Performance art pedagogy reflexively critiques those cultural practices that reproduce oppression. At the performative level, this pedagogy locates performances within these repressive practices, creating discourses that make the struggles of democracy more visible. In their performances, artists, teachers, students, and other cultural workers "invoke their personal memories and histories.... they engage in storytelling" (Garoian 1999:5). They perform testimonios. They "remember, misremember, interpret and passionately revisit ... [the] past and [the] present," and in so doing they invoke a "continuum of past performances, a history ... juxtaposed ... with existential experiences" (Diamond 1996:1). Through their coperformances, cultural workers critique and evaluate culture, turning history back in upon itself, creating possibilities for new historical ideas, new images, new subjectivities, new cultural practices (Garoian 1999:6; Diamond 1996:2).

To build on Giroux's (2000a:138) arguments, these forms of democratic practice turn the political into a set of performance events. Occurring in the here and now, these performances contest situations of oppression. They make things happen. They are consequential. They initiate and model change. In these events, performers intervene in the liminal and politicized spaces of the culture (Garoian 1999:50).

These events, or happenings, "reclaim the political as pedagogical" (Giroux 2000a:138; see also Giroux 1992:150, 1994:87). As sites of resistance, they connect "mystory" performances to popular, personal, and scholarly cultural texts.[19] These texts are located in their institutional and historical moments, the sites of power in everyday live. These performances join transnational and postcolonial narratives with storytelling about personal problems experienced at the local level. These interventions represent pedagogy done in the public interest, democratic art for by and of the people.

Bryant Keith Alexander (forthcoming) offers an example of such performances. Listen to his discussion of black barbershops as cultural spaces where identities and memories are infused with the past and the present:

> Black people enter these spaces for cultural maintenance and cultural proliferation. As I sit in the barber's chair my body, like my history, is in relation to other Black bodies. . . . Mr. Brown, Luke, Deanna and those who came before and those who will follow are simultaneously present. The fading, twisting, and weaving of hair, of voices, and life stories are a part of the process, a part of the experience, a part of me. But these are my stories. My hair tells its own story. (P. 17)

Everybody's hair tells a story, and in all of our stories culture is performed, and the political becomes personal and pedagogical.

❖ CONCLUSION

In this chapter I have argued that interpretive ethnography is at a crossroads. Ethnographers, pragmatists, symbolic interactionists, and critical race theorists face a challenge: how to reclaim the progressive heritage left by Du Bois, Mead, Dewey, Blumer, hooks, West, Diawara,

Hall, Jordan, Shange, Dove, and others. I have suggested that we need to craft an emancipatory discourse that speaks to issues of racial inequality under neoliberal forms of democracy and capitalism. This discourse requires a turn to a performance-based approach to culture, politics, and pedagogy. We need to explore performance autoethnography and performance art as vehicles for enacting a performative cultural politics of hope. In Chapter 2, I go more deeply into this project, offering a genealogy of the performance text and connecting that genealogy to an ethics for a performative cultural studies.

2

The Language
of Performance

All the world is not, of course, a stage, but the crucial ways in which it isn't are not easy to specify.

—Erving Goffman, *The Presentation of Self in Everyday Life,* 1959

Given that the logic of privatization and free trade . . . now odiously shapes archetypes of citizenship . . . [and] manages our perceptions of what constitute the 'good society,' . . . it stands to reason that new ethnographic research approaches must take global capitalism not as an end point of analysis, but as a starting point.

—Joe L. Kincheloe and Peter McLaren, "Rethinking Critical Theory and Qualitative Research," 2000

I agree with Goffman, and with Kincheloe and McLaren. The ways in which the world is not a stage are not easy to specify, and global capitalism is one reason this is so. Indeed, if everything is already performative, staged, commodified, and dramaturgical, as I have suggested in the preceding chapter, then the dividing lines between person and character, between performer and actor, between stage and setting, between script and text, and between performance and performativity disappear. When these divisions disappear, critical ethnography becomes pedagogical and performative, and its topics become the politics of global capitalist culture and the effects of that politics on the dramas of daily life (Willis and Trondman 2000:10).

I seek a language, a theoretical framework through which to talk about the relationships among these terms, about the ways in which capitalism, race, gender, class, colonialism, postcolonialism, pedagogy, and performance (auto)ethnography are connected. I seek a way to talk about ethnographic texts turned into performance events, into poems, scripts, short stories, texts with narrators, drama, action, shifting points of view, plays that are read, dramaturgical productions coperformed with audiences—life, narrative, and melodrama under the auspices of late capitalism.[20]

At one level, performance (auto)ethnography is a genre within critical, postmodern ethnography, a variant on what Paget (1993:42) calls *ethnoperformance*, Mienczakowski (1992, 1994, 1995, 2001; Mienczakowski and Morgan 1993, 2001) labels *ethnodrama*, and Turner (1982:40) terms *reflexive anthropology*, the rendering "of ethnography in a kind of instructional theater" (p. 41).[21] Reflexive ethnography exists in a pedagogical borderland, in the spaces where rhetoric, politics, parody, pastiche, performance, ethnography, and critical cultural studies come together (Conquergood 1992:80).[22]

In this chapter, I read this genre critically, offering a vocabulary with which to discuss it, while tracing its genealogy in communications, sociology, and anthropology, locating it within performance studies and theories of critical pedagogy (Schechner 1998; Garoian 1999).[23] Emphasizing a critical pedagogical, postmodern performance aesthetic (Garoian 1999:10), I privilege those performance texts/events that focus on the construction and coperformance of improvised "mystories" (Ulmer 1989:209).[24] Mystories are reflexive, critical, multimedia tales and tellings. Each mystory begins with the writer's biography and body; mystories relate epiphanic moments, turning-point experiences, and times of personal trouble and turmoil—Turner's (1986b:34–35) "liminal experiences."[25]

Performed mystories move from epiphanic moments to those larger popular culture and scholarly texts that interpret and make sense of problematic personal experience, public explanations of private troubles (Mills 1959:11).[26] Mystories critique these larger systems of personal, popular, and expert knowledge (Ulmer 1989:209–11). As interventions into the popular, mystories create conditions that allow individuals to imagine a politics of hope and possibility (Madison 1998:277). I conclude this chapter with a discussion of the place of politics and ethics in a performative cultural studies, but first, some history.

❖ A GENEALOGY OF THE PERFORMANCE TEXT

The origins of the alliance among ethnography, personal narrative, pedagogy, and performance studies can be traced to many sources and told in many different ways. Each telling establishes a different history, a different story of origin (Conquergood 1992:80; Jackson 1993; Stern and Henderson 1993:9–16; Strine 1998; Miller 1998:51; Doyle 1998:77; Pineau 1998:129; Worley 1998:138–39 Hill 1998; Hantzis 1998; Langellier 1998; Lockford 1998; Smith 1998; McCall 2000:421). I focus briefly here on four origin stories.

The Turn to Language and Narrative

Doyle (1998) begins with Nietzsche, connecting his view of the performative to "a number of productive 'turns' in twentieth-century critical thought" (p. 77), including the linguistic turn of Saussure (1966), which treats the world as a set of representations; the early Wittgenstein (1961), who advocated the pictorial turn in philosophy, an iconographic method for reading art and the world as a text; the narrative turn, which "historicizes the genres of oral anecdote, autobiography [and] personal narrative"; the cultural turn of Strine (1998), Turner (1986b), and Conquergood (1985), which sees culture as a performance; and, more recently, the performative-performance turn, shaped by the work of Butler and others, "the testing of theory by performance and performance by theory" (p. 78).[27]

Two more twists, or turns, must be added to Doyle's linguistic, pictorial, narrative, cultural, and performative turns. These are the simultaneous moves within cultural and performance studies to bring critical pedagogy and feminist and Marxist theory into the ethnographic project (see Freire 2001; Garoian 1999:45; Kincheloe and

McLaren 2000:297–98; Carspecken 1996; Giroux 2000a:137; McLaren 1998a, 2001; Clough 1998; Willis and Trondman 2000). The argument was brief, but powerful: The performative is pedagogical, and the pedagogical is political (see below).

Each of these turns is predicated on a different model or view of performance and the performative, including the performance as something to do, or go through; as a way to develop a set of skills; as a methodology, a means by which "students [can] explore texts more deeply and understand them more richly" (Dailey 1998a:xi); as a way of knowing; and as a way of being. At various moments the field of performance studies has been defined by each of these models of performance. It has moved from voice-centered studies to text-centered studies of interpretation, to chamber and reader-response models of performing literature, to performance art and performance ethnography (Miller 1998:51; Denzin 1997:104–7).

The Dramaturgical Turn

Another origin story, which I have reviewed elsewhere (Denzin 1997:102–3), is the dramaturgical story. In 1959, Erving Goffman proposed to read society dramaturgically, to look at those parts of daily life that are staged and to place an emphasis on the similarities between reality and appearance. Kenneth Burke (1969:43) extended this metaphor, suggesting that anthropologists examine the rhetorical nature of their own field and that anthropology be imported (in part) into rhetoric. Victor Turner (1986a) called for an anthropology of performance and offered a theory of drama and ritual. Stanford Lyman (1990:221) suggested that in the United States, the metaphor of a dramaturgical society had become an interactional reality. Today we understand everyday life through mass-mediated performances that make the hyperreal more real than the real.

Conquergood (1991:190) has extended the performance model into a performative, dramatic framework, viewing culture as a verb, not a noun; fieldwork as a collaborative process, a performance; and knowledge as performative, not informative. Turner's and Conquergood's calls to perform ethnographic narratives were anticipated by Paget's (1990a, 1990b, 1993) concept of "verbatim theater" and the notion of a performance science—that is, scholars performing ethnographic texts (see McCall 2000). In a parallel vein, Mienczakowski's (2001) ethnodrama represents an important extension of Boal's ([1979] 1985, 1995) method of forum theater. Mienczakowski uses postperformance discussions with informants and audience members as a way of making the performance of ethnographic texts more responsive to the demands of praxis and social critique.

Too often missing from the dramaturgical model is any sustained consideration of the politics of gendered, global capitalist culture. It is as if culture and its performances stand outside political economy and the structures of neoliberalism and the state apparatus.[28] Here is where another origin story becomes relevant.

Performance Art and Performance Studies

McCall (2000) begins her history of performance ethnography with a discussion of performance art.[29] She observes that "the term *performance* entered art critical and academic discourses in the 1970s, to name a new visual art form and to distinguish dramatic scripts from particular productions of them—that is, from performances onstage" (p. 421). Performance art as a movement predates, while running alongside, the crisis of representation in the human disciplines. It can be traced to the futurists of the 1910s and continued with the dadaist cabaret movement of the 1920s, the surrealism movement (1924 to the mid-1930s), and Brecht's experiments with a theater of the mind, culminating in the mid-1960s in an interdisciplinary, often multimedia kind of production that has come to be labeled "performance art" (McCall 2000:421; Garoian 1999:25; Sayre 1990:93; Stern and Henderson 1993:383).[30] Transformations in this movement focused on the gendered body, dissolving, fragmenting, blurring, and displacing its centered presence in performance (Birringer 1993:220–21; Garoian 1999:26).

These changes continued into the 1970s and 1980s as visual and theater artists developed two forms of performance art: body art and elaborate spectacles utilizing new media technologies (McCall 2000:423). The literal body was challenged, replaced by a gendered, autobiographical, confessional body text, cries and whispers onstage, a body in motion working against itself and its culture (Birringer 1993:221). This body and its representations were supplemented by a globalizing, electronic, postmodern video technology and experimental theater performances, including visual opera (i.e., persons listening to pictures; McCall 2000:423).

McCall (2000) extends this history into the social sciences, noting that "in the late 1980s and early 1990s, sociologists began to turn their ethnographic field notes into performances, and theater artists and academics in performance studies began to produce or adapt ethnographies in order to perform them" (pp. 423–24). Conquergood at Northwestern University and Schechner at New York University led this movement (see Schechner 1998). Thus was born performance ethnography, offspring of two disciplines: From social science, it inherited an emphasis on ethnography; from the arts and humanities, it inherited an emphasis on performance and interpretation.[31]

It remained for politics and the pedagogical to enter the picture, to show how the performative is political (Garoian 1999:28). This is the province, in part, of people's theater and Third World popular theater. In people's theater, members of the local community who have previously been denied power—such as the elderly, members of ethnic minority groups, women, the handicapped, and the imprisoned (Capo 1983:34)—become performers of their own stories of oppression (see also Boal [1979] 1985, 1995). Third World popular theater—that is, theater "used by oppressed Third World people to achieve justice and development for themselves" (Etherton 1988:991)—extends these critical views of what theater (and ethnography) can do politically. The International Popular Theatre Alliance, organized in the 1980s, uses existing forms of cultural expression to fashion improvised dramatic productions that analyze situations of poverty and oppression. This grassroots approach uses agitprop and sloganizing theater (theater pieces devised to foment political action) to create collective awareness and collective action at the local level. This form of theater remains popular in Latin America, Africa, India, and parts of Asia, and among Native populations in the Americas.

The Pedagogical Turn

Garoian (1999), Pineau (1998), and Hill (1998) have established the necessary links between performance studies and critical performative pedagogy.[32] Garoian (1999), drawing on Freire's oppositional pedagogy, suggests that "the resistance to cultural domination represents the performance of [a] political strategy to challenge the body politic" (p. 46). Freire (2001) describes this as a two-stage process. In the first stage, the oppressed unmask the forms of pedagogy that create oppression; they "unveil the world of oppression and through praxis commit themselves to its transformation" (p. 54). In the second stage, the reality of oppression "ceases to belong [only] to the oppressed" (p. 54). The pedagogy of oppression has been reversed. It now "becomes a pedagogy of all people in the process of permanent liberation" (p. 54). A critical performative pedagogy is thus always dialectical.

A performance-centered pedagogy uses performance as a method of investigation, as a way of doing ethnography, and as a method of understanding, a way of collaboratively engaging the meanings of experience (Hill 1998:142–43). Invoking Foucault's (1980a) concept of the disciplined body, Pineau (1998) argues that "the fusion of critical pedagogy and performance praxis" (p. 130) reveals how educational, ethnographic, and performing bodies are disciplined and ideologically trained in the classroom and in society at large (p. 128).

Worley (1998:139) goes one step further, contending that all classroom learning is embodied, performative, politicized, and based on negotiated authority. Drawing on the work of McLaren and Giroux, he advocates a critical, collaborative, performance pedagogy centered on the primacy of experience, the concept of voice, and the importance of turning classrooms into democratic public spheres. Thus critical performance pedagogy informs educational and ethnographic practice, which in turn helps to create the pedagogical conditions necessary for emancipatory schooling. In this regard, it is useful to maintain McLaren's (2001:121) distinction between critical and revolutionary pedagogy: Critical pedagogy is a dialectical and dialogic process, whereas revolutionary, radical (and reflexive) performance pedagogy critically situates agency, identity, and discourse within and against a broader historical landscape (see below).

Each of the origin stories related above is required. In hindsight, we can now see that each turn, from the linguistic to the narrative, the cultural, and the dramaturgical, needed to be taken. Each turn moved interpretive ethnography closer to its current critical performative, pedagogical moment. Each turn created a new space, a new set of openings; each space unsettled what had come before.

Most important, ethnography had to be taken out of a purely methodological framework and located first within a performative arena and then within the spaces of pedagogy, where it was understood that the pedagogical is always political. We can now see that interpretive ethnography's subject matter is set by a dialectical pedagogy. This pedagogy connects oppressors and the oppressed in capitalism's liminal, epiphanic spaces. I turn now to a discussion of relevant terms and assumptions.

❖ INTERPRETIVE ASSUMPTIONS

Experience is how lived reality presents itself to consciousness (Bruner 1986:6). Experience as lived consciousness cannot be studied directly. It can be studied only through performance, a form of representation. However, what counts as experience is shaped by a politics of representation and hence is "neither self-evident nor straightforward; it is always contested and always therefore political" (Scott 1993:412; see also Peterson and Langellier 1997:136). Representations of experience are performative, symbolic, and material. Anchored in performance events, they include drama, ritual, and storytelling.

This view of experience and the performative makes it difficult tom sustain any distinction between "appearances and actualities" (Schechner 1998:362). Further, if, as Butler (1993a:141) reminds us, there are no original performances, then every performance establishes itself performatively as an original, a personal and locally situated production. A quotation from Goffman (1959) summarizes my position:

> The legitimate performances of everyday life are not "acted" or "put on" in the sense that the performer knows in advance just what he is going to do, and does this solely because of the effect it is likely to have. The expressions it is felt he is giving off will be especially "inaccessible" to him . . . but the incapacity of the ordinary individual to formulate in advance the movements of his eyes and body does not mean that he will not express himself through these devices in a way that is dramatized and pre-formed in his repertoire of actions. In short, we all act better than we know how. (Pp. 73–74)

Persons are performers, but each person is unique, a universal singular, summing up and universalizing in his or her lifetime a particular segment of human history (Sartre 1981:ix). In their performances, all persons reproduce shreds and pieces of the epochs to which they belong. Behind and in front of their masks and performances, persons are moral beings, already present in the world, ahead of themselves, occupied and preoccupied with everyday doings and emotional practices, defined in and through their presence. Two performative levels of the person can thus be distinguished: the surface and the deep, imitation and the original, the image and an underlying reality (see Denzin 1984:91).

Now to address ethnography. *Traditional ethnography* represents attempts to write and inscribe culture for the purposes of increasing knowledge and social awareness. *Performance ethnography* represents and performs rituals from everyday life, using performing as a method of representation and a method of understanding. *Autoethnography* reflexively inserts the researcher's biographical experiences into the ethnographic performance project. *Critical and reflexive performance ethnography* dialectically situates the researcher and those he or she studies within capitalist culture, in a dialogue or exchange that reframes and reposes the "question of understanding itself" (McLaren 2001:121). *Radical performance ethnography* "goes further still . . . creating a narrative space set against the . . . daily poetics of agency, encounter, and conflict" (McLaren 2001:121–22).[33]

As Kincheloe and McLaren (2000:297) describe them, radical, critical performance autoethnographers work to expose the ways in which power and ideology shape self, desire, and human consciousness in concrete institutional and interactional sites. The everyday culture that critical performance autoethnographers interrogate is discursive, material, and embedded in the naturalized commonsense realities of capitalism, the media, and the neoliberal corporatist state (p. 304).

Critical performance autoethnography is catalytic; it moves persons to action, helping them to understand their world and its oppressions in new ways (Lather 1993). Critical ethnographers go beyond thick description of local situations to resistance performance texts/events that urge social transformations. Critical performance ethnography is doubly reflexive. Self-consciously locating the researcher in the research process, it challenges any notion that an easy identification between observer and observed can be forged. The critical ethnographer questions and then forfeits any claim to universal authority (Kincheloe and McLaren 2000:301; Visweswaran 1994). Still, to quote McLaren (2001), the final arbiter of any critical ethnographic practice is "its power to affect the world through praxis" (p. 125). Performance is praxis; words have material effects in the world. Baraka ([1969] 1998:1502) says:

We want a black poem, and a Black

World.

Let the world be a Black Poem.

Liminality, Ritual, and the Structure of the Epiphany

The postmodern world stages existential crises. Following Turner (1986b), the ethnographer gravitates to these narratively structured, liminal, existential spaces in the culture. In these dramaturgical sites people take sides, forcing, threatening, inducing, seducing, cajoling, nudging, loving, abusing, and killing one another. In these sites, ongoing social dramas with complex temporal rhythms occur (Turner 1986a:35). They are storied events, narratives that rearrange chronology into multiple and differing forms and layers of meaningful experience (Turner 1986a:35).

The critical autoethnographer enters those strange and familiar situations that connect critical biographical experiences (epiphanies) with culture, history, and social structure. He or she seeks out those narratives and stories people tell one another as they attempt to make sense of the epiphanies, or existential turning-point moments, in their lives. Epiphanies are experienced as social dramas, as dramatic events with beginnings, middles, and endings. Epiphanies represent ruptures in the structure of daily life.[34] Turner (1986b) reminds us that the theater of social life is often structured around a fourfold processual ritual model involving *breach, crisis, redress,* and *reintegration* or *schism.* Each of these phases is organized as a ritual, thus there are rituals of breach, crisis, redress, reintegration, and schism. Redressive rituals, for example, "include divination into the hidden causes of misfortune, conflict, and illness" (p. 41).

Many rituals are associated with life-crisis ceremonies, "particularly those of puberty, marriage, and death." Turner (1986b) contends that redressive and life-crisis rituals "contain within themselves a liminal phase, which provides a stage . . . for unique structures of experience" (p. 41). Liminal phases of experience, which are detached from daily life, are characterized by the presence of ambiguous and monstrous images, sacred symbols, ordeals, humiliation, gender reversals, tears, struggle, joy, and remorse (p. 41). The liminal phase of experience is a kind of no-person's land, "on the edge of what is possible" (Broadhurst 1999:12), "betwixt and between the structural past and the structural future" (Turner 1986b:41).

Epiphanies are ritually structured liminal experiences connected to moments of breach, crisis, redress, and reintegration or schism, crossing from one space to another. Mary Weems (2002:xx) reads this sign as she crosses the state line between Indiana and Illinois:

"The People of Illinois Welcome You"

comes right after the LYNCH ROAD sign

and the LYNCH ROAD sign comes right after

I see a thin road strung with the bodies

of black men like burned out lights

their backs twisting in the wind,

the road littered with try out ropes,

gleaned chicken parts, and cloth napkins

soiled wiping the lips of the audience.

I know roads don't hang,

but the welcome sandwiched between

the word like bread

cuts off my air

and I pull to the side of the road

loosen my collar

and search for bones.

The storied nature of epiphanic experiences continually raises the following questions: Whose story is being told (and made) here? Who is doing the telling? Who has the authority to make the telling stick? As soon as a chronological event is told in the form of a story, it enters a text-mediated system of discourse in which larger issues of power and control come into play (Smith 1990a). In this text-mediated system, new tellings occur, and the interpretations of original experience are now fitted to this larger interpretive structure (Smith 1990b).

This larger, text-based interpretive system reproduces the cultural logics of capitalism and literary naturalism. This is realism writ large, the attempt to reproduce accurately a real, external world of objects, to map and represent that world accurately, with a high degree of verisimilitude. This is the space entered by the performance text, which attempts to expose and challenge these larger systems of realistic interpretation and meaning.

Hence performance autoethnography inhabits a postmodern culture "with nearly invisible boundaries separating theatre performance from dance, music, film, television, video, and the various performance art 'disciplines'" (Birringer 1993:182). The performance text-as-an-event is situated in a complex system of discourse where traditional and avant-garde meanings—of the real, the hyperreal, mimesis and transgression, audiences, performances, performance video, and performance art pedagogy—all circulate and inform one another. Aesthetic theories (naturalism, realism, modernism, postmodernism) collide with positivist, postpositivist, and poststructural epistemologies, and hypertexts intersect with traditional print and performance forms of representation.

The reflexive performance text contests the pull of traditional "realist" theater and modernist ethnography, wherein performers and ethnographers reenact and re-create a "recognizable verisimilitude of setting, character and dialogue" (Cohn 1988), where dramatic action reproduces a linear sequence, a "mimetic representation of cause and effect" (Birringer 1993:196). An evocative epistemology demands a postmodern performance aesthetic that goes beyond "the already-seen and already-heard" (Birringer 1993:186). This aesthetic criticizes the ideological and technological requirements of late-capitalist social realism and hyperrealism (Birringer 1993:175).

Performances always return to the lived body (Garoian 1999:17). The body's dramaturgical presence is "a site and pretext for . . . debates about representation and gender, about history and postmodern culture" (Birringer 1993:203). The late-postmodern body, and the discourses that surround it, must be represented, from the AIDS body to the oversized body and the undersized anorexic body, from the pornographic to the erotic and the sexually abused, from the gay and lesbian to the transgendered and straight body, from the sporting body to Haraway's (1985) cyborg, and from cyborgs to the bombed, mutilated bodies of little children.

These texts-as-performances challenge the meanings of lived experience as simulated performance. They interrogate, as did Brecht, the concepts of theater and specularity, reconceptualizing the central features that define the material apparatuses of the stage, including audience member, director, actor, costume, script, sound, and lighting, even performance itself (see Benjamin 1968b).

Performance ethnography answers Trinh's (1991:162) call for works that seek the truth of life's fictions and in which experiences are evoked, not explained. The performer seeks a presentation that, like good fiction, is true *in* experience, but not necessarily true *to* experience (Lockford 1998:216). Whether the events presented actually occurred is tangential to the larger project (Lockford 1998:216; see also Benjamin 1968a:90). As dramatic theater, with connections to Brecht (epic theater) and Artaud (theater of cruelty), these texts turn tales of suffering, loss, pain, and victory into evocative performances that have the ability to move audiences to reflective, critical action, not just emotional catharsis (on Brecht's theater, see Kellner 1997:89; see also Benjamin, 1968b).[35]

In the moment of performance, these texts have the potential to overcome the biases of a positivist, ocular, visual epistemology. They undo the gazing eye of the modernist ethnographer, bringing audiences and performers into a jointly felt and shared field of experience. In this field memory operates. Each participant enters the ongoing performance from the standpoint of his or her own past experiences. These works also unsettle the writer's place in the text, freeing the text and the writer to become interactional and existential productions (see Gingrich-Philbrook 2000:ix).

The performed text is lived experience, interpretation, and this in two senses (Pelias 1998:20). The performance doubles back on the experiences previously represented in the writer's text. It then re-presents those experiences as an embodied performance. It thus privileges immediate experience, the evocative moment when another's experiences come alive for the self. As Conquergood (1985) notes, performances are always "enmeshed in moral matters. . . . [They] enact a moral stance" (pp. 2, 4; see also Conquergood 1986:56). In them, performers critically bring the spaces, meanings, ambiguities, and contradictions of late-capitalist culture alive. The performed text operates in the liminal spaces of culture.

❖   A CRITICAL POSTMODERN
     PERFORMANCE VOCABULARY

A family of contested concepts and terms, all blurred together, define the critical autoethnographic performance perspective. Dramatic performances occur within the public and democratic spaces of *auto-ethnographic theater*, a safe, sacred aesthetic place, a space where texts, performers, performances, and audiences come together to participate in shared, reflexive performances. This theater may be anywhere—a stage organized for performances or an improvised space, such as a classroom, a church basement, a lecture hall, a street corner. In this space, participants perform a narrative involving delineated characters (speaking parts) in plotted dramatic action. Such performance events involve audience members as coparticipants in the interpretive process, not as spectators (see Garoian 1999:8). These dramatic scripts are *pedagogical performance narratives*. They edit experience (see McCall and Becker 1990:118). They draw on multiple personal and group experiences and often include composite characters. They criticize existing social formations and imagine utopian alternatives. They are fragmentary and personal, and they stitch themselves into the many fabrics of popular and political culture.

An *autoethnographic performance* is an interpretive event, a way of projecting understanding about the self and its situations and experiences (Pelias 1999:ix). This performance event is the moment when *performativity* (being) brings a performance narrative alive (Langellier 1998:208). A *personal performance narrative* is a radically contextualized self-story or personal story (mystory) about something that happened to the storyteller or to a group to which the storyteller belongs (Langellier 1998:208). It is poetic, nuanced, and evocative. It mediates, interprets, and hence represents experience (Lockford 1998:216). Written in the first person, a personal narrative disavows any claim of being "the objective research report [or] the factual history" (Pelias 1999:xi).

Several different types of personal performance narratives can be distinguished. A *personal experience story* is a narrative that relates the self of the teller to a significant set of personal experiences that have already occurred (see Denzin 2001b:61). A *self-story* is a narrative that creates and interprets a structure of experience as it is being told. Self-stories deal with the past, the present, and the future simultaneously; personal experience stories deal with the past. As forms of autobiographical discourse, personal experience stories and self-stories often generate sequels—one story, one performance, reflexively builds on another. This creates what Alexander (2000:98) calls a *generative autobiographical performance*, a narrative and performance event that bridges the gaps that separate stories, performers, and audiences.

Hartnett (1998:290) merges these three narrative forms in the opening lines of his poem "Democracy Is Difficult":

Through fogged charter bus windows and wary talk of choke-holds I watch as the Chicago branch of the National

Coalition Against Control Unit Prisons Caravan rolls down
Indiana state road 41

an urban messenger carrying the underclass's rage . . .

to forgotten rural hell-holes

the new supermax prison at Wabash Valley

Personal histories are reconstructions of individuals' lives based on interviews, conversations, self-stories, and personal experience stories (see Denzin 2001b:61). A personal history may focus on the life or biography of a single person, group, or institution. A personal history embeds self-stories and personal experience stories within a larger narrative structure—that is, the story of a life. Often, one can glean the full meaning of a personal experience story or self-story only by locating the story in the biography of the speaker.

A *testimonio* is a first-person text with political content, told by a narrator who is the protagonist or a witness to the events reported upon. Testimonios report on torture, imprisonment, social upheaval, colonization processes, and other struggles for survival. These works are intended to produce change while providing records of social injustices. In so doing, they reinforce the desire for solidarity (Beverley 2000:555). Their truth is contained in the telling of the events recorded by their narrators (Beverley 2000:556).

The forms of personal performance narrative described above are also forms of storytelling. They are didactic. They entertain, instruct, and maintain and reproduce institutions and discourses through and across generations. During the moment of performance, they invoke style and character by interweaving aesthetics, politics, and history (Langellier 1998:207).

Personal performance narratives are studied as situated performance practices, as performance events, as sites where performativity and performance interact (Langellier 1998:208). The performance, the telling of the story, is the event. Narrators and audience members as coperformers are constituted in and through the rituals of performativity, in the spaces, words, and lines of the stories as they are told—that is, performed (Langellier 1998:208). As Alexander (2000) puts it, an "affirmative aesthetic of unification" operates, connecting the "audience's subjective involvement . . . with . . . the performance" (p. 103). In this aesthetic transaction, coperformers construct a shared emotional experience. The performance enlivens, enhances, and represents experience.

Performativity locates experience, its narratives and performances, within larger networks of discourse and power (Langellier 1998:208). Thus the personal performance narrative politicizes the personal.

As Gentile (1998) has noted, postmodern performance artists (and ethnographers) often compose personal narrative texts "for performance that later are published as poetry [or] fiction, blurring the boundary between 'literature' [ethnography] and 'performance script'" (p. 72). Performed literature/ethnography, often referred to as *spoken-word performance*, allows audience members to become active players in the staging and interpretation of a narrative and the experiences it represents. Mienczakowski's (2001) call for ethnodrama extends this impulse to give the ethnographic text back to readers and "informants in the recognition that we are co-performers in each other's lives" (p. 468).

A Postmodern Performance Aesthetic

A postmodern performance aesthetic privileges a pragmatic, or commonsense, approach to texts, performers, and performances (see McCall 2000:430; Broadhurst 1999:22–25; Mamet 1997) while drawing upon more traditional presentational and representational aesthetics (Donmoyer and Yennie-Donmoyer 1995; McCall 2000:430; see also Broadhurst 1999:22–25).[36] Pragmatic theater, or commonsense theater—my name for playwright David Mamet's (1997) performance aesthetic—is action based. Mamet asserts that "to act means to perform an action, to do something" (p. 72). For Mamet, the words in a play do not carry the meaning. Action carries meaning; words are set and unchanging. Mamet asks the actor to "accept the words as is, and speak them simply and clearly in an attempt to get what you want from another actor" (p. 63). He asserts: "It is the job of the actor to show up, and use the lines and his or her will and common sense, to attempt to achieve a goal similar to that of the protagonist. And that is the end of the actor's job" (p. 12; quoted in McCall 2000:430).

Mamet's action-based approach challenges representational theater, the theater of illusion. Modernist theater enacts the logic of naturalistic realism by creating onstage verisimilitude.[37] Mamet's perspective extends presentational, postmodern theater, in which there is little pretense of illusion.[38] Performers in such theater act as though they are reading from scripts. They may "assume a variety of roles ... interact with imaginary characters, and [often] manipulate non-existent or partial props" (Donmoyer and Yennie-Donmoyer 1995:427). Mamet's action-based aesthetic creates the space for a politics of resistance. This space allows audience members to separate their personal and political reactions to a performance from the performance event.[39]

My students and I use a version of Mamet's model at the University of Illinois. Influenced by Mienczakowski's ethnodrama framework and Mamet's theory of acting, students write and coperform personal performance narratives. These performances enact a pedagogy of resistance. In their performances, the students make little attempt to adhere to a representational or presentational performance aesthetic. Meaning is lodged in performativity, in the action involved in speaking the words. Each performance event becomes an occasion for the imagination of a world where things can be different, a radical utopian space where a politics of hope can be experienced.

The students' narratives are based on epiphanic moments in the writers' lives, moments that connect self-awareness with critical racial consciousness. A given narrative may take one of several forms: It may be poetry, a short story, a memoir, a play, or a performance text made from transcriptions of interviews (see Smith 1993, 1994). The performance may take one of several forms as well; it may be an improvisational ethnodrama (see Mienczakowski 2001), a rehearsed reading, or an improvised reading in which a stage director (the author) hands parts of the script to members of the audience, who then read on cue.[40]

Under this postmodern performance aesthetic, the traditional audience disappears. The postmodern audience is both an interactive structure and an interpretive vehicle. Audience members are citizens from the local community, performers who bring their own interpretive frameworks to a performance event. As existential collaborators, they are co-constructed by the event, by an aesthetic of affirmation (see Gingrich-Philbrook 2000:ix; Alexander 2000:102). The performance event "interrogates specific political and social processes" (Madison 1998:281). A cultural politics is at work. This politics enacts a performance of possibilities, a performance that directs citizens down a path of collective action and social change (Madison 1998:281). Thus postmodern audience members are neither voyeurs nor spectators; they are not passive recipients of a performance event. Rather, audience members are participants in a dialogic performance event, an event that is emancipatory and pedagogical (Garoian 1999:52). They engage in a spoken-word performance and become part of the performance event. As voices build upon one another, choruslike, all participants experience a new performance narrative, one that is now part of the original text.

So conceptualized, audience members function in a variety of different ways: as audience to each other's performance, as witnesses to the experiences reported upon in the story, as therapists and emotional supporters of the storyteller, as cultural critics commenting on the events that produced the story, and as narrative analysts of the systems of discourse embedded in the narrative (Langellier 1998:210). In these ways, performers are both inside the performance and observers of it.

Thus in postmodern autoethnographic theater there are only writers and performers, cultural teachers pedagogically staging and performing narratives drawn from their own and other persons' life experiences. I return now to the mystory and the study and performance of those cultural moments that leave indelible marks on people, their bodies, and their biographies.

❖ THE MYSTORY TEXT AND ITS PERFORMANCE

A critical, performative cultural studies attempts to put in place subversive performance texts that carry forward Trinh's (1991:203–4) agenda for the retelling of stories that the sciences of the human disciplines have reduced to fiction or minor literature, or marginalized, stigmatized, and paternalized as politically correct multicultural performances.[41] These works interrogate the realities they represent, locate the tellers' stories in the histories presented, make the audience members responsible for their own interpretations, foreground difference rather than conflict, oppose dichotomies, and use multiple voices in their tellings.

These texts invoke and then criticize standard social science methods of research; for example, some involve parodies of the interview as a tool for gathering objective data about the world of the other. Some texts mock the scientific journal article as a vehicle for presenting knowledge about the world; some criticize ethnographers for their so-called objective methods of truth seeking. These texts undermine the concept of a unified subject.

The writer of a mystory seeks a form of writing and performing that opens new ways of presenting the plural self in its multiple situations. The goal is to create a text that will produce a sudden awakening on the part of the viewer, who, as audience member, is also a performer. This means that the performed text will be ever changing. It will constantly work against those textual strategies (such as verbatim transcriptions) that would allow readers and listeners to assimilate the performance as a realist text. These are the aesthetic and epistemological features that partially define a postmodern performance sublime.

Mystory as Montage

The mystory is simultaneously a personal mythology, a public story, a personal narrative, and a performance that critiques. It is an inter-active, dramatic performance. It is participatory theater, a version of one of Brecht's learning plays (Ulmer 1989:210); it is presentational, not representational, theater (Donmoyer and Yennie-Donmoyer 1995). A mystory performance is a performance, not a text-centered interpretive event; that is, the emphasis is on performance and improvisation, not on the reading of a text.

The mystory is a montage text, cinematic and multimedia in shape, filled with sounds, music, poetry, and images taken from the writer's personal history. This personal narrative is grafted onto discourses from popular culture. It locates itself against the specialized knowledges that circulate in the larger society. The audience coperforms the text, and the writer, as narrator, functions as guide, commentator, and coperformer.

Following is an excerpt from a mystory, Hugo Campuzano's per-formance narrative "In the Name of Tradition" (2001):

Speaker One: In the name of tradition, how much tradition should I follow? . . . I have been in this country for 24 years. I have grown up watching the Cosby show, wearing Payless shoes. . . . I have lived with my Mexican family in a Mexican Community. I have grown up eating tortillas, believing in La Virgen de Guadalupe.

Speaker Two: Don't get me wrong I love being Mexican. . . . But I have to tell you, it is tough being Mexican. Take mar-riage for example. My mom has told me . . . that when I get married, I should go to Mexico and find myself a nice Mexican girl. . . . she means I should go to Mexico . . . and find a nice quiet girl who knows how to cook and clean. . . . how do I tell my mom I do not want someone like her?

Speaker Three: *Must tradition go on in the name of tradition?*

Speaker Four: My mom's insistence that I marry a nice Mexican girl also makes me think about my sisters. Would she want my sisters to be nice Mexican girls? They have certainly been in training all their lives. . . . I remember a conversation I had a few years back with my siblings. We were talking about marriage and future families in this all-night conversation, everything that was coming out of our mouths was how we were not going to follow in our parents' footsteps. My brother and I were saying we were not going to be like our father, an authoritarian machista who uses the name of tradition to do things the way he wants to. My sisters were saying that they were not going be like our mother, a passive woman who in the name of keeping the family together . . . participated in her own silencing. I guess there's just no room for tradition in my family.

Speaker Five: *Must tradition go on in the name of tradition?*

By splitting his voice into five speaking parts, Campuzano moves his narrative through a complex space. There are improvised elements in the performance. Each speaker brings a gendered presence and personal style of speaking to the text. At the same time, every person in the room, speaker or listener, brings to this text a set of personal memories involving family, tradition, marriage, mothers, fathers, daughters, and sons. Campuzano's mystory get tangled up in other people's lives, unsettling and troubling the deep cultural narratives and myths surrounding duty, tradition, and family.

The mystory performance event does not take place on a stage per se; the invisible "fourth wall" that usually separates performers and audience does not exist, because all parties to the performance are also performers. The script puts into words the world of experiences, actions, and words that are, could be, and will be spoken. The script, like Campuzano's, brings this world and its ethnodramas alive, reports on it in some fashion, and then criticizes the structures of power that operate therein. Campuzano asks, "Must tradition go on in the name of tradition?"

The mystory text delineates specific characters who are caught up in some dramatic conflict that moves to some degree of resolution by the end of the narrative. Simplistic characterizations based on traditional oppositions (such as male/female) are avoided; difference, not conflict, is privileged (Trinh 1991:188). A mystory can include as many characters as there are participants available to read the parts. A given participant can read all the words of one character or the words of different characters. Every performance event is different, with different participants, different lines, and different meanings and interpretations, yet in every instance a story is told and performed, a story with political consequences, a story that shows how the world can be changed.

Of course, the mystory text is not easily constructed. Writing a mystory involves the hard interpretive work of editing personal, biographical reality (McCall and Becker 1990:118; Jackson 1993:26). In editing his or her biographical experience, an individual often will dramatically reinterpret what he or she has felt and lived in moments of crisis and pain. What a person will edit is determined by what he or she remembers and has collected or written down, perhaps in notes to the self—the "*Rashomon* effect" turned inside out. From the several layers and versions of the biographical field text, the writer aims to tell a story with some degree of dramatic power. Editing, or crafting, the text involves many decisions, such as what words to put in the mouths of which characters, who the characters will be, how many readers there will be. The focus is always on showing rather than telling. Minimal interpretation is favored; less is more.

The mystory text begins with the moments that define the crisis in question, a turning point in the person's life. Ulmer (1989) suggests the following starting point: "Write a mystory bringing into relation your experience with three levels of discourse—personal (autobiography), popular (community stories, oral history or popular culture), [and] expert (disciplines of knowledge). In each case use the punctum or sting of memory to locate items significant to you" (p. 209; see also Ulmer 1989:xii, 139). The sting of memory locates the moment, the beginning. Once located, this moment is dramatically described, fashioned into a text to be performed. This moment is then surrounded by those cultural representations and voices that define the experience in question. These representations are contested, challenged.

Mystories, Liminality, and Utopia

Focusing on epiphanies and liminal moments of experience, the writer imposes a narrative framework on the text. This framework shapes how the writer's experience will be represented, using the devices of plot, setting, characters (protagonists and antagonists), characterization, temporality, and dialogue; the emphasis is on showing, not telling. The narration moves through the four-stage dramatic cycle of breach, crisis, redress, and reintegration or schism. Following Victor Turner's model, this narrative model stresses conflict, tension, crisis, and the resolution of crisis.

Jameson (1990) reminds us that works of popular culture are always already ideological and utopian. Shaped by a dialectic of anxiety and hope, such works revive and manipulate fears and anxieties about the social order. Beginning with a fear, problem, or crisis, these works move characters and audiences through the familiar three-stage dramatic model of conflict, crisis, and resolution. In this way they offer kernels of utopian hope. They show how these anxieties and fears can be satisfactorily addressed by the existing social order (Jameson 1990:30). Hence the audience is lulled into believing that the problems of the social have in fact been successfully resolved.

The mystory occupies a similar ideological space, except it functions as critique. The mystory is also ideological and utopian; it begins from a progressive political position that stresses the politics of hope. The mystory uses the methods of drama and personal narrative to present its critique and utopian vision. It presumes that the social order has to change if problems are to be resolved successfully in the long run. If the status quo is maintained—if only actors change, and not the social order—then the systemic processes producing the problem remain in place.

Troy Anthony LaRaviere (2001) begins his mystory this way:[42]

> *My first memory is my mother's first memory of me.*
>
>> *'She's told me this story so many times that I feel like I'm telling the story from my own memory. As if I remember being in the delivery room . . .*
>
> "Boy I remember that labor I had with you!
>
> Lord Jesus! You was the worst of all of 'em."
>
> "You came out weighing ten pounds and five ounces."

"And once you came out, the doctors and the nurses just

looked at you like they was in shock. Then they kept calling

other doctors in to come and look at you."

"But they wouldn't let me see you. My legs was propped up with

sheet in the way. So I couldn't see nothin'" . . .

Doctor: "We never seen anything like this!"

"And they just kept calling more doctors in, and all the doctors

kept saying the same thing. . . . But they still wouldn't let me see you.

Finally I just started yelling, 'let me see my child. What's wrong with my baby?!'"

"The doctor finally looked at me and said 'Ma'am, this is the cleanest baby

I've ever seen.' They gave you to me and you didn't have fluid or blood on you.

Not one drop."

perhaps all the blood was used up from hundreds of years of doing nothing

but bleeding.

When the doctor cut the umbilical cord, cutting me off from the source of all

that was life-giving; my mother.

How different was that cut from the cut his great, great, great, great, great-

grandfathers made when they cut us off from our African mother culture and all in it that was life-giving to us. . . . All that was life-giving to me?

> *But it wasn't at my birth that the cord was torn*
>
> *it was severed from me long before I was born . . .*
>
> I remember the work I must do to insure my name is called.

Remembering his birth, as told to him by his mother, LaRaviere connects this birth memory to the struggles of all African Americans to maintain a living connection to family and a mother culture. Ending on a utopian note, he bitterly criticizes the larger culture that has cut African Americans off from their mother culture.

In another mystory, Ruoyun Bai (2001) remembers the stories her grandmother told her:

> Last summer I returned to China under the pretext of a research project and found myself listening to Grandma tell her stories most of the time. The picture stays in my mind of Grandma rocking in her bamboo chair, waving her self-made paper fan, emphatically at times, and talking in her naturally loud voice. Grandma does not have a big repertoire so she would soon end up sharing with me the same stories again and again, adding, changing and skipping details casually.
>
> Grandma has two "enemies" in her life—Grandpa and Father. I've never seen Grandpa, but I know he was "evil"—evil, because he spent all the money Grandma earned, he beat her, and he wanted Mother to drop out of middle school. Grandma opposes herself against Father because he throws out her collections of empty bottles . . . and complains that she's turned his home into a dumping ground. . . . When I was still a high school girl, I joined my father in his crackdowns. . . . I believed that Father was right—Grandma was crude and unwomanly. . . .
>
> But Grandma has one treasure—her stories. Nobody can take them from her. I would complain, "Grandma, you have told this a thousand times!" and she would smile bashfully. . . . Grandma's stories have a touch of valor, hilarity and humor. . . .
>
> Grandma . . . was never modest. She boasts of her appetite, her only daughter, and her grandchildren. . . . Going over Grandma's stories, I realize how diagonally opposite she has been to the concept of a "good" woman. A good woman does not fight with

men, and a good mother-in-law doesn't fight with the son, but Grandma does both, with her naturally loud voice. . . . I don't have a say in whether or not Grandma will go to heaven after death, but I know that at the age of 88, she enjoys excellent health, a big heart and her stories. God bless you, Grandma.

In the performance of these memories and stories, Bai finds support for a new conception of a "good" woman. She locates her experiences and struggles within the stories told by her grandmother. Following Trinh (1989b:141), Bai seeks to recover her grandmother's stories. In so doing, she folds her story into her grandmother's, thereby creating a new story that carries deep meaning for herself and for others.[43]

Life in the United States After September 11, 2001

After the terrorist attacks on the World Trade Center and the Pentagon on September 11, 2001, a number of interpretive social scientists wrote about the events and the meanings of the events in their lives. Many of these personal narratives could be performed within the mystory format.

Michelle Fine's (2002) narrative text about the aftermath of the September 11 attacks, titled "The Mourning After," opens thus:

12. September

You can tell who's dead or missing by their smiles. Their photos dot the subways, ferries, trains and Port Authority Terminal, shockingly alive with joy, comfort and pleasure. They died before they could know what we now know. The not-dead travel on subways and trains filled with hollow eyes; no smiles; shoulders down. Five thousand dead and still counting, and that's without the undocumented workers whose families can't tell, the homeless men and women whose families don't know.

Each evening, millions of nightmares startle and awaken, alone and dark, throughout the metropolitan area.

The air in the City chokes with smoke, flesh, fear, memories, clouds and creeping nationalism. . . . Now a flood of flags, talk of God, military and patriotism chase us all. (P. 137)

Two days later, Fine writes:

The Path train stopped. In a tunnel. No apparent reason. I couldn't breath. Anxiety. . . . Is this an ok way to die? . . .

Lives and politics; grief and analysis. Those of us in New York seem to be having trouble writing. . . . U.S. politics then and now, racial profiling and anxious worries about what's coming next. . . . Death, ghosts, orphans, analyses of U.S. imperialism, Middle East politics, and the terrors of terrorism sit in the same room.

How do you write the meaning of the present when you have never before experienced the nightmares and terror that define the present? Laurel Richardson (2002b) writes:

September 11, 2001:

When I hear of the airplanes and the towers, my first thoughts are—the children. . . .What will the children be told? . . .

And then I see that the children are being told, as the adults are, through television cameras and media voices. The children are seeing the airplane and the second tower, and the airplane/tower, airplane/tower over and over until it's All Fall Down. And All Fall Down again and again.

I call my children. I call my stepchildren. I call my grand-children. . . . My heart breaks for the children whose lives are broken. . . . What can I say? What can anyone say? My email Listservs are repositories for quick fixes, ideological purity. . . . I can't join the discussion. I refuse to intellectualize, analyze, or academize. I don't have any answers. . . .

I call my grandson's mother to see how Akiva is doing. She tells me that he was afraid an airplane would hit his school. . . . On Rosh Hashanah the rabbi said "Choose Life." I meditate on our small world. I pray. I write this piece. (P. 25)

In a piece titled "Grief in an Appalachian Register," Yvonna S. Lincoln (2002) speaks for those for whom the expression of grief does not come easily:

For two weeks now, we have watched the staggering outpouring of grief, shock and horror as a nation struggles to come to terms with the attacks on the World Trade Center towers and the Pentagon. . . .

And I, too, have sat numb with shock, glued to the television screen, struggling with the incomprehensibility of these acts, overwhelmed by the bewildering world view which could have led people to commit such atrocities. But I have been numb for another reason, and it will be important to see my reasons as another part of the phenomenon which has struck so deeply at the heart and soul of the United States. I sat numb because my reactions to grief are always usually private. They are always delayed. . . .

My people—my family (of English and Dutch and Scottish stock) were born and raised, as were their parents before them, in the southern Appalachian mountains. . . . Mountain people . . . keep their emotions to themselves, especially those of a most private nature. . . . The end result, I have come to realize, is a human being who lives with his or her grief for all their days. The future, like tears, never comes. (Pp. 146–48)

Turning to Annie Dillard, I seek my own meaning in these events (Denzin 2002e). Dillard (1974) says that divinity is not playful, that the universe was not made in jest, but in "solemn incomprehensible earnest. By a power that is unfathomably secret, and holy and fleet" (p. 270), and violent. I choose to believe this.

In "The Peace of Wild Things," Wendell Berry (1998:30) says that when

Despair for the world grows in me . . .

I go and lie down where the wood drake

rests in his beauty on the water, and the great heron feeds.

I come into the peace of wild things . . .

For a time I rest in the grace of the world, and am free.

I follow Berry's advice.

Noon, September 15: Mattis Lake, Champaign, Illinois: Fishing pole in hand, I parked and walked over a small hill to Mattis Lake, which is near my home. The lake is not large. It is surrounded by walking paths and small picnic areas. An apartment complex hovers in the distance. Reeds, rushes, and willows grow in the corners of the lake and along its banks. Two tall maples shade the water where I stop. Rocks jut out into the water. Bull rushes sway in the wind. Grasshoppers sun themselves on blades of green grass. The noon sun dances off the water. Waves ripple as the wind comes over the hill. I bait my hook with an old earthworm and cast my line into the water. Just as my red-and-white bobber settles on the surface, a tall sand crane makes a delicate landing on the grassy shoreline. As if on stilts, this elegantly awkward bird walks in an easterly direction, head darting back and forth, up and down, looking for I know not what.

My line is tugged sharply; I jerk my rod upward. A large bass jumps in the air. It jerks its head and then dives down into deeper water. I set the hook and begin to reel in the line. The bass comes back to the surface, drawing near to the shore. I reach town and touch the fish, it must be over 12 inches long and weighs over 2 pounds. I cradle the fish in my palm. Holding it in the water, I reach over with my other hand and remove the tiny hook from its jaw. I then put the fish back in the water, and with a violent twist of its body, it disappears into the depths.

As I stand to catch my breath, the sand crane, which has been watching me, flies off in haste, and on the distant shore ducks glide quietly into the hidden waters beneath a regal oak tree.

Each of the mystory texts excerpted above attempts, in its own way, to function as a form of critical pedagogy. Each narrative moves back and forth between private troubles and public discourse, self and other. Each text troubles race, ethnicity, popular culture, cultural politics, the mass media, religion, global world order, terror, fear, life, and death. Each text takes the truth of fiction as a starting point for social criticism, a cultural politics that defines itself through a performative ethnography of hope and possibility (Giroux and McLaren 1989:xxxv).

As William Kittredge (1987) has observed, in the United States today,

we are struggling to revise our dominant mythology, and to find a new story to inhabit. Laws control our lives, they are designed to preserve a model of society based on values learned from mythology. Only after reimagining our myths can we coherently remodel our laws, and hope to keep our society in a realistic relationship to what is actual. (P. 87)

The writers of these mystories are struggling to revise the dominant myths that organize daily life in the many small worlds that proliferate and splinter under the nightmares of late capitalism. Each writer seeks a new model of society, a new set of traditions, new stories that will bring the present in line with utopian dreams of liberation, freedom, and justice, life without terror.

❖ ETHICS FOR A PERFORMATIVE, PEDAGOGICAL CULTURAL STUDIES

Every time a text is written and performed, a performance ethics is enacted. As Stucky (1993:176) argues, ethnographers as writers and performers need to take responsibility for their interpretations of the life experiences of others. These interpretations are shaped by a variety of factors, including what the ethnographer selects to perform, whose point of view the ethnographer represents, what the ethnographer reveals about the other in the performance, and the ranges of actions, meanings, and intentions the ethnographer attributes to other individuals (Stucky 1993:176–77).

Blew (1999) says that students in her writing classes often ask, "What can you decently write about other people? Whose permission do you have to ask? What can you decently reveal about yourself?" (p. 7). Blew's answer is blunt: "I can speak only for myself. I own my past and my present. Only I can decide whether or how to write about it" (p. 7). Once you have written about the past, it is forever changed; you will "never remember it in quite the same way" (p. 7).

Of course, if I write about my past, that involves writing about others, those who shared and shaped my past—my mother, my father, my grandparents. Do I have permission to write about the dead? Blew hesitates on this point, noting, appropriately, "I feel an uneasy balance between writing about the dead as their lives 'really' were and writing about them as a projection of my own experiences" (p. 6). I am comfortable treating the dead as projections of my own experiences, as they impinged on my life. I understand, however, that they would tell their stories differently, that the emotional truths I seek would not be the truths they would seek. I restrict myself to what I know happened, concrete events, and details. I seek a liminal writing space that is fluid and murky, but, like Blew, when "I speculate, I say so" (p. 7).

Writers may at times reassess how they have written in the past about the dead and their relationships with them. In "Letter, Much Too Late" Wallace Stegner ([1989] 1992a) writes to his mother:

Mom, listen,
In three months I will be 80 years old, thirty years older than you were when you died. . . .
In the more than fifty years that I have been writing books and stories, I have tried several times to do you justice, and have never been satisfied with what I did. The character who represented you in *The Big Rock Candy Mountain* and *Recapitulation*, two novels of a semiautobiographical kind, is a sort of passive victim. I am afraid I let your selfish and violent husband, my father, steal the scene from you and push you into the background in the novels as he did in life. Somehow I should have been able to say how strong and resilient you were, what a patient and abiding and bonding force, the softness that proved in the long run stronger than what it seemed to yield to. (Pp. 22–24)

And so Stegner attempts to set the record straight by telling another story about his mother (and father).

There is always a tension between an ethnographic writer-performer's intentions and his or her ability to recognize and understand what defines other individuals' worlds. In every instance, the researcher must ask and answer the question raised by Prattis (1985): "Just what are we doing in other people's culture?" (p. 277). This question (and its answer) is doubly problematic in performance work. As Conquergood (1985:2) observes, the performer is unable to maintain aesthetic distance from the experiences being performed and interpreted. Empathic performances intensify the participatory nature of fieldwork. They challenge attempts to create intellectual or epistemological barriers that would separate the writer from those he or she is studying. Performances do not "proceed in ideological innocence and axiological purity" (p. 2).

As a writer and a performer of mystories, I must attempt to avoid four particular ethical pitfalls, morally problematic stances toward the representation of others' experiences. Conquergood (1985) labels these four pitfalls "the Custodian's Rip-Off," "the Enthusiast's Infatuation," "the Curator's Exhibitionism," and "the Skeptic's Cop-Out" (p. 4).

Cultural custodians, or cultural imperialists, ransack their own biographical pasts looking for good texts to perform and then perform them for profit, often denigrating family members or cultural groups who regard as sacred the experiences they discuss. The enthusiast, or superficial, writer (and performer) fails to become deeply involved in the cultural setting that he or she reperforms. As Conquergood (1985:6) notes, this trivializes the other because the writer neither contextualizes nor well understands the experiences of the other. To modify Conquergood's definition of the skeptic this writer values detachment and a cynical viewpoint. He or she may ridicule or criticize the other because of past personal experiences, as Stegner did with his father and mother. Such a writer may also take the position that only he or she can talk about this other, because only the writer really knows that person. As Conquergood puts it, this position refuses to face up to the "ethical tensions and moral ambiguities of performing culturally sensitive materials" (p. 8). Finally, the curator, or sensationalist, like the custodian, is a performer who sensationalizes the cultural characteristics that supposedly define the world of the other. He or she stages performances for the voyeur's gaze, perhaps telling stories about an abusive, hurtful other. This is "the Wild Kingdom approach to performance that grows out of a fascination with the exotic, primitive, culturally remote . . . the Noble Savage" (p. 7).

These four stances make problematic the question, How far into the other's world can the performer and the audience go? Of course, one person can never know the mind of another person; we know others only by their performances. We can know only our own minds, and sometimes we don't know those very well.

This means that the writer-performer must always respect the differences between him- or herself and the other that define the other's world. There is no null point in the moral universe (Conquergood 1985:8–9). The other always exists, as Trinh would argue, in the spaces on each side of the hyphen (Conquergood 1985:9). The performance text can only ever be dialogic, a text that does not speak about or for the other, but rather "speaks to and with" the other (Conquergood 1985:10). It is a text that reengages the past and brings it alive in the present. The dialogic text attempts to keep the dialogue, the conversation, among text, the past, the present, performer, and audience ongoing and open-ended (Conquergood 1985:9). This text does more than invoke empathy; it interrogates, criticizes, and empowers. This is dialogic criticism. The dialogic performance is the means for "honest intercultural understanding" (Conquergood 1985:10).

If this understanding is to be created, several elements need to be present. Scholars must have the energy, imagination, courage, and commitment to create these texts (see Conquergood 1985:10). Audiences must be drawn to the sites where these performances take place, and they must be willing to suspend normal aesthetic frameworks so that coparticipatory performances can be produced. In these sites, shared emotional experiences are created, and in these moments of sharing, critical cultural awareness is awakened.

The coperformed cultural studies text aims to enact the feminist, communitarian moral ethic. As I have noted in Chapter 1, this ethic presumes a dialogic view of the self and its performances. It seeks narratives that ennoble human experience, performances that facilitate civic transformations in the public and private spheres. This ethic ratifies the dignities of the self and honors personal struggle. It understands cultural criticism to be a form of empowerment that begins in that ethical moment when individuals are led into the troubling spaces occupied by others. In the moment of coperformance, lives are joined and struggle begins anew.

❖ CONCLUSION

Of course, there are more ways to "do" a text than simply to read it to an audience. A text can be performed in a straightforward way—for example, the writer might read a poem aloud—or a reading may be supplemented by other devices. An author might use slides or photographs, or show a film, or use other audiovisual aids; he or she might bring in music or a sound track, or lip-synch words set to a musical text. An author might even bring the audience into the performance—setting up a sing-along, handing out scripts, giving audience members speaking parts—to make a communal experience out of the scholarly text. Within the performance, the author can assume multiple places—be the ethnographer, the subject in the field, the audience member, a representative from the scholarly community who asks, "What is going on here?"

In this chapter I have attempted to answer that question. What is going on here is something new, a new language of performance. Ethnography has crossed the liminal space that separates the scholarly text from its performance. The text is now given back to those to whom it has always belonged, the readers, the others, who find in these texts parts of themselves, parts of others just like them. We are all coperformers in our own and others' lives. This is what the performance text does.

3

The Cinematic
Society and
the Reflexive Interview

Think of how much we learn about contemporary life by way of interviews. Larry King introduces us to presidents and power brokers. Barbara Walters plumbs the emotional depths of stars and celebrities. Oprah . . . and Geraldo invite the ordinary, tortured and bizarre to "spill their guts" to millions of home viewers.

—James A. Holstein and Jaber F. Gubrium,
The Active Interview, 1995

We inhabit a secondhand world, one already mediated by cinema, television, and other apparatuses of the postmodern society.[14] In this world, culture is driven less and less by the technological innovation of the written word, and more and more by the interactive conventions of dramaturgy, performance, and the media. We have no direct access to this world; we only experience and study its representations. A reflexive sociology studies society as a dramaturgical production. The reflexive interview is a central component of this interpretive project.

In this chapter and the next, I examine the nexus of the cinematic society and the interview society. I show how postmodern society has become an interview society, how our very subjectivity "comes to us in the form of stories elicited through interviewing" (Holstein and Gubrium 2000:129; see also Atkinson and Silverman 1997). The interview, whether conducted by social researchers, mass-media reporters, television journalists, therapists, or counselors, is now a ubiquitous method of self-construction (Holstein and Gubrium 2000:129).

I will discuss the concept of the active, dialogic interview, anchoring this complex formation in the postmodern, cinematic society (Holstein and Gubrium 1995; Gubrium and Holstein 1997; Jackson 1998; Denzin 1995a, 1995b, 1997; Scheurich 1995). The reflexive interview is simultaneously a site for conversation, a discursive method, and a communicative format that produces knowledge about the self and its place in the cinematic society—the society that knows itself through the reflective gaze of the cinematic apparatus. A cinematic sociology requires a concept of the reflexive interview.

A single two-part question organizes my argument: First, how does the postmodern, cinematic world mediate the ways in which we represent ourselves to ourselves? And second, what is the place of the interview-interviewer relationship in this production process? I begin the discussion by outlining the central features of the postmodern, cinematic-interview society. I then show how the interview and the interviewer, as a voyeur, are basic features of this society. I thicken this argument by demonstrating how popular media representations shape and define situated cultural identities. I show how these representations become anchor points for the postmodern self—that is, how they occupy a central place in the background of our cultural consciousness. They mediate structures of meaning in the cinematic-interview society. A circular model of interpretation is thus created. Interviews, interviewers, and storytellers are defined in terms of these dominant cultural images and understandings. Thus the cinematic society structures the interview society and vice versa. I conclude with a series of epistemological observations on the significance of the relationship between the cinematic society and the reflexive interview (see also Mishler 1986; Heyl 2001; Burawoy 1998; Bourdieu 1996).

❖ THE POSTMODERN, CINEMATIC SOCIETY

Members of the postmodern society know themselves through the reflected images and narratives of cinema and television. On this, Altheide (1995) observes, "Culture is not only mediated through mass media . . . culture in both form and content is constituted and embodied by the mass media" (p. 59). The postmodern landscape is distinguished, as Gottschalk (2000) argues, by "its constant saturation by multiple electronic screens which simulate emotions, interactions, events, desires. . . . From TV screens to computer terminals, from surveillance cameras to cell phones, we increasingly experience everyday life, reality . . . via technologies of spectacle, simulation and 'telepresence'" (p. 23).

Consider the following exchange between ESPN sports journalist Sal Paolantonio and Kurt Warner, quarterback of the St. Louis Rams, who was named Most Valuable Player in the 2000 Super Bowl:

Sal: There's a minute and 54 seconds left in the game. The Titans have just tied the score. Now look, let me show you your 73-yard winning pass to Isaac Bruce. Kurt, what were you thinking when Isaac caught that pass?

Kurt: [Looks up at replay] We'd called the same play earlier and Isaac was open. So we thought it would work. It was a go route. We thought we could get a big one right off the bat. I just thought it was meant to be, it was meant to work.

Sal: This has been a terrific year for you. Five years ago you were sacking groceries in the IGA. Two years ago you were playing arena football in Cedar Rapids, Iowa. This is better than a Hollywood script. Tell me how you feel about what has happened to you this year?

Kurt: I don't think of it as a Hollywood story. It's my life. I take it one day at a time.

Sal: It has not been easy, has it?

Kurt: I was getting to the point of thinking how much longer am I going to have before people say he is too old to give him an opportunity. It has been tough for us until this last year. Even when I was playing arena football we did all right, but a lot of tough decisions . . . . When I first started dating my wife, she was on food stamps, and I was in between jobs. That is why I ended up stocking shelves; I had to do something at nights so I could work out and keep my chances in football. A lot of things like that have helped keep things in perspective, even though we are not making a million dollars, we are very fortunate to be where we are at, in this position, and don't look beyond that, don't take anything for granted.

Sal: Thanks Kurt. Is there anything else you want to say?

Kurt: I'm truly blessed. If I can be a source of hope to anybody, I'm happy to be a part of it. The good lord has blessed me. I am on a mission. He has called me to do this. I can only share my testimony with others. Thank you Jesus. (*SportsCenter*, ESPN, January 31, 2000; see also Vecsey 2000)

Kurt's self-narrative is grafted onto the replay of the winning touchdown pass. Indeed, this Super Bowl victory symbolizes the larger-than-life-triumph that he has experienced over the course of the preceding 5 years. Sal elicits this self-story by asking Kurt how he feels about his award-winning year, comparing it to a Hollywood script. Kurt complies by giving him a socially acceptable answer; indeed, Sal's questions establish Kurt's right to give this extended account of his life and what it means (see also Holstein and Gubrium 2000:129). The viewer shares in this experience vicariously.[45]

The ingredients of the postmodern self are modeled in the media. The postmodern self has become a sign of itself, a double dramaturgical reflection anchored in media representations on one side and everyday life on the other. These cultural identities are filtered through the individual's personal troubles and emotional experiences in interactions with everyday life. These existential troubles connect back to the dominant cultural themes of the postmodern era. The electronic media and the new information technologies turn everyday life into a theatrical spectacle where the dramas that surround the decisive performances of existential crises are enacted. This creates a new existential "videocy," a language of crisis coded in electronic, media terms.

The media structure these crises and their meanings. A 38-year-old male alcoholic is standing outside the door to a room where Alcoholics Anonymous (A.A.) meetings are held. He asks:

How do I get into one of those A.A. meetings? What do I say? I
seen them in the movies. That Michael Keaton in *Clean and Sober*.
He went to one of them. He just stood up and said he was an alcoholic. Do I have to do that? I ain't even sure I am one, but I drank
a fifth of Black Jack last night and I started up agin this mornin'.
I'm scared. (Quoted in Denzin 1995b:260)

This is a postmodern story waiting to be heard, already partially told
through the figure of Michael Keaton, himself an actor, playing a
fictional character (Daryl Poynter) who goes to a fictional A.A. meeting
in a Hollywood film. Texts within texts, movies, everyday life, a man
down on his luck, A.A., a door into a room where meetings are held,
anxiety, fear. The everyday existential world connects to the cinematic
apparatus, and our drunk on the street hopes to begin a story that will
have a happy ending, like Michael Keaton's.

❖ THE BIRTH OF CINEMATIC SURVEILLANCE

In the space of the period from 1900 to 1930, cinema became an integral
part of American society. Going to the movies became a weekly pastime for millions of Americans. Motion pictures became a national
institution. Hollywood stars became personal idols, fan clubs were
formed, and movie theaters, with their lighted marquees, were a
prominent part of virtually every American community.

The cinematic, surveillance society soon became a disciplinary
structure filled with subjects (voyeurs) who obsessively looked and
gazed at one another, as they became, at the same time, obsessive listeners, eavesdroppers, persons whose voices and telephone lines could
be tapped, voices that could be dubbed, new versions of the spoken
and seen self. A new social type was created: the voyeur, or Peeping
Tom, who would, in various guises (ethnographer, social scientist,
detective, psychoanalyst, crime reporter, investigative journalist, innocent bystander, sexual pervert), elevate the concepts of looking and
listening to new levels.

With the advent of color and sound in film in the mid-1920s, there
was a drive toward cinematic realism. This impulse to create a level of
realism that mapped everyday life complemented the rise of naturalistic realism in the American novel and the emergence of hard-nosed
journalistic reporting by the major American newspapers and radio

(and later TV) networks (Denzin 1997:21–22). During the same period, an ethnographic, psychoanalytic, and life history approach was taking hold in the social sciences and in society at large. Like journalists, sociologists, market researchers, and survey researchers were learning how to use the interview to gather and report on the facts of social life (Fontana and Frey 1994:362, 2000; Denzin 1997:129).

Robert E. Park (1950), a founder of the Chicago school of ethnographic research (Vidich and Lyman 1994:32–33), clarifies the relationships among journalism, social science, and the use of the interview:

> After leaving college, I got a job as a reporter. . . . I wrote about all sorts of things. . . .
>
> My interest in the newspaper had grown out of the discovery that a reporter who had the facts was a more effective reformer than an editorial writer. . . .
>
> According to my earliest conception of a sociologist he was to be a kind of super-reporter. . . . He was to report a little more accurately, and in a little more detail. (Pp. v, vii–ix)

And so, although sociologists and journalists both used interviews, the duties and practices of the two occupational groups were separated, and the groups organized surveillance in distinctly different ways.

The Interview Society

The interview society emerges historically as a consequence, in part, of the central place that newspapers and cinema (and television) came (and continue) to occupy in daily life. The media, human services personnel, market researchers, and social scientists "increasingly get their information via interviews" (Holstein and Gubrium 1995:1). The interview society has turned the confessional mode of discourse into a public form of entertainment (Atkinson and Silverman 1997:309–315; Holstein and Gubrium 2000:129). The world of private troubles, the site of the authentic, or real, self, has become a public commodity.

The Interview Goes to Hollywood

It remained for Hollywood to authorized the interview as a primary method of gathering information about social issues, selves, and the meanings of personal experience. Soon Hollywood was telling stories about newspaper reporters (*The Front Page*, 1931), detectives and private eyes (*The Maltese Falcon*, 1931, 1941), psychoanalysts and psychiatrists (*Spellbound*, 1945), spies and secret agents (*Saboteur*, 1942), and market researchers (*Desk Set*, 1957; *Sex and the Single Girl*, 1964). More recently, the movies have offered spoofs of sociologists (*The Milagro Beanfield War*, 1988) and anthropologists (*Krippendorf's Tribe*, 1998).

Each of these film genres glamorized the interview as a form of interaction and as a strategy and technique for getting persons to talk about themselves and others (see Holstein and Gubrium 1995:3). Journalists, detectives, and social scientists were presented as experts in the use of this conversational form. Hollywood led us to expect that such experts will use this form when interacting with members of society. Furthermore, it led us to expect that persons, if properly asked, will reveal their inner selves to such experts.

And thus the key assumptions of the interview society were soon secured. The media and Hollywood cinema helped to solidify the following cluster of beliefs: Only skilled interviewers and therapists (and sometimes the person) have access to the deep, authentic self of the person; sociologists, journalists, and psychoanalysts know how to ask questions that will produce disclosures, often discrediting, about the hidden self; members of the interview society have certain experiences that are more authentic then others, and these experiences are keys to the hidden self (these are the experiences that have left leave deep marks and scars on the person); adept interviewers can uncover these experiences and their meanings to the person; nonetheless, persons also have access to their own experiences, and this increases the value of first-person narratives, which are the site of personal meaning.

When probing for the inner self, or when seeking information from an individual, an interviewer is expected to use some method to record what is said in the interview. In the film *True Crime* (1999), Clint Eastwood plays Steve Everett, a burned-out, alcoholic reporter who becomes convinced that Frank Beachum, a black man due to be executed within 24 hours, is innocent. Eastwood tracks down Mr. Porterhouse, the man whose testimony led to Beachum's conviction. Everett and Porterhouse meet in a café and the following exchange unfolds:

Everett: Let me get this straight, you didn't really see the murder?

Porterhouse: I never said I did.

Everett:	What did you see?
Porterhouse:	I can't tell you how many times I've been over this. I went into Pokeums to use the phone. My car had over-heated. Beachum jumped up from behind the counter. He was covered with blood and had a gun in his hand. He was bending over, stealing her necklace. He got one good look at me and then he ran out the store. My concern was for the girl. So I immediately dialed 911. I figured why should I run after a killer, when the police should do their job.
Everett:	And they sure did it, didn't they.
Porterhouse:	Aren't you gonna take some notes, or somethin'? Or use a tape recorder? Usually when I'm talkin' to a reporter they wanta keep some sort of record of what I've been sayin'.
Everett:	I have a photographic memory [points to head]. I have a notebook right here [pulls a notebook and pen out of his jacket pocket].

Everett refuses to write anything in his notebook, and Porterhouse challenges him: "I did some checking on you. You're the guy who lead the crusade to get the rapist released. That lying what's his name? Had all your facts straight on that one too, didn't you?"

Everett next interviews Beachum in his prison cell. Beachum's wife, Bonnie, is there too. (The reporter who had originally been assigned to the case was killed in a car accident.)

Beachum:	I guess you wanta hear how it feels to be in here.
Everett:	Yeah, it's a human interest piece.
Beachum:	I feel isolated. I feel fear, pain, fear of prison, fear of being separated from my loved ones. All those fears rolled up into one.
	[Everett takes notebook out of pocket.]
Beachum:	I want to tell everyone that I believe in Jesus Christ, our Lord and Savior.
	[Everett scribbles on page of notebook: BLV, JC.]

Beachum:	I came into my faith late in life. Did a lot of bad things. . . . I believe that the crooked road remains straight, that's what the Bible says.
	[Everett scribbles on page of notebook: LORD, SAV, CARO, STRAIT.]
Beachum:	Is there any more that you want?
Everett:	You don't know me. I'm just a guy out there with a screw loose. Frankly I don't give a rat's ass about Jesus Christ. I don't even care what's right or wrong. But my nose tells me something stinks, and I gotta have my faith in it, just like you have your faith in Jesus. . . . I know there's truth out there somewhere. . . . I believe you.
Bonnie Beachum:	Where were you?
Everett:	It wasn't my story.

Beachum clearly expected Everett to ask him how he felt about being on death row. He expected to tell a reporter a deeply personal story about what this experience means to his inner, authentic self. Indeed, Everett's presence in the prison elicits such a story from Beachum. To paraphrase Holstein and Gubrium (2000:129), the prison interview with a journalist is now a natural part of the death row identity landscape. But Everett, through his note taking, mocks this assumption. He has no desire to record the inner meaning of this experience for Beachum. This is unlike the desire illustrated in the excerpt from the *SportsCenter* interview above, in which Sal Paolantonio sought and got from Kurt Warner a self-validating, self-congratulatory story about hard work and success in American life.

The Interview Machine as an Epistemological Apparatus

The interview society uses the machinery of the interview methodically to produce situated versions of the self. This machinery works in a systematic and orderly fashion. It structures the talk that occurs in the interview situation. There is an orderly mechanism "for designating who will speak next" (Holstein and Gubrium 2000:125). Using the question-answer format, this mechanism regulates the flow of conversation. Talk occurs in question-answer pairs, for the asking of a question requires an answer. Turn taking structures this give-and-take. The rule of single speakership obtains: One persons speaks at a time. Interviews, in this sense, are orderly, dramaturgical accomplishments. They draw on local understandings and are constrained by those understandings. They are narrative productions; they have beginnings, middles, and endings.

The methodology of asking questions is central to the operation of this machine. Different epistemologies and ideologies shape this methodological practice. Four epistemological formats can be identified: the objectively neutral format, the entertainment and investigative format, the collaborative or active interview format, and the reflexive, dialogic interview format.[46] In each format, the asking of a question is an incitement to speak, an invitation to tell a story; in this sense the interview elicits narratives of the self (Holstein and Gubrium 2000:129).

The place of the interviewer in this process varies dramatically. In the *objectively neutral format*, the interviewer, using a structured or semistructured interview schedule, attempts to gather information without influencing the story that is being told. Holstein and Gubrium (2000) correctly observe that the demands of ongoing interaction make the "'ideal' interview a practical impossibility, because the interview itself always remains accountable to the normative expectancies of competent conversation as well as to the demand for a good story to satisfy the needs of the researcher" (p. 131).

In the *entertainment and investigative format*, the interviewer often acts as a partisan, seeking to elicit a story that will sell as an entertainment commodity or can be marketed as a new piece of information about a story that is in the process of being told. In this format, the interviewer asks leading, aggressive questions as well as friendly questions, questions that allow the subject to embellish on a previous story or to give more detail on the meanings of an important experience. Paolantonio's interview with Warner employs the entertainment format. This is a friendly interview that shows both participants in a good light. Steve Everett's interview with Mr. Porterhouse in *True Crime* illustrates the investigative version of this format. Everett is aggressive and hostile; he seeks to discredit Porterhouse as a witness.

In the *collaborative or active format*, interviewer and respondent tell a story together (see Holstein and Gubrium 1995:76–77). In this format a conversation occurs. Indeed, the identities of interviewer and respondent disappear. Each becomes a storyteller, or the two collaborate in telling a conjoint story. The *SportsCenter* interview excerpt above also illustrates this format, as together Sal and Kurt tell a story about the meaning of this victory for Kurt's life.

In the *reflexive interview format*, two speakers enter into a dialogic relationship with each other. In this relationship, a tiny drama is played out. Each person becomes a party to the utterances of the other. Together, the two speakers create a small dialogic world of unique meaning and experience. In this interaction, each speaker struggles to understand the thought of the other, reading and paying attention to such matters as intonation, facial gestures, and word selection (see Bakhtin 1986:92–93).

Consider the following dialogue excerpted from the 1982 film *Chan Is Missing*, directed by Wayne Wang. Set in contemporary San Francisco, the film mocks popular culture representations of stereotypical Asian American identities. It also mocks social science and those scholars who point to language as an answer to cultural differences. The following Lily Tomlin–like monologue is central to this position. In the monologue, racial and ethnic identities are constructed. This construction is directly connected to the use of the objective interview format. The speaker is a female Asian American attorney. She is attempting to find Mr. Chan, who had an automobile accident just days before he disappeared. She is speaking to Jo, a middle-aged Chinese American cab driver, and Jo's young "Americanized" nephew, Steve. They are at Chester's Cafe. The young attorney is dressed in a black masculine-style suit, with a white shirt and dark tie.

You see I'm doing a paper on the legal implications of cross-cultural misunderstandings. [nods head] Mr. Chan's case is a perfect example of what I want to expose. The policeman and Mr. Chan have completely different culturally related assumptions about what kind of communication [shot of Steve, then Jo] each one was using. The policeman, in an English-speaking mode, asks a direct factual question—"Did you stop at the stop sign?" He expected a yes or a no answer. Mr. Chan, however, rather than giving him a yes or a no answer, began to go into his past driving record—how good it was, the number of years he had been in the United States, all the people that he knew—trying to relate different events, objects, or situations to what was happening then to the action at hand. Now this is very typical. . . . The Chinese try to relate points, events, or objects that they feel are pertinent to the situation, which may not to anyone else seem directly relevant at the time. . . . This policeman became rather impatient, restated the question, "Did you or did you not stop at the stop sign?" in a rather hostile tone, which in turn flustered Mr. Chan, which caused him to hesitate answering the question, which further enraged the policeman, so that he asked the question again, "You didn't stop at the stop sign, did you?" in a negative tone, to which Mr. Chan automatically answered, "No." Now to any native speaker of English, "No" would mean "No I didn't stop at the stop sign." However to Mr. Chan, "No I didn't stop at the stop sign" was not "No I didn't stop at the stop sign [Jo shakes head, looks away]. It was "No, I didn't not stop at the stop sign." In other words, "Yes I did stop at the stop sign." Do you see what I'm saying? [camera pans room]

Then, in a voice-over, Jo comments, "Chan Hung wouldn't run away because of the car accident. I'm feeling something might have happened to him" (see Denzin 1995a:105).

Here the speaker, the young attorney, attempts to dialogically enter into and interpret the meanings that were circulating in Mr. Chan's interview with the policeman. In so doing, she criticizes the concept of cross-cultural communication, showing through her conversation that meanings are always dialogic and contextual.

This text from Wang's film is an example of how the reflexive, dialogic interviewer deconstructs the uses and abuses of the interview—uses that are associated with the objectively neutral and entertainment/investigative formats. This text suggests that interpretations based on the surface meanings of an utterance sequence are likely to be superficial. To paraphrase Dillard (1982:46), serious students of society take pains to distinguish their work from such interpretive practices.

At another level, reflexively oriented scholars, such as Bakhtin, contend that there is no essential self or private, real self behind the public self. They argue that there are only different selves, different performances, different ways of being a gendered person in a social situation. These performances are based on different interpretive practices. These practices give the self and the person a sense of grounding, or narrative coherence (Gubrium and Holstein 1998:165). There is no inner or deep self that is accessed by the interview or narrative method. There are only different interpretive (and performative) versions of who the person is.

Steve Everett embodies one version of the reflexive interviewer. He has no interest in the inner self of the person he is interviewing, no interest in right or wrong. He only seeks the truth, the truth that says an injustice may have been done. Wang's Asian American attorney is another version of this interviewer; she understands that the self is a verbal and narrative construction.

The Interview and the Dramaturgical Society

The text from the Kurt Warner interview presented above suggests that the metaphor of the dramaturgical society (Lyman 1990:221), or "life as theater" (Brissett and Edgley 1990:2; Goffman 1959:254–55), is no longer a metaphor. It has become interactional reality. Life and art have became mirror images of each other. Reality, as it is visually experienced, is a staged, social production.

Raban (1981) provides an example of how life and television coincide. In a TV ad "beamed by the local station in Decorah, an Iowa farmer spoke stiffly to the camera in testimony to the bags of fertilizer that were heaped in front of him" (p. 123). Here the personal testimony of the farmer, a hands-on expert, authorizes the authenticity and value of the product. This message is carried live, staged in the frame of the TV commercial; a real farmer says this product works. The farmer's awkwardness comes, perhaps, from the fact that he must look at himself doing this endorsement, knowing that if he sees himself looking this way, others will as well.

The reflected, everyday self and its gendered presentations are attached to the cinematic/televisual self. Blumer (1933) provides an example. An interview respondent connects her gendered self to the Hollywood screen:

Female, 19, white, college freshman.—When I discovered I should have this coquettish and coy look which all girls may have, I tried to do it in my room. And surprises! I could imitate Pola Negri's cool or fierce look. Vilma Banky's sweet and coquettish attitude. I learned the very way of taking my gentlemen friends to and from the door with that wistful smile, until it has become a part of me. (P. 34)

Real, everyday experiences are judged against their staged, cinematic, video counterparts. The fans of Hollywood stars dress like the stars, make love like the stars, and dream the dreams of the stars. Blumer provides an example:

> *Female, 24, white, college senior.*—During my high-school period I particularly liked pictures in which the setting was a millionaire's estate or some such elaborate place. After seeing a picture of this type, I would imagine myself living such a life of ease as the society girl I had seen. My day-dreams would be concerned with lavish wardrobes, beautiful homes, servants, imported automobiles, yachts, and countless suitors. (P. 64)

With this dramaturgical turn, the technology of the media "disengages subjects from their own expressions. . . . Individuals become observers of their own acts. . . . Actions come to be negotiated in terms of a media aesthetic, both actor and spectator live a reality arbitrated by the assumptions of media technicians" (Eason 1984:60). Altheide and Snow (1991) provide an example from Richard Nixon's presidency. In a memo to H. R. Haldeman dated December 1, 1969, Nixon wrote:

> We need a part- or full-time TV man on our staff for the purpose of seeing that my TV appearances are handled on a professional basis. When I think of the millions of dollars that go into one lousy 30-second television spot advertising deodorant, it seems to me unbelievable that we don't do a better job of seeing that Presidential appearances [on TV] always have the very best professional advice. (Quoted p. 105; see also Oudes 1989:46)

And because of the same media aesthetic, Kurt Warner has learned how to talk the form of sports talk that Ron Shelton mocks in his 1988 film *Bull Durham*. So, too, does Frank Beachum expect Steve Everett to record his moral story.

The main carriers of the popular in postmodern society have become the very media that are defining the content and meaning of the popular; that is, popular culture is now a matter of cinema and the related media, including television, the press, and popular literature. A paradox is created, for the everyday is now defined by the cinematic and the televisual. The two can no longer be separated. A press conference at the 1988 Democratic National Convention is reported thus:

> A dozen reporters stood outside CBS's area, and as was so often the case at the convention, one began interviewing another. A third

commented wryly on the interview: "Reporter interviews reporter about press conference." (Weiss 1988:33–34; quoted in Altheide and Snow 1991:93)

Reporters are reporting on reporters interviewing reporters.

❖ STUDYING THE INTERVIEW IN THE CINEMATIC SOCIETY

The cinematic apparatuses of contemporary culture stand in a twofold relationship to critical inquiry. First, the cultural logics of the postvideo cinematic culture define the lived experiences that a critical studies project takes as its subject matter. How these texts structure and give meaning to the everyday must be analyzed. At the same time, critical ethnographies of the video-cinematic text must be constructed, showing how these texts map and give narrative meaning to the crucial cultural identities that circulate in the postmodern society.

Consider race, the racial self, and Hollywood cinema. Lopez (1991) reminds us that "Hollywood does not represent ethnics and minorities; it creates them and provides an audience with an experience of them" (pp. 404–5). Consider her argument in terms of the following scene from Spike Lee's highly controversial 1989 film *Do the Right Thing*. Near the film's climax, as the heat rises on the street, members of each racial group in the neighborhood hurl vicious racial slurs at one another:

Mookie: [to Sal, who is Italian, and Sal's sons, Vito and Pino] Dago, wop, guinea, garlic breath, pizza slingin' spaghetti bender, Vic Damone, Perry Como, Pavarotti.

Pino: [to Mookie and the other blacks] Gold chain wearin' fried chicken and biscuit eatin' monkey, ape, baboon, fast runnin', high jumpin', spear chuckin', basketball dunkin' ditso spade, take you fuckin' pizza and go back to Africa.

Puerto Rican man: [to the Korean grocer] Little slanty eyed, me-no speakie American, own every fruit and vegetable stand in New York, bull shit, Reverend Sun Young Moon, Summer 88 Olympic kick-ass boxer, sonofabitch.

White policeman: You goya bean eatin' 15 in the car, 30 in the apartment, pointy red shoes wearin' Puerto Ricans, cocksuckers.

Korean grocer: I got good price for you, how am I doing? Chocolate egg cream drinking, bagel lox, Jew asshole.

Sweet Dick Willie: [to the Korean grocer] Korean motherfucker . . . you didn't do a goddamn thing except sit on your monkey ass here on this corner and do nothin. (See Denzin 1991:129–30).

Lee wants his audience to believe that his speakers are trapped within the walls and streets of a multiracial ghetto that is the Bedford-Stuyvesant area of New York City. Their voices reproduce current (and traditional) cultural, racial, and sexual stereotypes about blacks (spade, monkey), Koreans (slanty eyed), Puerto Ricans (pointy red shoes, cock-suckers), Jews (bagel lox), and Italians (dago, wop). The effects of these in-your-face insults are exaggerated through wide-angle, close-up shots. Each speaker's face literally fills the screen as the racial slurs are hurled.[47]

Lee's film presents itself as a realist, ethnographic text. It asks the viewer to believe that it is giving an objectively factual, authentic, and realistic account of the lived experiences of race and ethnicity. The film performs race and ethnicity (e.g., Pino talking to Mookie) and does so in ways that support the belief that objective reality has been captured. The film "realistically" reinscribes familiar (and new) cultural stereo-types—for example, young gang members embodying hip-hop or rap culture. Lee's text functions like a documentary film.

The Cinematic Society and the Documentary Interview

It is this documentary impulse and its reliance on the objectively neutral interview format that I now examine through an analysis of Trinh T. Minh-ha's 1989 film *Surname Viet Given Name Nam*. This is a film about Vietnamese women, whose names change or remain constant depending on whether they marry foreigners or other Vietnamese. In this film, Trinh has Vietnamese women speak from five different subject positions, representing lineage, gender status, age status, leadership position, and historical period. This creates a complex picture of Vietnamese culture (see Trinh 1992:144).

The film is multitextual, layered with pensive images of women in various situations. Historical moments overlap with age periods (childhood, youth, adulthood, old age), rituals and ceremonies (weddings, funerals, war, the market, dance), and daily household work (cooking) while interviewees talk to offscreen interviewers. There are two voice-overs in English, and a third voice sings sayings, proverbs, and poetry in Vietnamese (with translations into English appearing as texts on the screen). There are also interviews with Vietnamese subtitled in English and interviews in English synchronized with the onscreen images (Trinh 1992:49). The interviews are reenacted in Trinh's film by Vietnamese actresses, who are then interviewed at the end of the film about their experiences of being performers in the film (Trinh 1992:146).

Trinh's film allows the practice of doing reflexive interviews to enter into the construction of the text itself, thus the true and the false, the real and the staged intermingle; indeed, the early sections of the film unfold like a traditional, realist documentary (Trinh 1992:145). The viewer does not know that the women onscreen are actresses reenacting interviews. Nor does the viewer know that the interviews were conducted in the United States, not Vietnam (this becomes apparent only near the end of the film).

In using these interpretive strategies, Trinh creates a space for the critical appraisal of the politics of representation that structures the use of interviews in the documentary film. In undoing the objectively neutral interview as a method for gathering information about reality, Trinh takes up the question of truth (see Trinh 1992:145). Whose truth is she presenting—that given in the onscreen interview situation or that of the women-as-actresses who are interviewed at the end of the film?

Trinh begins by deconstructing the classic interview-based documentary film, which enters the native's world and brings news from that world to the world of the Western observer. In its use of the traditional, nondialogic interview method, documentary film starts with the so-called real world and the subject's place in that world. It uses an aesthetic of objectivity and a technological apparatus that produces truthful statements (images) about the world (Trinh 1991:33). Trinh (1991:39) argues that the following elements are central to this apparatus:

❖ The relentless pursuit of naturalism, which requires a connection between the moving image and the spoken word
❖ Authenticity—the use of people who appear to be real and locating these people in "real" situations
❖ The filmmaker/interviewer presented as an observer, not as a person who creates what is seen, heard, and read
❖ The capture only of events unaffected by the recording eye
❖ The capture of objective reality
❖ The dramatization of truth
❖ The presentation of actual facts in a credible way, with people telling them

Along with these elements, the film-interview text must convince spectators that they should have confidence in the truth of what they see. These aesthetic strategies define the documentary interview style, allowing the filmmaker-as-interviewer to create a text that gives the viewer the illusion of having "unmediated access to reality" (Trinh 1991:40). Thus naturalized, the objective, documentary interview style has become part of the larger cinematic apparatus in American culture, including a pervasive presence in TV commercials and news (Trinh 1991:40).

Trinh brings a reflexive reading to these features of the documentary film, citing her own texts as examples of dialogic documentaries that are sensitive to the flow of fact and fiction, to meanings as political constructions (see Trinh 1991:41). Such texts reflexively understand that reality is never neutral or objective, that it is always socially constructed. Filmmaking and documentary interviewing thus become methods of "framing" reality.

Self-reflexivity does not translate into personal style or a preoccupation with method. Rather, it centers on the reflexive interval that defines representation, "the place in which the play within the textual frame is a play on this very frame, hence on the borderlines of the textual and the extra-textual" (Trinh 1991:48). The film becomes a site for multiple experiences.

A responsible, reflexive, dialogic interview text embodies the following characteristics (Trinh 1991:188):

❖ It announces its own politics and evidences a political consciousness.
❖ It interrogates the realities it represents.

❖ It invokes the teller's story in the history that is told.
❖ It makes the audience responsible for interpretation.
❖ It resists the temptation to become an object of consumption.
❖ It resists all dichotomies (male/female and so on).
❖ It foregrounds difference, not conflict.
❖ It uses multiple voices, emphasizing language as silence, the grain of the voice, tone, inflection, pauses, silences, repetitions.
❖ It presents silence as a form of resistance.

Trinh creates the space for a version of the cinematic apparatus and the interview machine that challenges mainstream film. She also challenges traditional ethnography and its use of objective and investigative interview formats.

Reflexive texts question the very notion of a stable, unbiased gaze. They focus on the pensive image, on silences, on representations that "unsettle the male apparatus of the gaze " (Trinh 1991:115). This look makes the interviewer's gaze visible. It destabilizes any sense of verisimilitude that can be brought to this visual world. In so doing, it also disrupts the spectator's gaze, itself a creation of the unnoticed camera, the camera that invokes the image of a perfect, natural world, a world with verisimilitude (Trinh 1991:115). In using these interpretive strategies, Trinh creates the space for the viewer (and listener) to appraise critically the politics of representation that structures the documentary text.

Cultivating Reflexivity

Learning from Trinh, I want to cultivate a method of patient listening, a reflexive method of looking, hearing, and asking that is dialogic and respectful. This method will take account of my place as a co-constructor of meaning in this dialogic relationship. As an active listener (Bourdieu 1996), I will treat dialogue as a process of discovery. I will attempt to function as an empowering collaborator. I will use the reflexive interview as a tool of intervention (Burawoy 1998). I will use it as a method for uncovering structures of oppression in the life worlds of the persons I am interviewing. As a reflexive participant, I will critically promote the agendas of radical democratic practice. In so doing, I hope to cultivate a method of hearing and writing that has some kinship with the kinds of issues Gloria Naylor (1998) discusses in the following passage:

Someone who didn't know how to ask wouldn't know how to listen. And he coulda listened to them the way you been listening to us right now. Think about it: ain't nobody really talking to you. . . . Really listen this time; the only voice is your own. But you done just heard the about the legend of Saphira Wade. . . . You done heard it in the way we know it, sitting on our porches and shelling June peas . . . taking apart the engine of a car—you done heard it without a single living soul really saying a word. (P. 1842)

But this is also a sociology that understands, here at the end, that when we screen our dreams and our crises through the canvases and lenses that the cinematic and electronic society makes available to us, we risk becoming storied versions of somebody else's version of who we should be.

4

Toward a Performative Social Science

Performative writing refuses an . . . easy and . . . false distinction between performance and text, performance and performativity. . . . writing as doing displaces writing as meaning.

—Della Pollock,
"Performing Writing," 1998

This book is a "writing performance."

Ronald J. Pelias, *Writing Performance:
Poeticizing the Researcher's Body*, 1999

What most influences [me] . . . is . . . how an interview text works as a physical, audible, performable vehicle. Words are not an end in themselves. They are a means to evoking the character of the person who spoke them.

—Anna Deavere Smith,
Twilight: Los Angeles, 1992, 1994

I have argued that we perform culture; we do not write it.[48] Furthermore, our performances are not innocent practices. They are always ideological, carrying the traces and scars of global capitalism and white patriarchy (Pelias 1999:138; hooks 1990:4). Still, if we know the world only through our representations of it, then to change the world, we must change how we write and perform it.

As noted in Chapter 3, throughout the twentieth century the transcribed interview was the basic information-gathering tool and one of the major writing forms used by scholars in the social sciences. This model presumed a view from outside society and the possibility of an objective observer. The transcribed interview allowed the writer to create a discourse that suspended, even did away with, the presence of a real subject in the world. It made social experience and human character irrelevant to the topic at hand. It created an interpretive structure that said social phenomena should be interpreted as social facts. It shifted discussions about agency, purpose, and meaning from the subject to the phenomena being discussed. It then transformed these phenomena into texts about society, giving the phenomena a presence that rested in the textual description (Smith 1989:45.) Real people entered the text as a figment of discourse in the form of excerpts from field notes and transcribed interviews (Denzin 1997:55; Smith 1989:51). Transcribed words did this work.

Performance writing challenges this model of inquiry. Building on the performance interviews of Anna Deavere Smith (1993, 1994, 2000), in this chapter I introduce the concept of performance interviewing. I connect this form of the interview to performance writing and to public-voice and performance ethnography (see Pollock 1998a:74). This chapter is a "writing performance" (Pelias 1999:xiv); in these pages, I take up the multiple ways in which writing can perform itself.

I begin the chapter with a discussion of the performative sensibility and the interview as an interpretive practice. I then turn to the topics of the performance interview, performative writing, ethnodrama, and public-voice and performance ethnographies (Pollock 1998a; Pelias 1999; Sedgwick 1998; Schechner 1998; Mienczakowski 1992, 1994, 1995, 2001; Mienczakowski and Morgan 1993, 2001; Heyl, 2001). I next explicate Anna Deavere Smith's project, especially her concepts of performance and the poetic text. I move from Smith's arguments to a performance text of my own based on a reflexive interview with a woman who led the battle to desegregate the schools in her city in the mid-1960s. I conclude the chapter by returning to my utopian themes, the promises of performance writing and the reflexive interview for helping to nurture a free and just society.

This chapter is a part of a utopian project. I search for a new interpretive form, a new form of the interview, which I call the *reflexive, dialogic,* or *performative* interview. The reflexive interview is not an information-gathering tool per se. It is not a commodity that one person can hire another to collect or pay someone to produce. It belongs to a moral community. On this point I borrow from Leopold (1949), who says of the land, "We abuse land because we regard it as a commodity belonging to us. When we see land as a community to which we belong, we may begin to use it with love and respect" (p. viii). We do not own the land; the land is a community to which we belong. Substitute the words *interview* and *research* for the word *land.* As researchers we belong to a moral community. Doing interviews is a privilege granted to us, not a right that we have. Interviews are living things that belong to everyone. They should not be bought and sold. Interviews are part of the dialogic conversation that connects all us to the larger moral community. Interviews arise out of performance events. They transform information into shared moral experience.[49]

This reflexive project presumes that words and language have a material presence in the world; that is, words have effects on people. Recall the words of Mary Weems (2002:4) in her poem, "This Evolution Will Not Be Televised," part of which I have quoted in Chapter 1:

One million poems, and blood

paintings pressed between fingers

not leaving prints. . . .

Our image, our braids, our music, our mistakes,

our asses, our rhythms are played on TV

like a long 78 album in commercial after commercial.

Words matter.

Those who perform culture critically are learning to use language in a way that brings people together. The goal is to create critically empowering texts that "demonstrate a strong fondness . . . for freedom and an affectionate concern for the lives of people" (Joyce 1987:344). These texts do more then move audiences to tears—they criticize the world the way it is and offer suggestions about how it could different.

❖ INTERPRETIVE FRAMEWORK

I want to reread the interview, to look at it not as a method of gathering information, but as a vehicle for producing performance texts and performance ethnographies about self and society (see Richardson 1997:135–36). I want to locate this reading within the seventh moment of inquiry, a postexperimental period of writing and representation.[50] The present moment is defined by a performative sensibility, by a willingness to experiment with different ways of presenting interview texts. The performative sensibility turns interviews into performance events, into poetic readings, spoken-word poetry. It turns interviewees into performers, into persons whose words and narratives are then performed by others. As Richardson (1997:121) argues, in the postexperimental period no discourse has a privileged place, and no method or theory has a universal and general claim to authoritative knowledge.

The Interview as Interpretive Practice

The interview, as an interpretive practice, has had a different set of meanings in each historical period. Its meanings, forms, and uses change from moment to moment, moving from the structured, semi-structured, and open-ended objective formats of the traditional and modernist periods to the feminist criticisms of these formats in the third and fourth moments (see Oakley 1981; Reinharz 1992), to autoethnographic uses of the method in the fifth and sixth moments (DeVault 1999), as well as the more recent postexperimental performative turn. The present moment is further defined by increased resistance from persons of color to the interviews done by white university and government officials. The modernist interview no longer functions as an automatic extension of the state, as an interpretive practice to which persons willingly submit.

The interview is a way of writing the world, of bringing the world into play. The interview is not a mirror of the so-called external world, nor is it a window into the inner life of the person (see Dillard 1982:47, 155). The interview is a simulacrum, a perfectly miniature and coherent world in its own right (see Dillard 1982:152). Seen thus, the interview functions as a narrative device that allows persons who are so inclined to tell stories about themselves. In the moment of storytelling, teller and listener, performer and audience, share the goal of participating in an experience that reveals their shared sameness (Porter 2000).

The interview's meanings are contextual, improvised, and performative (Dillard 1982:32). The interview is an active text, a site where meaning is created and performed. When performed, the interview text creates the world, giving the world its situated meaningfulness. Seen thus, the interview is a fabrication, a construction, a fiction, an "ordering or rearrangement of selected materials from the actual world" (Dillard 1982:148). But every interview text selectively and unsystematically reconstructs that world, tells and performs a story according to its own version of truth and narrative logic.

As I have argued previously, we inhabit a performance-based, dramaturgical culture where the dividing line between performer and audience is blurred and culture itself has become a dramatic performance. This is a gendered culture with nearly invisible boundaries separating everyday theatrical performances from formal theater, dance, music, MTV, video, and film (Butler 1990:25, 1997:159, 1999:19). But the matter goes even deeper than blurred boundaries. The performance has become reality. On this, speaking of gender and personal identity, Butler (1990) is certain. Gender is performative, gender is always doing, "though not a doing by a subject who might be said to preexist the deed. . . . there is no being behind doing. . . . the deed is everything. . . . there is no gender identity behind the expressions of gender. . . . identity is performatively constituted by the very 'expressions' that are said to be its results" (p. 25). Further, the linguistic act is performative, embodied, a bodily act, and words can hurt (Butler 1997:4).

Gender performances in the interview are shaped performatively, through the acts, gestures, and symbols persons use to bring a gendered self into play. The coherence of the self is given in these performances; that is, "body, sex and gender are all performed [and regulated] through the fiction of heterosexual coherence" (Butler 1990:137; see also Clough 2000b:760). Power, Foucault (1980b:93) reminds us, is a process located in a field of forces. Power works through unstable systems of discourse, producing, according to Butler, gendered differences, differences that have the potential to bring about disruption and political change (Clough 2000b:760).

Performance interviews are situated in complex systems of gendered discourse. Behind every interview, in the figure of the interviewer, lurks the power of the state. And in the figure of the interviewee lurks the illusion of a reflexive, unified self reporting on his or her opinions and beliefs. The meanings of lived experience and subjectivity are inscribed and made visible in these dramaturgical illusions.

Ethnodramas and Public Voice Ethnography

Mienczakowski (1992, 1994, 1995, 2001) and Mienczakowski and Morgan 1993, 2001) locate the performance interview within the framework of ethnodrama. Ethnodrama, or what they call *public-voice ethnography*, is a form of ethnographic theater involving "participant and audience empowerment through forum reconstruction and 'dialogical interactions'" (Mienczakowski 1995:361). Ethnodramas enact performance writing through a particular type of ethnographic theater.

According to Mienczakowski (2001), ethnodrama is organized by the proposition "that performed ethnography may provide more accessible and clearer public explanations of research than is frequently the case with traditional, written report texts" (p. 471). Coperformers read performance scripts based on fieldwork and interviews. Mienczakowski and Morgan use verbatim ethnographic accounts taken from a variety of health care settings, including a drug and alcohol withdrawal center.[51] They fashion these accounts into scripts, plays in which the characters represent different types of staff members and clients within these settings. Before they stage a performance, Mienczakowski and Morgan distribute copies of the script and invite individuals to comment on it. The script and the commentary it provokes provide the basis for education workshops and for evaluations of the setting in question. Because Mienczakowski and Morgan write their scripts in a public voice, in an accessible and unassuming form, the scripts "are instantly open to interpretation by nonacademics" (Mienczakowski 1995:368). Such scripts and performances can help to correct negative public stereotypes and thereby may influence, inform, and help to change public health care policy. This is the "public voice purpose of ethnodrama" (Mienczakowski 1995:372).

Mienczakowski (2001) believes that these ethnodramas provide emancipatory opportunities for health informants and health professionals. He notes that ethnodramas and other ethnographic performances are "about *the present moment* and seek to give the text back to readers and informants in the recognition that 'we are all co-performers in each other's lives'" (p. 468). Mienczakowski and Morgan use postperformance discussions with staff members, informants, and audience members as a way of reworking texts and performances to make them more responsive to the demands of praxis and social critique. The processes of participant and audience empowerment through forum reconstruction and dialogic interactions give health consumers control over the meanings of their own experiences (Mienczakowski 1995).

Mienczakowski (1995) explains that the ethnodrama process is "sensitive to the pedagogy of teaching. . . . by using the words, stories and advice of people involved in alcohol dependency or other mental health issues, the ethnodrama methodology seeks to tell the truth as they see it, so as to give them voice" (p. 367). Ethnodramas differ from other forms of performance ethnographic practice in that "it is their overt intention . . . to be a form of public voice ethnography that has emancipatory and educational potential" (Mienczakowski 2001:469).

Ethnodramas trouble the boundaries and barriers that separate health care recipients, professionals, policy makers, and the general public (Mienczakowski 2001:469). Grounded in local understandings and experiences, these texts provide the basis for the critical evaluation of existing programs. They return the ownership of programs to immediate stakeholders. They address audiences previously ignored or unmoved by more traditional approaches (p. 470). This is ethnographic research that turns program evaluation into a participatory-performative process. In so doing, it provides, in its own small way, "limited grounds for Habermas's notion of human communicative consensus/ competence" (p. 470).

Ethnodramas focus on crises and moments of epiphany in the culture. Suspended in time, they are liminal moments. They open up institutions and their practices for critical inspection and evaluation.

A Politics of Possibility

Recall my description in Chapter 1 of Madison's (1998) case study of the development of a performance based on the story of striking cafeteria workers at the University of North Carolina; that is an example of a performance ethnography that helped to enact a politics of resistance and possibility. Like Anna Deavere Smith, D. Soyini Madison, and Jim Mienczakowski and Stephen Morgan, I want a performative social science, a social science and a public ethnographic theater that embraces racial diversity and social difference (see Denzin 1997:123; Turner 1986a). Borrowing from Smith (1993), this social science asks: "Who has the right to ask whom what questions?" "Who has the right to answer?" "Who has the right to see what?" "Who has the right to say what?" "Who has the right to speak for whom?" (p. xxviii). The questions Smith raises are the ones that "unsettle and prohibit a democratic theatre in America" (p. xxix). Bringing together "these relationships of the *unlikely* . . . is crucial to American theater and culture if theater and culture plan to help us assemble our obvious differences" (p. xxix). Perhaps more deeply, these are the questions that unsettle the discourses of a democratic social science in North America and the rest of the world today. Can performance (auto)ethnography do what Smith asks of theater?

❖ PERFORMING THE
INTERVIEW, PERFORMING SOCIETY

Interviews are performance texts. A performative social science uses the reflexive, active interview as a vehicle for producing moments of performance theater, a theater that is sensitive to the moral and ethical issues of our time (Smith 1993:xxix). This interview form is gendered and dialogic. In it, gendered subjects are created through their speech acts. Speech is performative. It is action. The act of speech, the act of being interviewed, becomes a performance itself (Smith 1993:xxxi; see also Butler 1990:25).[52] The reflexive interview, as a dialogic conversation, is the site and occasion for such performances; that is, the interview is turned into a dramatic, poetic text.[53] In turn, these texts are performed, given dramatic readings. In such events, as Phelan (1998) puts it, "performance and performativity are braided together by virtue of iteration; the copy renders performance authentic and allows the spectator to find in the performer 'presence' . . . [or] authenticity" (p. 10).

Listen to Laurel Richardson's (1997:131) Louisa May introduce her life story:

> The most important thing
>
> to say is that
>
> I grew up in the South.
>
> Being Southern shapes
>
> aspirations shapes
>
> what you think you are . . .
>
> . . .
>
> I grew up poor in a rented house
>
> in a very normal sort of way

on a very normal sort of street

with some very nice middle-class friends.

Louisa May comes alive as a person in these lines. She comes off the page, and if her words are spoken aloud softly, with a middle-Tennessee twang, you can feel her presence in the room.

The reflexive interview is simultaneously a site for conversation, a discursive method, and a communicative format that produces knowledge about the cinematic society. This interview form furnishes the materials that are fashioned into critical performance texts, critical narratives about community, race, self, and identity (Smith 1993:xxiii).

One of the young black men whom Smith (1994:xxv–xxvi) interviewed after the 1992 Los Angeles riots reflects on the meanings of race, ethnicity, and identity in his life:

Twilight is the time of day between day and night

limbo, I call it limbo,

and sometimes when I take my ideas to my homeboys

they say, well Twilight, that's something you can't do right

now . . .

I affiliate darkness with what came first,

because it was first,

and relative to my complexion,

I am a dark individual

And with me being stuck in limbo

I see the darkness as myself.

The Interview Society

Atkinson and Silverman (1997) remind us that the postmodern is an interview society, a society of the spectacle, a society of the personal confession. The interview society, according to these authors, is characterized by the following features and beliefs:

1. The confessional mode of discourse has become a form of public entertainment.

2. The private has become a public commodity.

3. Persons are assumed to have private and public and authentic selves, and the private self is the real self.

4. Skilled interviewers and therapists (and sometimes the person) have access to this real self.

5. Certain experiences, epiphanies, are more authentic then others, leaving deep marks and scars on the person.

6. Persons have access to their own experiences.

7. First-person narratives are very valuable; they are the site of personal meaning. (Pp. 309-15)

The reflexive interviewer deconstructs these uses and abuses of the interview (Atkinson and Silverman 1997; Holstein and Gubrium 2000:227–28).[54] Indeed, to paraphrase Dillard (1982:46), serious students of society take pains to distinguish their work from these interpretive practices. In the surveillance society, journalists, social scientists, psychiatrists, physicians, social workers, and the police use interviews to gather information about individuals. Interviews objectify individuals, turning lived experiences into narratives. The interview is the method by which the personal is made public. The interview turns transgressive experience into a consumable commodity. These narratives are bought and sold in the mass-media and academic marketplaces. Thus the interview society affirms the importance of the speaking subject and celebrates the biographical. Nothing is private any longer.

Of course, there is no essential self or private, real self behind the public self. There are only different selves, different performances, different ways of being a gendered person in a social situation. These performances are based on different narrative and interpretive practices. These practices give the self and the person a sense of grounding, or narrative coherence (Gubrium and Holstein 1998). There is no inner or deep self that is accessed by the interview or narrative method. There are only different interpretive (and performative) versions of who the person is. At this level (to borrow from Garfinkel 1996:6), there is nothing under the skull that matters.

Narrative Collage and the Postmodern Interview

The postmodern or contemporary modernist interview builds on narrative collage, the shattering of narrative line.[55] Dillard (1982) compares narrative collage to cubism:

> Just as Cubism can take a roomful of furniture and iron it into nine square feet of canvas, so fiction can take fifty years of human life, chop it to bits and piece these bits together so that, within the limits of the temporal form, we can consider them all at once. This is narrative collage. (P. 21)

In the postmodern interview, storied sequences do not follow a necessary progression. Narrative collage fractures time; speakers leap forward and backward in time. Time is not linear; it is not attached to causal sequences, to "fixed landmarks in orderly progression" (Dillard 1982:21). Time, space, and character are flattened out. The intervals between temporal moments can be collapsed in an instant. More than one voice can speak at once, in more than one tense. The text can be a collage, a montage, with photographs, blank spaces, poems, mono-logues, dialogues, voice-overs, and interior streams of consciousness.

In *montage*, the artist makes a picture is by juxtaposing several dif-ferent images. In a sense, montage is related to pentimento, in which something painted out of a picture (an image the painter "repented," or denied) becomes visible again, creating something new. What is new is what had been obscured by the previous image.

Montage and pentimento, like jazz, which is improvisation, create the sense that images, sounds, and understandings are blending together, overlapping, forming a composite, a new creation. The images seem to shape and define one another, and an emotional, gestalt effect is produced. Often the images in film montages are com-bined in swiftly paced sequences, with dizzily revolving collections of images around a central or focused picture or sequence. Directors often use such effects to signify the passage of time.

In narrative collage or montage, the narrative can "shatter time itself into smithereens" (Dillard 1982:22). Points of view and style col-lide, switch back and forth, commingle. Now and then the writer intrudes, speaking directly to the reader. Sentences may be reduced to numbered lines. As Dillard (1982) puts it, the "arrow of time shatters, cause and effect may vanish and reason crumble" (p. 22). No one can say which sequence of events caused what, and the text makes no pretense about causality. Time, effect, and cause operate, as Borges would say, in a "garden of forking paths" (Dillard 1982:22). Space is no longer fixed, confined to walled-in, three-dimensional sites. It moves back and forth, sometimes randomly, between the public and private realms, which may be only temporary resting places. As space shifts, so too do forms of discourse, character, voice, tone, prose style, and visual imagery (Dillard 1982:22–23).

In these ways narrative collage allows the writer, interviewer, and performer to create a special world, a world made meaningful through the methods of collage and montage. These uses lay bare the structural and narrative bones of the reflexive, postmodern interview. In text and in performance, this form announces its reflexivity. No longer does the writer-as-interviewer hide behind the question-answer format, the apparatuses of the interview machine.

The Interview and the World

The interview elicits interpretations of the world, for it is itself an object of interpretation. But the interview is not an interpretation of the world per se. Rather, it stands in an interpretive relationship to the world that it creates. This created world stands alongside the so-called bigger and larger world of human affairs, of which this creation is but one tiny part. The lifelike materials of the interview absorb us and seduce us. They entice us into believing that we are seeing the "real world" being staged. But this is not so—there is no real world. There are no originals. There is no original reality that casts its shadows across the reproduction. There are only interpretations and their performances.

Nonetheless, the reflexive interviewer gives special attention to those performances, spaces, and sites where stories that cross and recross the borders and boundaries of illness, race, class, gender, religion, and ethnicity are told (Gubrium and Holstein 1998). I turn now to a consideration of the work of Anna Deavere Smith.

❖ ANNA DEAVERE SMITH'S PROJECT

Anna Deavere Smith knows how to listen. She says of her project, "My goal has been to find American character in the ways that people speak. When I started this project, in the early 1980s, my simple introduction to anyone I interviewed was, 'If you give me an hour of your time, I'll invite you to see yourself performed'" (Smith 1993:xxiii). Smith has transformed her project into the production of a series of one-woman performance pieces about race in America (Smith 1994:xvii). She is drawn to those racialized moments, spaces, and places where there is tension "between those on the margins and those in the center" (Smith 1993:xxxviii). In those liminal spaces, she seeks to find American character, asking whether the tension experienced in such sites will be productive or explosive, and if it explodes, will it "kill and maim those who happen to be in the wrong place at the wrong time" (1993:xxxvii).

In her search for American character, Smith observes, she has found that Americans lack a language that incorporates and transcends racial difference, a language that would bring communities together in productive ways while honoring difference. We need, Smith (1994:xxii) contends, a theater that will show us how to create and embrace diversity, a theater that includes new characters of color, characters previously excluded.

Over the past 10 years, Smith has created performances based on actual events in a series she has titled "On the Road: A Search for American Character." As Smith (1994) describes her process, each of these performances "evolves from interviews I conduct with individuals directly or indirectly. . . . Basing my scripts entirely on this interview material, I perform the interviewees on stage using their own words" (p. xvii). In May 1992, Smith was commissioned to create a performance piece about the recent civil disturbances in Los Angeles. *Twilight: Los Angeles, 1992*, is the result of her search "for the character of Los Angeles in the wake of the initial Rodney King verdict" (1994:xvii).[56]

Chronologically, Smith's *Fires in the Mirror* (1993) precedes her Los Angeles project. In *Fires*, she offers a series of performance pieces based on interviews with people who were involved in or otherwise connected to a racial conflict that took place in Crown Heights, Brooklyn, on August 19, 1991. The conflict was set in motion when a young black Guyanese boy was accidentally hit and killed by a car that was part of a police-escorted entourage carrying Lubavitcher Grand Rebbe Menachem Schneerson. Later that day, a group of black men fatally stabbed a 29-year-old Hasidic scholar. This killing was followed by a racial conflict that lasted 3 days and involved many members of the Crown Heights community. Smith's play has speaking parts for gang members, police officers, anonymous young girls and boys, mothers, fathers, rabbis, the Reverend Al Sharpton, playwright Ntozake Shange, and African American cultural critic Angela Davis.

The theater that Smith creates mirrors and criticizes society; she says that hers is a project that is "sensitive to the events of my own time" (Smith 1993:xxii). In fashioning her performance texts, she uses *dramaturges*, "persons who assist in the preparation of the text of a play and offer an outside perspective to those who are more active in the process of staging the play" (Smith 1993:xxii).[57]

Smith turns interview texts into scripts. She fashions an interview text "that works as a *physical, audible, performable* vehicle" (Smith 1993:xxiii). Words become a means or a method for evoking the character of a person. Smith has learned how to listen carefully. She has learned how to inhabit the words of the other, to use that person's manner of speech as a mark of individuality. She sees that a person can be completely present in his or her speech, and this is a gift (Smith 1993:xxvii, xxxi).

Here is how Smith (1993:19) renders her interview with the Reverend Al Sharpton:

James Brown raised me

Uh . . .

I never had a father.

My father left when I was ten.

James Brown took me to the beauty parlor one day

And made my hair like this.

And made me promise

to wear it like that

'til I die.

It's a personal family thing

between me and James Brown.

I always wanted a father

And he filled that void.

Smith (1993) says that her goal is to create "an atmosphere in which the interviewee would experience his/her own authorship" (p. xxxi). If this space is created, "everyone . . . will say something that is like poetry. The process of getting to that poetic moment is where 'character' lives" (p. xxxi).

Playwright, poet, and novelist Ntozake Shange reveals her character to Smith (1993:3) thus:

> Hummmm.
>
> Identity—
>
> it, is, uh . . . in a way it's, um . . . it's sort of, it's uh . . .
>
> it's a psychic sense of place
>
> it's a way of knowing I'm not a rock or that tree?
>
> I'm this other living creature over here?
>
> And it's a way of knowing that no matter where I put
>
> Myself
>
> that I am not necessarily
>
> what's around me.

Smith (1993) asserts that an unavoidable and painful tension exists in the United States today, a tension that has been taken up by women and people of color, a tension that surrounds race, identity, and gender; it is "the tension of identity in motion" (p. xxxiv). This tension turns, in part, as indicated above, on the question of "Who can speak for whom?" A profound danger exists, Smith (1993) points out: "If only a man can speak for a man, a woman for a woman, a Black person for all Black people, then we, once again, inhibit the *spirit* of theater, which lives in the bridge that makes unlikely aspects seem connected" (p. xxix), and we cannot construct a bridge that will connect diverse racial and gendered identities to discourse in the public arena. Democratic discourse and a new racial politics are threatened.

However, as I have argued above, there are no privileged identities, no deep or essential selves connected to inner structures of meaning (Gubrium and Holstein 1997:74). There are only different performances, different ways of being in the world. And so, in her performances,

Smith performs and presents the poetic texts of men and women of color. Smith's two plays document what she has learned and heard in these two sites of racial disturbance. Her performances reiterate what she has learned: It is the drama about the process that creates the problem in the first place, the drama surrounding racial identity (Smith 1993:xxiv).

As in Mienczakowski and Morgan's work, postperformance discussions with informants and audience members are important for Smith's project. These discussions, she reports, are often quite emotional and pedagogical. They are ethnodramas in their own right, and they are important for several different reasons (Smith 1994:xxiii). For one thing, Smith's performances often bring into theaters persons who would not normally be together, including whites, blacks, Latino/as, public officials, police officers, politicians, members of the press, and representatives of other mass media (1993:xxxviii). In these emotionally charged situations, interactants explore racial differences. They bring different interpretations to the experiences and events that Smith performs. These postperformance pedagogical exchanges provide Smith and her dramaturges with feedback. The interactions that take place bring participants into events that they may never have experienced directly. Participating in these performances gives them a form of ownership they would not otherwise have.

Cornel West (1993a) observes that *Fires in the Mirror* is a "grand example of how art can constitute a public space that is perceived by people as empowering rather than disempowering" (p. xix). Thus blacks, gang members, the police, and members of the Jewish community all come together and talk in this play. The drama crosses racial boundaries. As West observes, Smith's text shows that "American character lives not in one place or the other, but in the gaps between places, and in our struggle to be together in our differences" (p. xii).

In a scene from *Fires in the Mirror* (Smith 1993:79-80), one character, "An Anonymous Young Man # 1Wa Wa Wa," a Caribbean American with dreadlocks, describes the auto accident:

What I saw was

she was pushin'

her brother on the bike like

this,

right?

She was pushin'

him

and he keep dippin' around

like he didn't know how

to ride the bike . . .

So she was already runnin'

when the car was comin' . . .

we was watchin' the car

weavin',

and we was goin'

"Oh, yo

it's a Jew man.

He broke the stop light, they never get arrested."

In presenting this young man's words, Smith's text becomes performative; that is, the young Caribbean American narrates a street performance. The text works like a piece of montage, with many different things going on at once. It includes multiple points of view. Time moves back and forth, from past to present, present to past. More than one notion of causality (and blame) operates. In this text, Jews come up against blacks, young against old, as a small child's bike weaves its way down the sidewalk until it rolls in front of an oncoming car.

In Smith's public-voice theater there are no cultural custodians or identity police who assert that only blacks can understand and perform black experience (Conquergood 1985:8). Smith's antiessentialist performance aesthetic bridges the spaces that separate gender, race, and ethnic identity. It calls for a new identity politics, a different racialized and gendered version of the American dream (see Diawara 1996:303).

Performance Writing

Smith engages in a form of performance writing (see Pollock 1998a, 1998b; see also Phelan 1998:12–14). Using the methods of narrative collage, performance writing shows rather than tells. It is writing that speaks performatively, enacting what it describes. It is writing that does what it says it is doing by doing it. Performative writing "is an inquiry into the limits and possibilities of the intersections between speech and writing. . . . [It] evokes what it names" (Phelan 1998:13). Performative writing is not a matter of formal style per se, nor is it writing that is avant-garde or clever (Pollock 1998a:75). As Pollock (1998a:80–95) suggests, performative writing is evocative, reflexive, and multivoiced; it cuts across genres and is always partial and incomplete. But in performative writing things happen; it is writing that is consequential, and it is about a world that is already being performed.

A performance writing text may contain pictures, such as photographs or drawings. It may look distinctive on the page, perhaps set in double or triple columns and using unusual spacing between words and lines. It may be deeply citational, with footnotes or endnotes. It may be broken into sections that are separated by rows of asterisks or dingbats. It may combine several different types of texts, such as poetry, first-person reflections, quotations from scholarly works, and the daily newspaper.[58]

Performative writing requires performative reading, an active, collaborative form of reading. As Jones (1997) observes, performative reading creates a union between reader and writer that is "seriate, simultaneous, sketch-driven, improvisational, incorporative, circular, and transformative" (p. 72). In performative reading, the reader finds "a point of interest on the page, and lingers or moves on to another" (p. 72). The reader scans, fast-forwards, gazes at a line, and then turns back.

To say that Smith writes performatively and that she asks for performative readers is to say that her scripts (like Trinh's) allow persons to experience their own subjectivity in the moment of performance. Performance writing recovers what appears and then disappears, the performance itself, the original and the copy. In this sense, performance writing is behavior that is twice behaved (Schechner 1998:361). Even as it disappears into thin air, the performance has an afterlife; quietly resting in the text, it awaits its next performance.

Performance writing is poetic and dramatic, embodied. As Phelan (1998) notes, such writing lies at the "intersections between speech and writing" (p. 13). It is writing that is meant to be read, performed. It is transformative. It is a way of happening, a way of becoming (p. 10). It dwells in the spaces of liminality (pp. 8, 11). It is writing that refuses "the impossibility of maintaining the distinction between temporal tenses . . . between beginning and ending, between living and dying"

(p. 8). Performance writing transforms literal (and transcribed) speech into speech that is first person, active, in motion, processual. In such texts, performance and performativity are intertwined, the done and the doing; each defines the other. The performer's performance creates a space that the audience enters.

In this postmodern, liminal, posttheoretical age, performance writing teaches us how to rehearse events that have passed, allowing us to learn how to play the past when it happens again in the future (Phelan 1998:7). And in this sense, like all writing, performance writing is ideological. Transgressive performance texts, based on performance writing, politicize and criticize the violent worlds we inherit from global capitalism. Through mimicry, iteration, simulations, and repetition, twice-behaved behaviors interrupt the "strange temporal economy in which we live . . . [and] challenge the violence and illusionary seductions of colonialist and capitalist enterprises" (Phelan 1998:9).

I now present a performance text of my own.

❖ PERFORMING RACIAL MEMORIES

On July 28, 1966, Edge City desegregated its 10 elementary schools. According to the local newspaper, Edge City was the first town in Illinois to do this. In 1965–66 there were 456 African American children in elementary school in the district; 95% of these children attended the virtually all-black Martin School in the north end of town. To accomplish desegregation, the school district bused all but 100 of the African American students from Martin School to its 9 other previously all-white schools. It then sent 189 international children to Martin School. These children lived with their parents in a university housing complex. The school board called this "cross-busing," but the newspaper said that no white children were bused, just the kids from university housing (see Denzin et al. 1997).

Mrs. Anderson was the only woman member of the all-white school board that made the decision to desegregate. I had read stories about her in the local newspaper, seen her picture. I knew that she has been a secretary at one of the grade schools, and that she had worked at the Citizens Building Association. I did not know that she has been a single parent when she served on the board, nor did I know that her daughter eventually married a black man, making her the grandmother of biracial children. I learned these things later.

The newspaper said that Mrs. Anderson died in her home at 6:35 P.M. on November 10, 1996. She was 81 years old, a victim of old age and emphysema. For some time before her death, a long, clear-plastic air hose connected her to an oxygen machine. She breathed with great effort and had brief spells of intense coughing. She had the look of a patrician, a commanding presence, tall and graceful, but slow in her movements, held back by the hose. She had crystal-clear blue eyes. She was elegant in her velvet floor-length blue robe. Her chair faced a picture window that looked out on her small, well-cared-for backyard garden; from the window, she could see roses, bird feeders, evergreens, and a dying river birch.

There is a jar of jellybeans on the coffee table in front of the sofa, where I sit. I put the tape recorder next to Mrs. A's chair and pin its microphone to the collar of her robe, being careful not to disturb the oxygen tube.[59] She begins to speak, to tell her story about how desegregation happened in Edge City. Her story moves from the mid-1960s to the present. The point of view in her story changes as she takes on different voices.

It started with two people,

James and Marilyn Daniels.

They led a group of their neighbors

in the black neighborhood.

They said:

Look, you're moving all those kids

from university housing by bus to school.

Why don't you take Martin School

and bring them up here and take

King School kids out to the various neighborhoods?

[Pause]

And thirty years later

I look back and wonder

at what kind of courage it took

for those people to say that.

And so after some talking about it back and forth . . .

we had a six-to-one vote. . . .

But they came to us.

I don't think we were actually

aware of the fact that

there was a segregated school over there . . .

I think probably at heart

we didn't know how racist

we were behaving by allowing

the school to stay there.

She coughs. She gets up and goes to the kitchen and gets a glass of water. She comes back and looks out the window. The phone rings. She ignores it. She returns to her thoughts:

I remember the night

we voted on it. I remember—

It's stupid,

you remember what you thought,

not what you said.

I said,

Well we're only twelve years late.

Let's go.

And I said

Something

stupid and female,

like

I'd be honored.

I sat there and said to

myself,

This is historic.

We are doing something historic.

Of course this did not happen all at once.

There were community meetings

before the board voted,

one meeting involved the parents from university housing.

We met with people at Martin School.

That was ghastly.

We sat up front.

The board and the people

asked us questions and then they

got a little nasty.

I was not frightened,

but I was so unhappy.

A graduate student

stood up

and said,

"Those people

those African-

Americans

don't want to leave their homes

and

their schools . . ."

"Those people"

has haunted me for thirty years.

[Pause]

We only had one outspoken

racist

on the board

at that time

he is

dead now

and

we can speak ill of the dead.

He happened to be a National

Guard,

that was his

bread and butter.

The night we voted,

he had just come

back

from Chicago,

where the Guard had been sent

to hold down some of

the riots.

And he turned to me

and said,

"You haven't been in Chicago and

listened to those black bastards

calling you names."

No was his vote.

I had a different upbringing than many folks

I guess.

For years

I can remember my mother saying,

The happiest years of my life

were the 10 years we lived next door

to a Negro family down in Joliet.

And I don't know if that impressed me

that Negroes were people

or what,

but I remembered it and felt it

and

I have some black

friends today.

See the picture on the VCR?

I cross the room and remove the large family photo from the top of the VCR and hand it to Mrs. Anderson, who hands it back to me. It is one of those close-up color photos, a blow-up, of four people: mother and father in the back and two children, two little girls, in the front. The father is black, the children mixed, the mother white. Mrs. Anderson explains:

That is my older daughter

and her

husband

and

my two beautiful grandchildren.

Aren't they pretty?

I swear

they had the best of both worlds!

The young man

graduated from Columbia

and

played basketball for four years.

Now he's taking his M.B.A. at UCLA.

The young lady, my daughter,

graduated from Wesleyan.

She's now at Indiana University

in the school of law.

Another Set of Memories

As we prepared to leave Mrs. Anderson's house, one more question came to mind. It concerned the school board elections in 1968. I asked Mrs. Anderson about a black woman named Mrs. Caroline Adams Smith, who was part of an all-white coalition that ran against Mrs. Anderson and her fellow board members. The paper had said that Mrs. Smith's group felt that the incumbents on the board did business behind closed doors, that the busing decision had not been made in public. There were other issues as well. In the summer of 1968, the Martin parents walked out of a school board meeting because they felt that the board members were not considering their complaints. Mr. Daniels's group wanted more representation of African American teachers; the group also wanted an African American principal at Martin and more after-school programs for their children. In 1972, there was a report about desegregation and, according to Mr. Daniels, the report ignored the efforts of the Martin parents in the desegregation project. The president of the board apologized to Mr. Daniels. I reminded Mrs. Anderson that the newspapers called the summer of 1968 "Edge City's Summer of Discontent." She was quick to respond:

They must have taken the Summer of Discontent

from the John Steinbeck novel.

They had to have taken it from

someone.

They were not that clever.

Were you reading last night's paper?

I said that

the wrong way.

Still the same old things,

30 years later.

But I just flat out don't remember those complaints.

Caroline Adams Smith.

She never did like us very much.

I'm having a problem

bringing up the story though.

Probably

it was not nice and

I turned it off and

didn't want to remember it.

I have one habit

that is really very well

ingrained,

and that is if it was distasteful,

I put it away and don't remember it.

My mind is horrible. I don't remember this.

I'm remembering the report now.

But I pitched it.

Another Memory

Six days after the interview, Mrs. Anderson called me at home. It was early evening.

Hello, Dr. Denzin,

this is Alice Anderson.

After you left last week

I remembered

I kept a scrapbook of the years

I was on the school board.

I think you should have it.

I want someone

to tell my story,

now that I am getting so old.

You are welcome to it,

if you want it.

When I arrived at her home, she directed me to her kitchen table. There lay a large scrapbook, 12 by 14 inches, and two folders, as well as a large manila envelope with press clippings inside. The scrapbook carried the label "School board, 6/66–4/67" (the first year of her first term on the board). Two collie puppies were pictured on the cover of the scrapbook, one sitting in a red wheelbarrow. Out of the folders fluttered newspaper clippings, pictures, and notes that congratulated Mrs. Anderson on her victorious reelection to the board in 1968.

Mrs. Anderson had remembered what she had forgotten. She hadn't pitched her files. She had kept all of them. Her scrapbook was a record of the past. But not everything was there. She had indeed forgotten to clip those stories about the "Summer of Discontent," and she had no record of the 1972 desegregation report that ignored Mr. Daniels and his group. These were painful experiences, and Mrs. Anderson had the habit of not remembering distasteful things. Thirty years ago, a lot of distasteful things surrounded desegregation in Edge City.

Reading Mrs. Anderson's Performance

I have attempted to turn Mrs. Anderson's interview into a dramatic, poetic text. As Smith notes, such a text should evoke the character of the speaker; it should allow the speaker to be fully present in his or her speech.

Mrs. Anderson uses irony to convey her views of the world, a racist world she disdains. With her words she creates a narrative montage. Inside this world of jumbled images and memories she looks back, locating herself in the summer of 1966. Thirty years after the fact, she sees courage in the eyes and words of James and Marilyn Daniels. She sees that she and her colleagues allowed themselves to not see the segregated school "over there," and she applies the term *racist* to this gaze. But when she voted, she voted as a woman, and said something "stupid and female," as if a white woman in Edge City could not have a voice on race matters in 1966.

She recalls the graduate student who spoke harshly of "those people." She willingly speaks harshly herself of the one outspoken racist on the board. The 1966 Chicago race riots are evoked by the images behind the words she quotes, "You haven't been to Chicago and listened to those black bastards calling you names." So, for one man, Edge City's desegregation vote was a vote to give a voice to those "black bastards."

In her montage, Mrs. Anderson separates herself from other white people. Her mother had spoken to her of happy times living next door to a Negro family in Joliet, and she came to see that Negroes are people too. She passed this understanding along to her daughter, as the family photo dramatically demonstrates.

All did not go well in Edge City's desegregation experiment. There was a summer of discontent. The white school board ignored the black parents. Mrs. Anderson's scrapbook, with its pictures and clippings, tells part of this story, but the most painful part she did not keep. And in her obituary, there was no mention of her part in this history. The paper did not even record the fact that she had served on the school board.

❖ CONCLUSION

Anna Deavere Smith (1993) contends that Americans have difficulty "talking about race and talking about [racial] differences. This difficulty goes across race, class and political lines" (p. xii). There is, she says, "a lack of words. . . . we do not have a language that serves us as a group" (p. xii). Smith's plays are attempts to find that language. Her performance texts allow us to see more clearly the limits of the language we now use.

Performances like Mrs. Anderson's create spaces for the operation of racial memories. They create occasions for rethinking the politics of race and racism. Mrs. Anderson's text shows that in the 1960s a wide gulf existed between whites and blacks in Edge City. White male voices reproduced racial stereotypes. When a white women spoke out, she felt uncomfortable. But a white woman did speak out in 1966, and she crossed racial boundaries. Listening to Mrs. Anderson's story today reminds us that we still need performers (and performances) like her if we are ever to achieve the promise of a democracy for all races in the United States.

I seek an interpretive social science that is simultaneously autoethnographic, vulnerable, performative, and critical. This is a social science that refuses abstractions and high theory. It is a way of being in the world, a way of writing, hearing, and listening. Viewing culture as a complex performative process, it seeks to understand how people enact and construct meaning in their daily lives. This is a return to narrative as a political act, a social science that has learned how to use the reflexive, dialogic interview. This social science inserts itself into the world in an empowering way. It uses the words and stories that individuals tell to fashion performance texts that imagine new worlds, worlds where humans can become who they wish to be, free of prejudice, repression, and discrimination.

This is the promise of a performative social science in a postcinematic, postvisual society. This social science refuses to treat research as a commodity that can be bought and sold. As researchers, we belong to a moral community. The reflexive interview helps us to create dialogic relationships with that community. These relationships, in turn, allow us to enact an ethic of care and empowerment. This is the kind of ethic Mrs. Anderson sought to create in Edge City in the summer of 1966. In performing her interview, we learn a little more about how we can do the same in our own communities.

5

Reading and Writing Performance

Rules for "good" experimental ethnographic writing can now be established; at least what should be published as "good" experimental writing can be debated.

—Patricia Ticineto Clough, "Comments on Setting Criteria for Experimental Writing," 2000

I am concerned with the performance of subversive . . . narratives. . . . the performance of possibilities aims to create . . . a . . . space where unjust systems and processes are identified and interrogated.

—D. Soyini Madison, "Performances, Personal Narratives, and the Politics of Possibility," 1998

We recognize that performative ethnography can mirror and evoke the performative character of everyday life.

—Paul Atkinson, Amanda Coffey, and Sara Delamont, "Editorial: A Debate About Our Canon," 2001

How can aesthetics move . . . closer to engaged cultural history?

—Stephen Hartnett, "'Democracy Is Difficult':
Poetry, Prison, and Performative Citizenship," 1998

For qualitative researchers, the turn to experimental ethnographic texts poses the problem of the establishment of performative criteria—that is, how researchers should go about critically analyzing these texts and their performances in terms of their epistemological, aesthetic, and political aspects. In this chapter, building on the discussions of aesthetics and pedagogy provided by Giroux (2000a, 2000b) and Garoian (1999), I examine performative criteria in the seventh moment.[60] I foreground subversive, resistance narratives, dramatic, epiphanic performances that challenge the status quo.[61] My topics include the reading, writing, and judging of performances as well as the production of performances that move history.

I begin the chapter with a discussion of the problem of attempting to set criteria for experimental writing (Clough 2000a; Bochner 2000). I then turn to feminist, communitarian criteria, as they apply to resistance performance texts. I next discuss alternative ways of assessing narrative and performance texts, building on the recent arguments of Richardson (2000a, 2000b, 2002a), Bochner (2000), Ellis (2000), Bochner and Ellis (2002), and Clough (2000a). I conclude with some commentary on an aesthetic of color, critical race theory, and the politics of interpretation in the performance community.

❖   A CAVEAT

In the main, in this chapter I focus on North American discourse in sociology and cultural studies. Unfortunately, this has the effect of slighting the highly relevant work of several non-American scholars in other disciplines who have taken up the topics I discuss here. The areas I do not explicitly examine include related discussions of writing and rhetoric (Atkinson and Hammersley 1994; James, Hockey, and Dawson 1997; Spencer 2001), the ethnographic self (Coffey 1999), voice (Atkinson and Hammersley 1994:256–57), authenticity and authentic representations of experience (Atkinson and Silverman 1997), interpretive criteria (Atkinson, Coffey, and Delamont 1999; Delamont, Coffey, and Atkinson 2000), and indigenous, resistance performance texts (Marcus 1998; Smith 1999; Grande 2000; Brayboy 2000).

This complex literature is international, interdisciplinary, and in flux. North Americans are not the only scholars struggling to create postcolonial, nonessentialist, feminist, dialogic, performance texts, texts informed by the rhetorical, narrative turn in the human disciplines (Delamont et al. 2000). This international work troubles the traditional distinctions among science, the humanities, rhetoric, literature, fact, and fiction. As Atkinson and Hammersley (1994:255) observe, this discourse recognizes the "literary antecedents" of the ethnographic text and affirms the "essential dialectic" underlying these aesthetic and humanistic moves.

Moreover, this literature is reflexively situated in multiple historical and national contexts. It is clear that Americans' history with qualitative inquiry cannot be generalized to the rest of the world (Atkinson, Coffey, and Delamont 2001). Nor do all researchers embrace a politicized cultural studies agenda that demands that all interpretive texts advance issues surrounding social justice and racial equality.

The performance turn in Anglo-European discourse can surely benefit from the criticisms and tenets offered by Maori and other indigenous scholars and by a critical red pedagogy (see Chapter 1). Westerners have much to learn from indigenous epistemologies and performance theories.

After Atkinson, Coffey, and Delamont (2001:9), we must ask how the forces of history and culture structure those versions of everyday life that are mirrored and evoked in performance ethnography. Of course, the performance turn in Anglo-European theory has not been embraced everywhere, nor has there been a massive rush among researchers to take up postinterpretive, postfoundational evaluative paradigms. In the pages that follow, I present my interpretation of where this field is currently moving.

❖   SETTING CRITERIA FOR
      PERFORMANCE ETHNOGRAPHY

In the social sciences today there is no longer a God's-eye view that guarantees absolute methodological certainty. All inquiry reflects the standpoint of the inquirer. All observation is theory laden. There is no possibility of theory-free or value-free knowledge. The days of naive realism and naive positivism are over. In their place stand critical and historical realism and various versions of relativism. The criteria for evaluating research are now relative.[62]

Clough (2000a) rightly warns that if we set criteria for judging what is good and what is bad experimental writing or performance ethnography, we may only conventionalize the new writing "and make more apparent the ways in which experimental writing has already become conventional" (p. 278). More deeply, in normalizing this writing, and the performances connected to it, we may forget that this kind of writing was once "thought to be 'bad' writing, improper sociology. . . . It might be forgotten that experimental writing was strongly linked to political contentions over questions of knowledge" (p. 278). And the new writing, in one moment, was taken to be a form of cultural criticism, a way of also criticizing traditional ethnography.

Bochner (2000) elaborates, observing that today "no single, unchallenged paradigm has been established for deciding what does and what does not comprise valid, useful, and significant knowledge" (p. 268). Furthermore, it is impossible to fix a single standard for deciding what is good or bad, or right; there are only multiple standards, temporary criteria, momentary resting places (p. 269). Too often, criteria function as policing devices. The desire to authorize one set of standards can take our attention away from "the ethical issues at the heart of our work" (p. 269).

On this point, Clough (2000a) and Christians (2000) agree with Bochner: All inquiry involves moral, political, and ethical matters. Clough (2000a:283) goes one level deeper, however. With Atkinson, Coffey, Delamont, Lofland, and Lofland (2001:3), she reminds us that from the beginning, the criticisms of standard ethnographic writing in sociology were linked to identity politics and feminist theory, and in anthropology to postcolonial theory. These criticisms involved a complex set of questions, namely, Who has the right to speak for whom, and how?

The need to represent postcolonial hybrid identities became the focus of experimental writing in ethnography, just as there has been "an effort to elaborate race, classed, sexed, and national identities in the autoethnographic writings of postcolonial theorists" (Clough 2000a:285). These debates about writing, agency, self, subjectivity, nation, culture, race, and gender unfolded on a global landscape, involving the transnationalization of capital and the globalization of technology (p. 279). Thus from the beginning, experimental writing has been closely connected to gender, race, family, nation, politics, capital, technology, critical social theory, and cultural criticism—that is, to debates over questions of the representation and presentation of knowledge.

The drive to performance ethnography among Western scholars, the drive to the personal and the autobiographical, Clough (2000a) suggests, reflects a growing sensitivity to issues surrounding agency and the new media technologies. But the subjectivity and forms of selfhood performed and examined in the new autoethnography are linked to "the trauma culture of the teletechnological" (p. 287). Clough observes that much of the new autoethnography is performed by persons writing about the "experiences of drug abuse, sexual abuse, child abuse, rape, incest, anorexia, chronic illness, and death." She goes on, "Autoethnography is symptomatic of the trauma culture that has been most outrageously presented in television talk shows" (p. 287).

This trauma culture exposes and celebrates the erasure of the traditional barriers that have separated the public and the private in American life. In a pornography of the visible, the violent side of intimate family life is exposed, and the contradictions in capitalism as a way of life are revealed. Much of the new autoethnography focuses on trauma, on injuries, on troubled, repressed memories, on inabilities to speak the past, the search for a new voice, the search by shattered, damaged egos for new histories, new forms of agency. But in speaking from the spaces of trauma, Clough (2000a) asserts, autoethnographers do not "critically or self-consciously engage enough the technical substrata of their own writing form" (p. 287).

Clough does not mean to trivialize the trauma written about; rather, she wants to read it as symptomatic of something else that requires attention—namely, how new computer and media technologies, in conjunction with global capital on a transnational scale, are creating new forms of subjectivity. She states, "I think it is these figures of subjectivity appearing in autoethnography which cultural criticism must now attend" (p. 287). Thus she comes back to a single two-part criterion for evaluating experimental writing: cultural criticism and theoretical reflection. Staying close to these two standards allows "experimental writing to be a vehicle for thinking new sociological subjects, new parameters of the social" (p. 290). Clough is fearful that the search for new criteria will silence cultural criticism (p. 290), and I join her in that fear.

In seeking to conventionalize performative criteria, we must not forget Clough's and Bochner's warnings. As Atkinson, Coffey, and

Delamont (2001) note, "Orthodoxy . . . is not a stable category" (p. 11). Mindful of the above distinctions, I turn now to a discussion of criteria that move in three directions at the same time: toward the moral, the political, and the ethical; toward the literary and the aesthetic; and toward trauma and the politics of experience.

❖ FEMINIST, COMMUNITARIAN CRITERIA

To build on Clough's argument, in the seventh moment of inquiry, the understandings and criteria for evaluating critical performance events combine aesthetics, ethics, and epistemologies.[63] Several criteria can be outlined. Like hooks's (1990:111) black aesthetic and Giroux's (2000b:25) public pedagogy, these performance criteria erase the usual differences among ethics, politics, and power. This erasure creates possibilities for a practical, performative pedagogy, a call for performances that intervene and interrupt public life. Such interruptions are meant to unsettle and challenge taken-for-granted assumptions concerning problematic issues in public life. They create a space for dialogue and questions, giving voice to positions previously silenced or ignored (but see Bishop 1998:209; see also Smith 1999).

Ideologically, this performance aesthetic refuses assimilation to white middle-class norms and the traumas of white middle-class culture. It resists those understandings that valorize performances and narratives centered on the life crises of the humanistic subject (see Comolli and Narboni [1969] 1971). In contrast, this aesthetic values performance narratives that reflexively recognize, go against the grain of, and attack the dominant cultural ideologies connected to race, class, family, and gender. These performances expose ruptures in the ideological seams in these dominant cultural mythologies, both through political action and through their subject matter.

Richard Posner's public art functions this way (see Pitzl-Waters and Enstrom-Waters 2002:6). For example, his Berlin installation *Der Wider-Haken-Kräuter-Garten* (*The Garden of "Live Not on Evil"*) manipulates two swastikas made of broken glass. The first swastika, with its arms spinning clockwise, is a symbol from ancient temples representing the sun and its ability to sustain life. The second swastika, its arms spinning counterclockwise, is the Nazi *Hakenkreuz*, a symbol of prejudice. Posner located this installation on the site where a synagogue had previously stood. Destroyed by Allied bombers, the site had been turned into a toxic place, a public dump. Posner's art transforms this formerly toxic place into a site that honors the victims of the Holocaust, including members of Posner's family.

In a feminist, communitarian sense, this aesthetic contends that ways of knowing (epistemology) are moral and ethical (Christians 2000). These ways of knowing involve conceptions of who the human being is (ontology), including how matters of difference are socially organized. The ways in which these relationships of difference are textually represented answer to a political and epistemological aesthetic that defines what is good, true, and beautiful.

Three interconnected criteria shape these representations of the world. *Interpretive sufficiency* is the watchword (Christians 2000:145).[64] Accounts should possess the amount of depth, detail, emotionality, nuance, and coherence that will permit a critical consciousness, or what Paulo Freire (2001) terms *conscientization,* to be formed. Through conscientization, the oppressed gain their own voices and collaborate in transforming their cultures (Christians 2000:148). Second, these accounts should exhibit a *representational adequacy* and be free of racial, class, or gender stereotyping (Christians 2000:145). Finally, texts are *authentically adequate* when they meet three conditions: (a) They represent multiple voices, (b) enhance moral discernment, and (c) promote social transformation (Christians 2000:145). Multivoiced ethnographic texts should empower persons, leading them to discover moral truths about themselves while generating social criticism. These criticisms, in turn, should lead to efforts at social transformation (Christians 2000:147).

Lincoln (1995; see also Finley forthcoming) suggests five criteria for reading and assessing interpretive texts that elaborate Christians's criteria of authentic adequacy. Lincoln proposes that one should ask if a work (a) displays the author's positionality (the criterion of *positionality*); (b) addresses the community in which the research was carried out (*community*); (c) engages and gives voice to silenced or marginalized persons (*voice*); (d) explores the author's understandings during, before, and after the research experience (*critical subjectivity*); and (e) demonstrates openness between researchers and participants (*reciprocity*).

All aesthetics and standards of judgment are based on particular moral standpoints. Hence, for example, an Afrocentric feminist aesthetic (and epistemology) stresses the importance of truth, knowledge, and beauty ("Black is beautiful"). Claims made from this standpoint are based on a concept of storytelling and a notion of wisdom that is experiential and shared. Wisdom so conceived is derived from local, lived experience and expresses lore, folktale, and myth (Collins 1990). This is a dialogic epistemology and aesthetic. It involves give-and-take, an ongoing moral dialogue between persons. It enacts an ethic of care and an ethic of personal and communal responsibility (Collins 1990:214; Giroux 2000a:130). Politically, this aesthetic imagines how a truly democratic society—one free of race prejudice and oppression—might look. This aesthetic values beauty and artistry, movement, rhythm, color, and texture in everyday life. It celebrates difference and the sounds of many different voices. It expresses an ethic of empowerment.

This ethic presumes a moral community that is ontologically prior to the person. This community has shared moral values, including the concepts of shared governance, neighborliness, love, kindness, and the moral good (Christians 2000:144–49). This ethic embodies a sacred, existential epistemology that locates persons in a noncompetitive, nonhierarchical relationship to the larger moral universe. This ethic declares that all persons deserve dignity and a sacred status in the world. It stresses the value of human life, truth telling, and nonviolence (Christians 2000:147).

Under the principle of authentic adequacy (described above), this aesthetic enables social criticism and engenders resistance (see below). It helps persons imagine how things could be different. It imagines new forms of human transformation and emancipation and enacts these transformations through dialogue. If necessary, it sanctions nonviolent forms of civil disobedience (Christians 2000:148). In asking that interpretive work provide the foundations for social criticism and social action, this ethic represents a call to action.

This aesthetic understands that moral criteria are always fitted to the contingencies of concrete circumstances, assessed in terms of those local understandings that flow from feminist, communitarian understandings. This ethic calls for dialogic research rooted in the concepts of care and shared governance. One cannot predict how this ethic will work in any specific situation.

Properly conceptualized, performance autoethnography becomes a civic, participatory, collaborative project. It turns researchers and subjects into coparticipants in a common moral project. This is a form of participatory action research. It has roots in liberation theology, neo-Marxist approaches to community development, and human rights activism in Asia and elsewhere (Kemmis and McTaggart 2000:568). Such work is characterized by shared ownership of the research project, community-based analyses, and an emancipatory, dialectical, and transformative commitment to community action (Kemmis and McTaggart 2000:568, 598). This form of inquiry "aims to help people recover, and release themselves, from the constraints embedded in the *social media* through which they interact" (Kemmis and McTaggart 2000:598).

As a cultural critic, the researcher speaks from an informed moral and ethical position. He or she is anchored in a specific community of progressive moral discourse. The moral ethnographer-as-performer takes a side, working always on behalf of those who seek a genuine grassroots democracy (Hartnett 1998:288).

Moral Criticism and Taking Sides

It is proper for the ethnographer-as-performer, as cultural critic, to take a side, because this is what politically engaged theater does. The process of taking a side is complex (Becker 1967; Hammersley 2001). The performer-as-critic must make his or her own moral and political values clear, including the social constructions, values, and so-called objective facts and ideological assumptions that are attached to these positions. He or she must take care to represent alternative standpoints and claims to truth with minimal distortion. The performer-as-critic must assess these alternative standpoints and reveal how they disadvantage and disempower members of a specific group (Ryan et al. 1998). He or she must then show how a participatory, feminist, communitarian ethic addresses the situation through actions that empower and enable social justice. Advocates of the black arts movement in the 1970s, for example, insisted that art must function politically. They asked how much more beautiful a poem, melody, play, novel, or film made the life of a single black person (Gayle [1971] 1997:1876).

In a call to action, the researcher-as-performer engages in concrete steps that will change a given situation. The performer may show others how to bring new and sacred meanings to a previously marginalized and stigmatized public site, as Richard Posner did. Through performance, the performer demonstrates how particular texts directly and indirectly misrepresent persons and reproduce prejudice and stereotypes.

In advancing this utopian project, the performer seeks new standards and new tools of evaluation. For example, Karenga ([1972] 1997), a theorist of the black arts movement in the 1970s, argued that black art should be political, functional, collective, and committed. Politically and functionally, this art would be about blacks, made by blacks for blacks, and located in local black communities, as was Du Bois's (1926:134) black theater. This community art would support and "respond positively to the reality of a revolution" (Karenga [1972] 1997:1973). It would not be art for art's sake; rather, it would be art for persons in the black community, art for "Sammy the shoeshine boy, T. C. the truck driver and K. P. the unwilling soldier" (p. 1974). Karenga told blacks that "we do not need pictures of oranges in a bowl, or trees standing innocently in the midst of a wasteland . . . or fat white women smiling lewdly. . . . If we must paint oranges or trees, let our guerrillas be eating those oranges for strength and using those trees for cover" (p. 1974). Collectively, Karenga argued, black art comes from the people, and it must be returned to the people "in a form more beautiful and colorful than it was in real life. . . . art is everyday life given more form and color" (p. 1974). Such art is committed to political goals. It is democratic. It celebrates diversity as well as personal and collective freedom.[65] It is not elitist.

In asking whether a work is political, functional, collective, and committed, Karenga's black aesthetic complements the feminist, communitarian ethic and its concepts of interpretive sufficiency, representational adequacy, and authentic adequacy. We can now bring multiple criteria to our evaluation of a work. Is it political, functional, committed, and free of stereotype? Does it exhibit depth, nuance, detail, coherence, and emotion? Are multiple voices and ethical positions present in the work? Does the work create conditions for a critical consciousness?

Committed scholars implement these understandings in their performances. They show others how to fashion their own *grounded aesthetics* within the spaces of the everyday world (Willis 1990; Laermans 1993:156). Such aesthetics are at once political and personal. In the area of commodity consumption, these aesthetics deconstruct the images, appearances, and promises of happiness that marketers use to make objects attractive to consumers (Harms and Kellner 1991:49). These aesthetic practices speak to the complex interplay between resistance and consumption, between desire and pleasure. They articulate the many different ways in which consumers creatively use the resources of popular culture for personal and group empowerment (Laermans 1993:154–55).

The grounded aesthetic functions both as a vehicle and as a site of resistance. In the arena of consumption and race, for example, race scholars deconstruct negative racial representations, turning negative images into positive ones by inventing new cultural images and slogans. In these moves, they formulate a racially grounded practical aesthetic. In the sensuous enactment of this aesthetic, the consumer becomes an active player in the construction of new racial identities.

Critical scholars, of course, make their own values clear. At the same time, they listen to the perspectives and voices of many different stakeholders. In any given situation, they advocate for the underdog (Ryan et al. 1998). In so doing, they attempt to create a critical, reflexive moral consciousness on the part of the citizen-consumer. They argue that happiness is not necessarily connected to the possession of particular material objects, that in fact the desire to possess is a desire created by the manufacturer of the object in question (Harms and Kellner 1991:65).

Critical researchers demonstrate how particular consumption patterns and choices reproduce, for particular oppressed consumer groups (the poor, women, youth, members of racial and other minority groups), the normative ideologies of possessive materialism, designer capitalism, and current fashion. They show how an emphasis on the possession of material goods becomes an end in itself, not a means to attain specific nonmaterial ethical and moral goals. Moreover, critical scholars show how advertising reproduces gender, racial, sexual orientation, and social class stereotypes, and even contributes to consumer practices that are harmful to the personal health of individuals and the environment. In so doing, interpretive researchers engage in social critique and moral dialogue, identifying the different gendered relations of cultural capital that operate in specific consumption contexts.

But more is involved in a researcher's taking a side. The researcher-as-performer must evaluate specific programs and make recommendations concerning programs and practices, advocating lines of action that will maximize participatory democracy, citizen health, and autonomy. Such a commitment makes the researcher accountable for the moral and personal consequences of any particular line of action that he or she recommends.

❖   PERFORMATIVE NORMS AND CRITERIA

As I have argued elsewhere, the feminist ethical model produces a series of norms for the writing and performing project (Denzin

1997:282–83).[66] These norms elaborate four nonnegotiable journalistic norms: accuracy, nonmaleficence, the right to know, and making one's moral position known. The ethnographer-performer's moral tales are not written to produce harm for the innocent (Christians 1986:124) or for those who have been oppressed by the culture's systems of domination and repression (the principle of nonmaleficence). When harm would be produced otherwise, the ethnographer must always protect the identities of the persons about whom he or she writes. These tales are factually and fictionally correct; that is, they are organized under the rule that if something did not happen, it could have happened. When a writer-performer creates a text that includes fiction, or creative nonfiction, or that molds composite cases into a single story, he or she is under an obligation to report this to the reader or audience (see Christians, Ferre, and Fackler 1993:55; Eason 1984, 1986). The reader has the right to read what the ethnographer has learned, but the ethnographer must balance this right to know against the principle of nonmaleficence.

The writer must be honest with the reader.[67] The text must be realistic, concrete as to character, setting, atmosphere, and dialogue. The performance event, as in good ethnodrama, provides a forum for the search for moral truths about the self and the other. This forum explores the unpresentable in the culture, the discontents of daily life. The performer stirs up the world; objectivity is a fiction, and the writer-performer's story (mystory) is part of the tale that is told. The writer has a theory about how the world works, and this theory is never far from the surface of the text. Self-reflexive readers-viewers are presumed, individuals who seek honest but reflexive works that draw them into the many structures of verisimilitude that shape the story in question.

There remains a struggle to find a narrative and performative voice that writes against a long tradition that favors autobiography and lived experience as the sites for reflexivity and self-hood (Clough 1994:157). This form of subjective reflexivity is a trap that too easily reproduces normative conceptions of self, agency, gender, desire, and sexuality. And there is, to repeat, a pressing need for ethnographers to invent a reflexive form of writing and performing that turns autoethnography and experimental literary texts back "onto each other" (Clough 1994:162).

Always a skeptic, the performer-writer is suspicious of conspiracies, alignments of power and desire that turn segments of the public into victims. So these performance works trouble traditional, realist notions of truth and verification, asking always, "who stands to benefit from a particular version of the truth?" The public ethnographer-as-performer enacts an ethics of practice that privileges the client-public relationship. The ethnographer is a moral advocate for the public, although a personal moral code may lead an individual researcher to work against the so-called best interests of a client or a particular segment of the public.

The ethnographer's performance tale is always allegorical, a symbolic tale, a parable that is not just a record of human experience. This tale is a means of experience, a method of empowerment. It is a vehicle for readers to discover moral truths about themselves. More deeply, the performance tale is a utopian tale of self and social redemption, a tale that brings a moral compass back into the reader's (and the writer's) life. The ethnographer discovers the multiple "truths" that operate in the social world, the stories people tell one another about the things that matter to them. Like the public journalist, the ethnographer writes stories that create "pockets of critical consciousness ... discourse[s] of cultural diversity" (Christians 1997:11). These performance stories move oppressed people to action, enabling transformations in the public and private spheres of everyday life.

❖ LITERARY AND AESTHETIC CRITERIA

I turn now to the work of Ellis, Bochner, and Richardson. Collectively, these scholars offer a subtly nuanced set of criteria that emphasize the literary, substantive, and aesthetic dimensions of the new writing (and are consistent with the four nonnegotiable journalistic norms discussed above). In the main, these scholars and their students have focused on what Clough calls the experiences embedded in the culture of trauma. Their works (especially those of Ellis and Bochner) destigmatize the experiences of damaged egos.

Ellis's Literary Realism

Ellis (2000:273) offers a fully developed literary aesthetic. She wants writing that conforms to the criteria of interpretive sufficiency and authentic adequacy. She wants works that are engaging and nuanced, texts that allow her to feel and think with them. She wants stories that immerse her in other worlds, stories that stay with her after she has read them. She privileges evocation over cognitive contemplation. If a writer cannot write evocatively, she says, he or she should write in another genre. She asks that a story tell her something new, "about social life, social process, the experience of others, the author's experience, my own life. Is there anything 'new' here?" (p. 275).

To the criteria of interpretive sufficiency and authentic adequacy, Ellis adds a third, what might be called *literary value,* or what Richardson (2000a:254, 2000b:937) calls *aesthetic merit.* Ellis wants a story to have a good plot, to have dramatic tension, to be coherent and logically consistent, to exhibit balance, flow, and an authenticity of experience, to be lifelike. She asks that authors show and not tell. She asks that they develop characters and scenes fully, but that they avoid including too many characters and scenes. She wants careful editing, an economy of words, but vivid pictures, sounds, smells, and feelings. She wants conversations that feel like real life and surprise endings that challenge her to see things in a new way. She asks whether the author's analysis has been connected closely to the story and to the relevant literature. She asks if the story is worth fighting for, even if it is unconventional (p. 276).

Ellis wants to know what the author's goals are, what he or she is trying to achieve, and asks whether the goals are achievable and worthwhile. She asks whether another writing form would better serve the author's purposes. She wonders whether the writer learned anything new about him- or herself in the act of writing, or about other characters in the story, or about social processes and relationships (p. 275).

Ellis also raises ethical questions, but in a less detailed manner then required by the criteria of authentic adequacy. She does not explicitly ask that an author include multiple voices, moral discernment, or social transformation. She asks whether the author received permission to portray others and whether the others portrayed had a chance to contribute to their perspectives in the story. If these things did not happen, she wants to know why. She asks whether the story may cause pain for characters and readers.

Ellis also asks, Does the story help others "cope with or better understand their worlds? Is it useful, and if so, for whom? Does it encourage compassion for the characters? Does it promote dialogue? Does it have the potential to stimulate social action?" (p. 275). She does not specify the form or direction of social action.

Bochner's Narratives of Self

Ellis's literary realism complements Bochner's vision of poetic social science and alternative ethnography. Bochner also emphasizes issues surrounding interpretive sufficiency. For example, he asks whether narratives of self use language in a way that allows readers (and writers) to extract meaning from experience, "rather than depict experience exactly as it was lived" (Bochner 2000:270).

Bochner (2000) isolates seven criteria. First, he looks for abundant, concrete detail, for the "flesh and blood emotions of people coping with life's contingencies; not only facts but also feelings" (p. 270). Second, he likes structurally complex narratives, stories told in the curve of time, weaving past and present together in the nonlinear spaces of memory work. Third, he judges authors in terms of their emotional credibility, vulnerability, and honesty. He wants texts that comment on those "cultural scripts that resist transformation . . . squeezing comedy out of life's tragedies" (p. 270), texts that take the "measure of life's limitations" (p. 270). Fourth, he wants stories of two selves, stories of "who I was to who I am," lives transformed by crises. Fifth, he holds the writer to "a demanding standard of ethical self-consciousness" (p. 271). Like Ellis, he wants the writer to show concern for those he or she writes about, concern for their place in the story, and concern for how telling the story changes the writer's (and reader's) self, concern for the "moral commitments and convictions that underlie the story" (p. 271). Sixth, also like Ellis, Bochner wants a story that "moves me, my heart and belly as well as my head" (p. 271). He does not demean a story if it is confessional or erotic, or even pornographic, because every story is a dare, a risk. And seventh, consistent with the criteria of authentic adequacy, Bochner wants narratives of the self that can be used as "a source of empowerment and a form of resistance to counter the domination of canonical discourses" (p. 271). He values those works that devictimize stigmatized identities, works that "confirm and humanize tragic experience by bearing witness to what it means to live with shame, abuse, addiction, or bodily dysfunction and to gain agency through testimony" (p. 271).

Bochner's criteria do not actively engage the issues surrounding authentic adequacy, including ethical discernment and social transformation. It is perhaps not enough, Clough would argue, only to bear witness to tragic experience, to make public the traumas of the trauma culture.

Richardson's Five Criteria

Laurel Richardson asks for more, offering five criteria that move back and forth across the dimensions of interpretive sufficiency, representational adequacy, and authentic adequacy. Her first criterion is *substantive contribution:* Does the piece contribute to our understanding of social life? Is the work grounded in a social scientific perspective? Second, she asks whether the work has *aesthetic merit:* Does it succeed aesthetically? Is it artistically shaped? Is it satisfying, complex, not boring (2000a:254)? Her third criterion, *reflexivity,* involves several separate issues: Is the author familiar with the epistemology of postmodernism? How was the information in the text gathered? Were ethical issues involved in this process? Is the author's subjectivity in the text? That is, is the author's point of view clear, is there adequate self-awareness and self-exposure? Is the author held accountable to standards of knowing and telling (2000a:254)? Her fourth criterion addresses *impact.* Richardson asks how the work affects her, emotionally, intellectually, and as a scholar. She asks, Does it generate new questions? Does it move her to try new research practices? Does it move her to action? Fifth, she wants to know how the work *expresses a reality:* "Does this text embody a fleshed out, embodied sense of lived experience? Does it seem 'true'—a credible account of a cultural, social, individual, or communal sense of the 'real'?" (2000b:937).

Together, Ellis, Bochner, and Richardson offer a set of interpretive criteria that emphasize the literary and aesthetic qualities of a work as well as its substantive contributions to an area of knowledge. Ethically, they focus on the dialogic relationship between the writer the subject, requiring that this be an honest and open relationship. Each of these scholars wants to be moved emotionally and intellectually by a work. Each values reflexivity and texts that empower.

A new aesthetic criterion emerges in this reading of Ellis, Bochner, and Richardson. It might be termed the *dialogic requirement.* In asking that they be moved by a text, these writers are saying that they want works that invite them into other persons' worlds of experience. In privileging the reading experience, they bring new meaning to the writerly text. If writing is a form of inquiry, then these scholars want works that provoke self-reflection. And they do not want to be bored (see Richardson 2000b:923–24).

Clough privileges cultural criticism and theoretical reflection. These impulses are present in the criteria developed by Ellis, Bochner, and Richardson, but not privileged. Nor do the latter three scholars interrogate, as Clough asks, the technical substrate of the writing they evaluate. But they offer guidelines for the writing of aesthetically pleasing, elegant, and moving autoethnographies. We are privileged to be able to stand on their shoulders.

I turn now to another list. Building on the work of Christians, Ellis, Bochner, and Richardson, and risking Clough's and Bochner's ire, I offer a set of performative understandings and criteria for performance texts in the seventh moment of inquiry.

❖ PERFORMATIVE UNDERSTANDINGS IN THE SEVENTH MOMENT

The tales and performances of the seventh moment are organized by a counterhegemonic, or subversive, utopian anti-aesthetic (Foster 1983).[68] This anti-aesthetic enacts the feminist, communitarian ethic. It embodies the spirit of Clough's call for cultural criticism, for critical readings of the trauma culture. It works outward from critical race theory. Drawing on the aesthetic and literary guidelines presented by Ellis, Bochner, and Richardson, it is shaped by the following understandings:

- ❖ No topic is taboo, including sexuality, sexual abuse, death, and violence.
- ❖ These texts speak to women and children of color; to persons who suffer from violence, rape, and injustice based on and sex.
- ❖ In these texts ethics, aesthetics, political praxis, and epistemology are joined; every act of representation, artistic or research, is a political and ethical statement. An ethics of care is paramount.
- ❖ Claims to truth and knowledge in these texts are assessed in terms of multiple criteria, including asking whether they (a) interrogate existing cultural, sexist, and racial stereotypes, especially those connected to family, femininity, masculinity, marriage, and intimacy; (b) give primacy to memory and its connections to concrete lived experience; (c) use dialogue and an ethics of personal responsibility that values beauty, spirituality, and a love of others; (d) implement an emancipatory agenda committed to equality, freedom and social justice, and participatory

democratic practices; (e) emphasize community, collective action, solidarity, and group empowerment.

❖ These texts presume ethnographers, performers, and social researchers who are part of and spokespersons for local moral communities, communities with their own symbolism, mythology, and storytelling traditions.

❖ These texts draw upon the vernacular, on folk and popular culture forms of representation, including proverbs, music (work songs, spirituals, blues songs, jazz, rap, *corridos*), sermons, prayers, poems, choreopoems, folktales, paintings, plays, movies, photographs, performance art pieces, and murals (Denzin 2002d:182).

❖ These texts are produced by artists-researchers-writers who aim to speak to and represent the needs of particular communities (drug addiction, teenage pregnancy, murder, gang warfare, AIDS, high rates of school dropout).

❖ The authors of these texts understand that no single representation or work can speak to the collective needs of the community. Rather, local communities are often divided along racial, ethnic, gender, residential, age, and class lines.

Thus in the seventh moment we seek emancipatory, utopian performances, texts grounded in the distinctive styles, rhythms, idioms, and personal identities of local folk and vernacular culture. These performances record the histories of injustices experienced by the members of oppressed groups. They show how members of local groups have struggled to find places of dignity and respect in a violent, racist, and sexist civil society.

These performances are sites of resistance. They are places where meanings, politics, and identities are negotiated. They transform and challenge stereotypical forms of cultural representation—white, black, Chicano, Asian American, Native American, gay, or straight.

Performative Criteria

Given the normative understandings listed above, I value those autoethnographic texts that do the following things:

1. Unsettle, criticize, and challenge taken-for-granted, repressed meanings

2. Invite moral and ethical dialogue while reflexively clarifying their own moral positions

3. Engender resistance and offer utopian thoughts about how things can be made different

4. Demonstrate that they care, that they are kind

5. Show instead of tell, using the rule that less is more

6. Exhibit interpretive sufficiency, representational adequacy, and authentic adequacy

7. Present political, functional, collective, and committed viewpoints

In asking whether a given performance event does all these things, I understand that every performance is different. Further, audiences may or may not agree regarding what demonstrates caring, or kindness, or reflexivity, and some persons may not want their taken-for-granted understandings challenged. I turn now to a brief discussion of the politics of interpretation in the performance community. I want to connect this discussion to critical race theory.

❖ TRAUMA, RACE, AND
    THE POLITICS OF INTERPRETATION

Writing, Richardson (2002a:879) reminds us, is not an innocent practice, although in the social sciences and the humanities there is only interpretation. Nonetheless, as Marx ([1888] 1983:158) continues to remind us, we are in the business of not just interpreting but of changing the world. Clough asks that writers transcend the traumas celebrated in a mass-mediated trauma culture. She asks for works that go more deeply into cultural criticism, into the politics of interpretation. This requires a return to race and critical race theory, an aesthetic of color. In this section I want to work back and forth between variations on a Chicana/o (Gonzalez 1998; Pizarro 1998) and African American aesthetic (Davis 1998; hooks 1990, 1996) and the relationship between these practices and critical race theory (Parker 1998; Ladson-Billings 2000). I want to connect to the radical performance texts stemming from the black arts movement of the 1960s and 1970s (Baraka 1997; Harris 1998; Baker 1997).

These interconnections are now being established in the various black cultural studies projects of the new black public intellectuals and cultural critics (Hall, Gilroy, hooks, Gates, West, Reed, Morrison, Wallace, Steele). A current generation of blues, rap, hip-hop, and pop music singers, jazz performers, poets (Angelou, Dove, Jordan, Knight, Cortez), novelists (Walker, Morrison, Bambara), playwrights (Wilson, Shange, Smith), and filmmakers (Lee, Singleton, Burnett, Dash) are also making these links (see Christian 1997:2019–20; Harris 1998:1343–44).[69]

A Feminist Aesthetic of Color

A feminist Chicana/o and black performance-based aesthetic uses art, photography, music, dance, poetry, painting, theater, cinema, performance texts, autobiography, narrative, storytelling, and poetic, dramatic language to create a critical race consciousness, thereby extending the post–civil rights Chicana/o and black arts cultural movements into the current century (see Harrington 1999:208). These practices serve to implement critical race theory, which "seeks to decloak the seemingly race-neutral and color-blind ways ... of constructing and administering race-based appraisals ... of the law, administrative policy, electoral politics, ... political discourse [and education] in the USA" (Parker et al. 1998:5; see also Ladson-Billings 2000).

Thus Collins's (1990, 1998) Afrocentric feminist agenda for the 1990s moves into the 21st century; that is, theorists and practitioners enact a standpoint epistemology that sees the world from the point of view of oppressed persons of color. This aesthetic is also informed by the successive waves of movements devoted to equal rights for Asian Americans, Native Americans, women, and gay, lesbian, bisexual, and transgendered persons, movements that "use their art as a weapon for political activism" (Harris 1998:1384; see also Nero 1998:1973).

Theorists critically engage and interrogate the anti–civil rights agendas of the New Right (see Jordan 1998), but this is not a protest or integrationist initiative aimed solely at informing a white audience of racial injustice. It dismisses such a narrow agenda, and in so doing it rejects classical Eurocentric and postpositivist standards for evaluating literary, artistic, and research work.

Aesthetics and Cinematic Practices

Within the contemporary black and Chicana/o aesthetic communities, there are specific film, narrative, and visual cultural practices associated with this aesthetic project (for a review, see Denzin 2002d:183–86). These practices inform and shape the narrative and visual content of these experimental texts. They include the following:

- ❖ Experiments with narrative forms, folk ballads, and *corridos* that honor long-standing Chicana/o discourse traditions (Noriega 1992:152–53; Fregoso 1993:70–76)
- ❖ The use of improvisation, mise-en-scène, and montage to fill the screen with multiracial images and to manipulate bicultural visual and linguistic codes
- ❖ The use of personal testimonials, life stories, voice-over, and off-screen narration to provide overall narrative unity to a text (Noriega 1992:156–59)
- ❖ The celebration of key elements in Chicana/o culture—especially the themes of resistance, maintenance, affirmation, and neoindigenism, or *mestizaje* (Noriega 1992:150)—which challenges assimilation and melting-pot narratives
- ❖ The deconstruction of machismo, the masculine identity, and the celebration of works that give the Chicana subject an active part in the text while criticizing such timeworn stereotypes as the virgin, the whore, the supportive wife, and the homegirl (Fregoso 1993:29, 93–94)
- ❖ The rejection of essentializing approaches to identity; an emphasis on a processual, gendered, performance view of self and the location of identity within, not outside of, systems of cultural and media representation
- ❖ The refusal to accept the official race-relations narrative of the culture, which privileges the ideology of assimilation while contending that black and Hispanic youth pose grave threats to white society (Fregoso 1993:29)

These artistic representations are based on the notion of a radical and constantly changing set of aesthetic practices. As hooks (1990) observes, "There can never be one critical paradigm for the evaluation of artistic work. . . . a radical aesthetic acknowledges that we are constantly changing positions, locations, that our needs and concerns vary, that these diverse directions must correspond with shifts in critical thinking" (p. 111).

At this level, there is no preferred aesthetic. For example, realistic art is not necessarily better than abstract, expressionist, or impressionist

art. In the worlds of jazz, ragtime, New Orleans, classic, or swing is not
necessarily more or less politically correct or aesthetically better than
bebop, cool, hard bop, Latin, avant-garde, or fusion. Nor is Charlie
Parker less politically correct then Lester Young or Ben Webster, Ella
Fitzgerald, Nina Simone, Nancy Wilson, Billie Holiday, Bessie Smith,
John Coltrane, or Miles Davis.

But then, June Jordan (1998:199–200) might put it differently. In her
jazz prose poem "A Good News Blues" she pays homage to Billie and
Louis, Nina, and Bessie, to anyone who sings the blues. In the following
lines she praises Billie Holiday:

Since the blues left my sky

I'm runnin out on Monday

To chase down all my Sundays . . .

. . .

I'm liftin' weights and wearin sweats . . .

And thrillin through the night . . .

And if I want to rewrite

all the sorry-ass/

victim/passive/feminine/

traditional

propaganda

spinnin out here

    ain' nobody's business

    if I do.

Each text, each performance, should be valued for the collective
and individual reflection and critical action it produces, including conversations that cross the boundaries of race, class, gender, and nation.
We should ask how each performance text promotes the development
of human agency, "resistance . . . and critical consciousness" (hooks
1990:111).

This aesthetic also seeks and values beauty and looks to find
beauty in the everyday, especially in "the lives of poor people" (hooks

1990:111). Here is an illustration from bell hooks, who recalls the houses of her childhood, especially the house of Baba, her grandmother. Looking back into her childhood, hooks observes that she now sees how this black woman was struggling to create, in spite of poverty and hardship, an oppositional world of beauty. Baba had a clean house that was crowded with many precious objects. Baba was also a quilt maker. She turned everyday, worn-out clothing into beautiful works of art, and her quilts were present in every room of her small house.

Late at night, hooks would sit alone in an upstairs room in Baba's house. In the stillness of the night, in reflections from the moon's light, hooks came to see darkness and beauty in different ways. Now, in a different time, late at night, she and her sisters "think about our skin as a dark room, a place of shadows. We talk often about color politics, and the ways racism has created an aesthetic that wounds us, we talk about the need to see darkness differently. . . . in that space of shadows we long for an aesthetic of blackness—strange and oppositional" (hooks 1990:113).

Aesthetics, art, performance, history, culture, and politics are thus intertwined, for in the artful, interpretive production, cultural heroes, heroines, mythic pasts, and senses of moral community are created. It remains to us to chart the future—to return to the beginning, to reimagine the ways in which performance ethnography can advance the agendas of radical democratic practice, to ask where these practices will take us next.

❖ INTO THE FUTURE

A new postinterpretive, postfoundational paradigm is emerging. This framework is attaching itself to new and less certain interpretive criteria. A more expansive framework shaped by an aesthetics of color and critical race theory principles informs these criteria.

Epistemologies and aesthetics of color will proliferate, building on Afrocentric, Chicana/o, Native American, Asian American, and Third World perspectives. More elaborated epistemologies of gender (and class) will appear, including queer theory and feminisms of color. These interpretive communities and their scholars will draw on their group experiences for the texts they will write, and they will seek texts that speak to the logics and cultures of these communities. In so doing, they will challenge those representations that have come before (see Cook-Lynn 1996:37–38, 71). They will be committed to advancing the political, economic, cultural, and educational practices of critical race theory. These practices will be embedded in the everyday world, in the worlds of oppression. New forms of critical pedagogy will not be reduced to arguments or explanations "bounded by the Western tradition" (Bishop 1998:209).

This new generation of scholars will be committed not just to describing the world, but to changing it. Their texts will be performance based. They will be committed to creating civic transformations and to using minimalist social theory. They will inscribe and perform utopian dreams, dreams shaped by critical race theory, dreams of a world where all are free to be who they choose to be, free of gender, class, race, religious, and ethnic prejudice and discrimination. The next moment in qualitative inquiry will be one in which the practices of performance ethnography finally move, without hesitation or encumbrance, from the personal to the political.

In the end, then, to summarize: I seek an existential, interpretive social science that offers a blueprint for cultural criticism. This criticism is grounded in the specific worlds made visible in the writing process. It understands that ethnography is never theory- or value-free. There can be no objective account of a culture and its ways. Taking our lead from 20th-century African American cultural critics (Du Bois, Hurston, Ellison, Wright, Baldwin, Hines), we now know that the ethnographic, the aesthetic, and the political can never be neatly separated. Ethnography, like art, is always political.

Accordingly, after Ford ([1950] 1998), we seek a critical, civic, literary ethnography that evidences a mastery of literary craftsmanship, the art of good writing. It should present a well-plotted, compelling, but minimalist narrative, a narrative based on realistic, natural conversation, with a focus on memorable, recognizable characters. These characters should be located in well-described, "unforgettable scenes" (p. 1112). Such work should present clearly identifiable cultural and political issues, including injustices based on the structures and meanings of race, class, gender, and sexual orientation. The work should articulate a politics of hope. It should criticize how things are and imagine how they could be different. It should locate and represent the gendered, sacred self in its ethical relationships to nature. Finally, it should do these things through direct and indirect symbolic and rhetorical means. Writers who create such texts are fully immersed in the oppressions and injustices of their time. They direct their ethnographic energies to higher, utopian, morally sacred goals.

The truth of these new texts is determined pragmatically, through their truth effects, through the critical, moral discourse they produce, the "empathy they generate, the exchange of experience they enable, and the social bonds they mediate" (Jackson 1998:180). The power of these texts is not a question of whether "they mirror the world as it 'really' is" (Jackson 1998:180)—the world is always already constructed through our performances. Rorty (1980) is firm on this point. There is no mirror to nature.

And so we must learn how to enact an enabling, performative ethnography, an ethnography that aspires to higher goals. We can scarcely afford to do otherwise. We are at a critical crossroads in the histories of our disciplines and our nation. As Cornel West (1994) reminds us, "We simply cannot enter the twenty-first century at each other's throats" (p. 159). But, with West, we must ask, "Do we have the intelligence, humor, imagination, courage, tolerance, love, respect, and will to meet the challenge?" (p. 159).

PART II

Performance Texts

Bone Deep in Landscapes

The chapters that follow are meant to be read aloud as spoken-word texts, as coperformances. I present these autoethnographic performance texts to implement the arguments developed in the preceding chapters. In framing the chapters in this section, I draw on the work of Mary Clearman Blew (1977, 1990, 1991, 1994, 1999:25, 2000), who speaks of being "bone deep in landscape," of reaching for performative connections among her personal story, a style of writing, and the history of a family homestead on the banks of the Judith River in north-central Montana. Blew writes of being anchored to a place, of being bone deep in its landscape and its histories, the umbilical tangle that connects place, person, and writer (1999:6). Like Blew, I search for the proper storied relationship between my past and its landscapes.

For years, I wrote as an ethnographer, an interpretive interactionist, a cultural critic, an occasional social theorist. But then something happened. Like Blew, I came to a divide. I felt a hollowness that writing ethnography and theory could not fill (see Blew 1999:4). Three deaths within the space of as many years changed the way I thought of myself as a writer. In 1994, Carl Couch, my intellectual mentor, died; in 1995, my father died, and my mother died the following year. These three deaths located me in three different landscapes: rural central Iowa; Champaign, Illinois, where I currently live and work; and south-central Montana. A month before Carl Couch died, my wife and I bought a small cabin on Rock Creek, 4 miles outside Red Lodge,

Montana, 20 miles from the Wyoming border, and 69 miles and 10,942 feet up and over the Beartooth Highway to Yellowstone Park, the road that travel correspondent Charles Kuralt called "the most beautiful drive in America." The death of my parents brought me back to a family history I had repressed—a rural Iowa childhood marked by illness, addiction, violence, divorce, and death.

The cabin in Montana placed me in touch with a regional performance literature, a literature of landscapes, nature, national parks, Native American stories and myths, the Lewis and Clark journals, stories of early pioneers and the agricultural frontier, and travel accounts, the literature and poetry of modern Montana and the contemporary West: the stories of Abbey, Beer, Blew, Blunt, Coates, Doig, Ehrlich, Ford, Guthrie, Kingsolver, Kittredge, Maclean, McGuane, Momaday, Quammen, Stegner, Welch, and Terry Tempest Williams, the literature collected in that huge volume edited by Kittredge and Smith, *The Last Best Place: A Montana Anthology* (1988).[70]

Kittredge (1996:97) says that we need new stories about the West. He says that the West is a place for performances, a place where myth circulates with reality. I have accepted Kittredge's invitation. I have started to write about performing Montana (Denzin 1999a); I am telling Rock Creek stories (Denzin 2000c).

Today, I am in between landscapes. Westward looking, from my writing table in Champaign, telling Montana stories returns me to my youth, to the places of family legend and lore. I seek today to retell this Iowa childhood, to tell it through the words of a person who is writing himself into a new place, a new landscape, the places and sounds of south-central Montana. I want to re-vision, to reexperience these prairie landscapes, where I was bone deep in misery and pain.

So, with Blew (1999:21), I play my part in the Westward movement. I am drawn to my version of a personal frontier. Modifying Frederick Jackson Turner (1894), my version of the frontier is a meeting point between my past and my future. Turner's pioneers struggled against a primal wilderness shaped by European imagery of savage and pastoral landscapes, the unknown mirrored in the known. As Blew (1999:25) observes, this is the theory of landscape as symmetry, a hall of mirrors, the promise of the familiar in the unfamiliar.

But suppose the unfamiliar cannot be given meaning in the familiar. Suppose that landscape as symmetry is a false hall of mirrors. Suppose the challenge is to let go of the familiar, to seek new stories, to create new performances that do not reproduce the old myths. In this model the personal frontier resides on a horizon that is always just out of reach. Turner was wrong. The wilderness never comes to a close. We are constantly restaging our personal version of the primal struggle (Blew 1999:22).

I intend a writing form that moves from interpretation and emotional evocation to praxis, empowerment, and social change. Guided by Victor Turner's theories of ritual, liminal experience and the epiphanic, I move back and forth in the chapters in Part II from the personal to the political. Writing through my own experiences, I am seeking a representational form that invokes critical race consciousness, an autoethnographic fiction that exposes the social circumstances that reproduce racial stereotyping and racial injustice in postmodern culture. This performance-based writing should conform to the interpretive and aesthetic criteria outlined in Chapter 5. It should show, not tell. It uses the techniques of a dialogic minimalist fiction, focusing more on dialogue than on plot or characterization. However, it does not ignore the demand to impose narrative unity on the events described. It bends back and forth in time while exhibiting emotional credibility, vulnerability, and honesty. It does not parade its theoretical underpinnings, but it is saturated with theory, thoroughly conversant with the principles and assumptions of critical pedagogy, poststructuralism, performance ethnography, critical race theory, pragmatism, and symbolic interactionism (Richardson 2000b:926–29, 2002a:878–80; Conquergood 1998; Madison 1999; Denzin 2001b, 2001d, 2001e).

I seek a writing form that is part memoir, part essay, part autoethnography. I write from the scenes of memory, rearranging, suppressing, even inventing scenes, forgoing claims to exact truth or factual accuracy, searching instead for emotional truth, for deep meaning (see Stegner 1990:iv; Blew 1999:7). As Stegner has noted, translating experience and memory into "fictional truth . . . is not a transcription at all, but a re-making" (quoted in Benson 1996:114). By participating in such a remaking, I am creating writing that falls within the "boundaries of creative nonfiction," which "will always be as fluid as water" (Blew 1999:7). In this writing I claim ownership of my past, changing it as I write about it.

To steal from and paraphrase Kittredge (1992:238), I want to do this so I can feel at home in this crazy world I keep calling my own. In so doing, I hope to be able to see more clearly that I am part of what is sacred. Again borrowing from Kittredge (1992), this is my "only chance at paradise" (p. 238). But there is more involved then personal paradise. Kittredge (1987) again:

In the American West we are struggling to revise our dominant mythology, and to find a new story to inhabit. Laws control our lives, and they are designed to preserve a model of society based on values learned from mythology. Only after reimagining our myths can we coherently remodel our laws, and hope to keep our society in a realistic relationship to what is actual. (p. 67; also quoted in Slovic 1999:83)

In the United States today, in the brutally cruel, cold days since September 11, 2001, we are struggling to revise our dominant mythology. Just who are we as Americans? What stories about ourselves do we want to inhabit? Who are our storytellers, whose stories will we accept? Which laws will we allow to control our lives?

We want laws designed to preserve a model of a radically peaceful democratic society, a society that is nonviolent. We want laws and courts that operate based on a post–September 11 mythology. We want a new mythology for America. We must reimagine our myths. Only then can we coherently remodel our laws and hope to keep our society in a realistic relationship to our utopian democratic ideals. In a modest way, I intend the essays in Part II to speak to this new mythology.

❖   WRITING STORIES

I begin Part II with "Two-Stepping in the '90s," a story that mourns the death of my mother while invoking childhood memories of music and dance. I wrote the original version of this chapter for a session at the 1998 meetings of the Midwest Sociological Society that was held to honor the work of Laurel Richardson. In "Two-Stepping," I call for stories that interrogate the repressive structures of daily life, in this case middle-class ideologies surrounding family, mothers and sons, and death and dying. I locate this essay in a tradition associated with the autoethnographic works of Richardson, Clough, Ellis, Krieger, Behar, and Rosaldo.[71]

Chapter 7, "Mother and Mickey," bridges two landscapes and two time periods: my Iowa childhood and my current place in Red Lodge, Montana. In telling this family story I connect my childhood to American popular culture in the 1950s, in this case Mickey Mantle, a sports idol. Mickey died while my wife and I were in Montana, and listening to Bob Costas's eulogy for him took me back to repressed childhood memories.

Chapter 8, "Performing Montana," was my first Montana story, so to speak, and it announces a desire to take a performance turn in my own work. I wrote the original version of this chapter at the request of Barry Glassner and Rosanna Hertz (1999), who were assembling a series of essays on the topic of qualitative sociology as everyday life. Contributors were invited to write about how they use sociology in their own lives. This invitation came at just the right time. I was struggling to find a way to write about Montana, to return to the world in front of me without doing traditional ethnography.[72] "Performing Montana" reflects my desire to write about Montana, but in a different way. By moving in the direction of performance writing, I was able to write Montana stories without being a traditional ethnographer. I did not want to study the place where I was vacationing, but I felt a need to write. And, after all, I was part of performing Montana. By writing about these performances I could record my experiences in this new landscape.

"Performing Montana" created the space for the next story, "Rock Creek History." Inspired by Edward Abbey's radical views on the landscape of the American West, I take on the topic of pollution in Rock Creek, the river that runs by our Montana cabin. It is a story about how outsiders with a lot of money can spoil a pristine "natural" setting. These outsiders were enacting their version of the New West. Down the narrow country road they would parade, astride their silver-saddled horses with braided manes. Decked out in fancy cowboy boots, expensive chaps, vests, and hats, flashing turquoise jewelry, they would smile and nod at us, the local landowners. But in their performances, they destroyed the very thing they sought—that is, an authentic western experience that would evoke awe and respect on our part. Instead, they fueled our anger and disrespect, and on top of that their horses were despoiling Rock Creek.

Chapters 10 and 11, "Cowboys and Indians" and "Redskins and Chiefs," are about race relations in Red Lodge and in Urbana, Illinois. In the writing-story that follows the story that opens Chapter 10, I state that I had gone to Red Lodge to leave the problems of Illinois behind, but the two landscapes intersected in a racial performance in the Red Lodge Civic Auditorium. Memories and experiences from my childhood collided in that site, and this essay tells the story of that collision.

"Redskins and Chiefs" is my attempt at a complex montage, a mixed-genre work, with many different voices speaking at the same time. In these voices the same message is heard over and over again, in slightly different form: White people with good intentions believe they have the right to honor persons of color. White people can do this by appropriating symbols, images, and meanings that are associated with another group and its way of life. If the intentions of whites are honorable, then their actions are beyond reproach. Those who would criticize them are engaging in cultural politics, in a form of political correctness. Hence the views of such critics can be dismissed.

The performance of these discourses represents multiple forms of cultural racism, forms that operate simultaneously at the institutional, personal, discursive, and interactional levels. Well-intended persons cannot claim to be free of racism if their performances create negative racial stereotypes and experiences for those being "honored." When this happens, the symbols in question must be dismantled. Autoethnographic performance texts are uniquely suited for penetrating and exposing these interconnecting layers and forms of racism.

In "Searching for Yellowstone," the final chapter in Part II, I take up my relationships with my father and grandfather. In this chapter, I read these relationships in terms of a trip to Yellowstone National Park that I never took with my grandfather. In searching for Yellowstone, I search for myself and for the meanings this park has for me and my family history.

6

Two-Stepping in the '90s

The technologies of writing create gendered social texts in which desire, intimacy, power, class, race, ethnicity, and identity come alive.[73] The authors of autoethnographic performance texts use personal experience and memory as the point of departure for writing about things that matter in everyday life. Such texts allow writers to confront and interrogate the cultural logics of late capitalism, including those logics connected to the myths of motherhood, family, marriage, love, and intimacy. When effectively crafted, these texts create a sense of emotional verisimilitude for reader and writer, producing experiences of catharsis, self-renewal, and self-discovery.

This form of writing, especially when read aloud, demands active and reflexive readers and listeners, persons willing to be moved by personal stories of pain, disease, and personal hardship. At the same time, this writing form makes the social scientist accountable and vulnerable to the public. A new ethics of writing is advocated, an ethics of narrative that demands that writers put their empirical materials into forms that readers can use in their own lives (Ellis and Bochner 1996:27). In so doing, writers strip away the veneer of self-protection that comes with professional title and position. With nothing any longer to hide, writers are now free to excavate the personal in the name of the political.

Clearly, this ethical mandate blurs into a second function. These texts must also work as cultural criticism, as tools for critique and political action. At this level they join the personal with the political. They work as venues for ground-level criticism aimed at the repressive structures of everyday life, including those structures connected to the deaths of loved ones. Ivan Doig (1978:11) suggests there are a thousand ways to mourn a mother's death. Here is one more way.

My mother died at noon on October 24, 1997. She was cremated an hour later, no funeral. She gave nobody a chance to say good-bye. A message on the answering machine said she was gone. But then we weren't talking, hadn't talked for more than 3 years, so Mother knew that any good-bye risked being false, untrue. She left on her own terms.

I ranted and raved, sulked, pouted, and cried for several weeks. One day my wife said, "You know your mother did everybody a favor. If there had been a funeral, you and your brother would have been fighting the whole time. Her way, it, was all over, all at once. Maybe she was a smart woman." I didn't like that. Maybe I wanted one more fight with mother and my brother?

Every fall I teach an advanced qualitative research seminar. In September and October of 1997, we were reading the works of women who were writing about writing culture: Patricia Clough, Laurel Richardson, Carolyn Ellis, Ruth Behar, Carol Stack, Susan Krieger, Yvonna Lincoln. Mother died on Friday, and that Wednesday we had been talking about Susan Krieger's short story "The Family Silver" (1996:65–82) and Laurel Richardson's long autobiographical story "Vespers" (1997:217–38).

Krieger's and Richardson's stories are written from sites of memory, not from sites of lived experience. Each writer re-creates, in her mind's eye, a series of emotional moments and then retraces her life through those moments, writing about the past from the vantage point of the present. Krieger (1996) begins the "Family Silver" thus:

I have just come back from a trip to Florida to settle the affairs of my lover's aunt [Maxine], who died suddenly at the age of seventy. She was carrying her groceries up the stairs to her apartment when she dropped dead of a heart attack. . . .

. . . It was an otherworldly experience: going to Florida . . . to clean out the house of a woman I did not know—sorting through her clothes and jewelry, finding snapshots she recently took, using her bathroom, meeting her friends. (pp. 65, 68)

On her last day in Florida, Krieger finds Aunt Maxine's silver flatware inside an old accordion case in the back corner of a greasy kitchen cabinet. Maxine's silver is cheap. It had been a replacement set. It is tarnished, not the real thing, like the family silver Krieger's mother had gotten from her mother. Krieger asks, "What determines the value of a person's life, is value different if you are a woman, how do you separate a woman from the things she owns, leaves behind, her clothes, the cheap family silver?" (p. 70). This cheap set of silver flatware was not an adequate measure of Aunt Maxine.

Laurel Richardson's mother died of breast cancer in Miami Beach on June 8, 1968. Nearly 30 years later, Laurel (1997) wrote about her mother's death:

On June 8, I awoke determined to drive to Key West for the day. I sponge-bathed Mother, greeted the nurse, kissed my parents good-bye, and drove off in Father's Dodge Dart. When I got to Long Key, I was overwhelmed with the need to phone my parents. Mother had just died—less than a minute ago—Father said. (p. 234)

Of this news she observes, "I was grateful to have not witnessed her passing-on. I was thirty years old—too young to lose a mother, again" (p. 235).

Ten years after her mother's death, Laurel wrote a poem titled "Last Conversation" (1997:234). Two weeks after my mother died, we read this poem aloud in my seminar:

I want to hold your

weightless body to my

breasts, cradle you,

rock you to sleep.

Standing against the wall of the seminar room, hearing these words, I wanted to cry, even scream, for now I knew why I was so mad at my mother. I could only imagine her body—Was it weightless? Did her eyes still sparkle as I remembered them? Had her hair turned white and gray like mine, or was it still pitch black, with a hint of white?

Laurel's poem continues: "you want to be held, mother, tired of the dance" (p. 235).

And now a memory of my own. One summer night, when I was a clumsy 12-year-old, Mother and I danced around the dining room table in our little house on Third Avenue in Indianola, Iowa. Harry James was on the radio playing "Makin' Whoopee." We swirled around that table, doing the two-step, my big feet stepping on hers. The fan blew her hair and she smiled, light as a feather on her feet. We went from one length of that room to the other. I've never danced better.

Renato Rosaldo (1989:3–9) talks of the grief of Ilongot men, of the cultural practice of head-hunting, of taking another's life as a way of venting and expressing the rage that an individual feels when a family member dies. Three years after the death of his wife, Michelle, Rosaldo came to understand this cultural practice. Still grieving, still filled with rage, he writes, he longed for the "Ilongot solution" (p. 11). He needed a "place to carry [his] anger" (p. 11). By "writing of grief and a Headhunter's Rage" he found that place (pp. 10–11), not by taking another's life, but by writing about the meaning of a loved one's death.

I write my memories of my mother, the meanings of her death for me, through Aunt Maxine's family silver, through Laurel's poem about her mother, that weightless body, through Rosaldo's final acceptance of his wife's death, through my memory of my last dance with Mother—a son's rage folded inside the love one must always feel for one's mother, a love that gets tarnished, that steps on your feet, a love that lies to you, lies to itself.

One more dance, replay Harry James, find a little Philco radio from the 1950s in an antique shop, look for a dining room table like the one your parents had in Indianola. Dance with your wife to Art Tatum and Ben Webster doing their version of "Makin' Whoopee." That blushing, black-haired, blue-eyed girl laughing on the old Coca-Cola tray looks just like your mother.

Replayed lives, memories done all over again, meanings in motion, men and women doing the two-step in the '90s. Last picture shows, cinema paradiso. Laurel Richardson (1997) again:

After an absence of forty-two years, I returned to Olivet Camp on Lake Geneva. I walked along the shore path, crossed the gravel knoll, climbed up the wooden stairs . . . looked at the Recreation Room where I had attended vespers . . . and then walked up the hill to Bluebird cottage. I looked inside. The sleeping room and porch seemed unchanged. I took pictures. Four decades were like a fortnight. . . . I was welcomed as "Auntie Laurel." . . . I declined the invitation for church and potluck. I was eight again, and I began to write. (pp. 237–38)

Beginning to write is what this project is all about. Learning how to write a new way, to move from the scenes of memory to the present and back again, to reclaim a re-visioned present against a newly understood past.

Laurel and Susan and Renato helped me better understand what my mother's death meant, to understand that her refusal to have a funeral was her way of giving me the family silver, her way of saying, You are going to have to do the hard work of constructing a memory of me that will work for you, because I'm not doing that work for you.

Laurel's mother died as Laurel drove to Key West. About the time my mother was being cremated, I was at a memorial service listening to a classical jazz band play a version of Louis Armstrong's version of "When the Saints Come Marching In."

Laurel and I were both doing something else when our mothers died, and in our memories, we attempt to reclaim connections to these women who marked our lives so deeply. Writing culture in this way is more than using the personal in the service of the therapeutic, although the therapeutic is not to be diminished. Culture seen in the rear view of memory comes alive as a spectacle, a performance, a series of improvised doings, big people acting out their versions of being adults—the personal and the political interacting with one another, new and different ways of doing gender, emotion, meaning, death, the value of a woman's life, the last act, one more time.

If the social sciences are to live far into this new century, they need to confront rather than reject this kind of experimental writing. This new writing challenges each of us always to work outward and backward to remembered experience, to write improvised moral texts that continually revisit the old. These texts are always personal, but always cutting away at the corrosive edges of repressive social structures and social institutions. This is a personal social science, a moral ethnography that reads repression and pain biographically, existentially. It knows that behind every act of institutional repression lurks a flesh-and-blood human being who can be held accountable, at a deep, moral level, for his or her actions. The new writing asks only that we all conduct our own ground-level criticism aimed at the repressive structures in our everyday lives.

7

Mother and Mickey

I was putting another picture of Mickey Mantle up on the wall in my
bedroom about the time Dad came in the front door, slightly drunk.
This was the summer of 1952. We were living in a little rental house on
West Fourth Street in Indianola, Iowa. Dad was drinking a lot, and
mother was sick. Mark stayed in his bedroom most of the time. Dad
always came home after dark. I tried to stay out of his way.

Elvis Presley was singing about blue suede shoes, and I had a pair.
Mickey Mantle had just come up to the New York Yankees, and he was
hitting home runs right and left. That summer it seemed like every
other week his picture was on the front cover of *Time* magazine. Mickey
was my idol. He could bat right- or left-handed. So could I. He could
hit home runs. So could I. He had a big smile. So did I. He was happy.
I wasn't. I wanted my life to be like Mickey's.

I was pretty deep into sports idols. Dad and I had a falling out and
he wasn't my idol much anymore. He said I had a bad attitude. I
thought *he* did. Mostly I looked up to old New York Yankees as my
heroes, men like Babe Ruth and Lou Gehrig, but Joe DiMaggio and
Yogi Berra too—all those guys. The library at my grade school had a
big section of books on sports heroes and leaders of the world. I had
gotten into the books on sports, and every week I checked out two or
three. I branched out into football and track, and got caught up in Jim

Thorpe's life story. I watched Burt Lancaster play Jim in the movie. These were stories about heroes for boys in grade school. By the time we moved to Indianola I was hooked. I was in junior high then, and pretty big stuff. I couldn't wait for Mickey's life story to come out in a book. In the meantime, I had pictures of him up on my wall, along with all his statistics: runs batted in, batting average, number of home runs.

We lasted 3 years in Indianola. I was elected president of my seventh-grade class. Our junior high team won the Warren County Basketball Tournament. I was a forward, and I averaged 11 points a game. My girlfriend was a cheerleader. She'd lead a chant when I made a basket.

We had a housekeeper that Grandpa paid for. She cleaned, fixed meals, and did laundry. Dad was county agent for the Farm Bureau. He had a secretary and agents who worked for him. He got me a job as janitor at the Farm Bureau; I cleaned the building three times a week before school. He was drinking more and away most of the time. They transferred him to Muscatine, on the Mississippi River, 40 miles away from Grandpa's farm near Iowa City. He wasn't in charge of an office anymore. He was just another life insurance salesman. But he was good. He was in the Million Dollar Club.

So in the summer of 1955 we moved back to the farm, into the two-story, four-bedroom, white wooden house on the hill where Grandpa's parents had lived. There was a hundred-foot pine tree in the front yard. Huge oaks and maples shaded the house. There were two large red barns, a grain silo, corncribs, concrete feeding lots for the hogs, a chicken house, a machine shed for a garage. There were animals, too: a herd of 50 Black Angus cows, a black bull, 100 breed sows, sheep, and chickens. A lilac hedge ran along the north side of the house, next to a grape arbor that Grandma had planted soon after she and Grandpa were married. When you stepped outside the front door and looked south, the horizon was endless. It stretched across field after field of green corn waving in the wind. If you squinted, the greenness turned to blue, as the sky bent down and touched the fields of corn.

To the north, at the bottom of the hill, was a small creek that cut the pasture in half. I could see the creek from my bedroom window. Mickey was still my hero, and he was still hitting home runs. I had his pictures up on the wall over my bed in my new bedroom.

Grandpa fixed up the house for Mother. He put on an addition, with a new kitchen and a second bathroom. Mark went to the country school 3 miles away. I got into University High. That fall, I got a driver's permit to go back and forth to school. I drove to Iowa City, and Dad drove to Muscatine. We didn't see much of each other. We didn't seem to have much money—or else Mother wasn't a good cook. We ate a lot of chipped beef and gravy on white bread.

Dad was drinking more and coming home later every night. I think this was causing problems between Mom and Dad, but I never heard them talk about it. There was a lot of fighting going on, though. These were silent fights, the kind where people ignore each other when they walk through a room. Everybody was ignoring everybody. I never saw Dad touch Mother when he was angry. If he was really mad, he would just yell at her. When he did that, Mark and I would leave the room.

This all changed the night Dad took out after me. We were finishing up another dinner of chipped beef and gravy. It was pretty clear Dad had been drinking. I could smell beer on his breath. I hadn't cleaned my plate. Nobody was talking. Mark was trying to eat and read a book. Mother was crying. It was kind of a typical meal for that summer. I got up and said I had to go outside. Dad would have none of it. "Sit down and finish your dinner!" he shouted.

I got up and took my plate to the kitchen sink and started doing dishes. "Did you hear me?" he shouted. "Yes," I said. "You don't have to yell." "Don't talk back to me, young man!" and he got up from the table and came toward me. Mother yelled, "Kenneth, sit down!" "Shut up," he said.

I slammed a pan down in the sink and ran out of the kitchen, out the back door. The door banged shut behind me. Dad yelled, "Get back in here and sit down!" I kept walking, past the oak tree in the yard, down toward the machine shed. I stopped next to the gate that led to the feed lot and turned back toward the house. Mother came running out of the house. Dad was following her. He ran right past her and caught up with me at the gate. He grabbed my shoulder and spun me around. I turned and looked at him. I was shaking all over. I was sweating. My pulse was racing. I pushed him back. "Get your hands off of me." Mother pushed between us. "Don't touch my son!" she screamed. "Get out of my way!" Dad shouted, and he threw me to the ground. Mother flew at him. She spit at him. She scratched his face. "You monster," she said. "You're no father."

Dad swore, "Dammit Betty! I'll show you," and he bent slightly at the waist and put his arms around her body. As he raised up he hit her head with his chin. Her shoulders fell back across his arms. He lifted Mother off the ground, as if she was as light as a feather. He tried to throw her over the gate. She kicked against the top board and scratched at Dad's eyes with her bright red fingernails. Blood ran down his cheek.

Mark came running from down the hill. "Daddy, Daddy, stop hurting Mommy. Mommy, are you all right, Mommy? I love you."

I jumped on Dad's back. He fell to the ground, dropping Mother. She got up and kicked him. Mark ran over and kicked him too. Then Mark put his arms around Mother and hugged her. She kissed him and then turned to me. She stood between the two of us and said, "Here are the real men in my life. These are the men who love me." Arm in arm, the three us walked back to the house.

I looked back at Dad. He was walking slowly into the garage. A few minutes later, I heard the car go roaring out of the barnyard. I ran to the dining room window in time to see the car disappearing in a cloud of dust at the bottom of the hill. Dad never came home that night.

I went upstairs to my bedroom and started looking at Mickey Mantle on the wall. Mother came in and sat on the edge of my bed. She looked at Mickey with me. "You like him, don't you?" she said. I said, "Yes, I do." She said, "He seems like a nice gentle man."

Five years after this fight Dad left for good. That was the summer of 1960. By that time he had joined Alcoholics Anonymous. About a month after Dad left, Leon, his A.A. sponsor, came out to the house one Sunday afternoon. He took me aside and said, "I've heard from your Dad. He's not coming home. He told me to tell you." I looked down at the ground. I started to cry. Leon continued, "I don't think you knew that your father was fooling around with a woman who was also in A.A. Well he was, and he left with her."

I wanted to hit Leon for telling me this. Every night I waited for Dad's footsteps to come up the stairs. I looked for his shadow to fall across the hallway. Those were the things that said he was home. Now Leon had said these things were never to going to happen again.

Three years after Dad left, Mom got a divorce. Over the years, Mother and I talked about many things, but never about the night she and Dad and Mark and I fought in the barnyard. Dad and I eventually got back together. He never brought the fight up either.

Dad died 5 years ago, and Mother died a year later. Three summers ago, Mickey Mantle died. It turned out his life had not been a bed of roses either. People talked of his carousing and his alcoholism and the pain he caused his family, especially his wife and his sons. Mickey had stopped being my hero sometime after Dad left us. Around that time, I lost faith in heroes more generally.

Five days after Mickey died, Bob Costas, the NBC television sports analyst, spoke at a memorial service held by the Mantle family. He talked in glowing terms about Mickey: about the high arch of the ball when he hit home runs; about his switch-hitting ability; about his grace and elegance on the field; about the poetry in his movements when he caught a ball, stole a base, or made a throw to home plate; about his being a man who lived a hard life and paid for it; about his being a man who got a second chance and turned some things around.

I thought about all these things as I listened to Costas's eulogy for Mickey on the car radio. I was with my wife in a rented car in Red Lodge, Montana. We were up on the West Bench, above town, watching the sun as it set on the Beartooth Mountains. The sky was a beautiful orange, purple, and deep blue, and the mountains seemed to glow. If you squinted it looked like a Chinese landscape, with mountain peaks and soft white clouds touching each other. Then it got dark.

I came between Mother and Dad that night because of Mickey. He was my hero, and he would not let this happen. Mother thought Mickey was a gentle man. But Mother was married to a man who could be violent when he had too much to drink. Mother never knew the dark side of Mickey. Nor did I.

8

Performing Montana

In the outdoor sports of the New West, the dreams of baby boomer childhood and the dreams of baby boomer middle age coincide. Performed in the landscape associated with televised Western adventure . . . the New West provides an essential setting to play hide-and-seek with time. . . . Americans wanting the West to be a remedy, a cure, and a restorative, wanting the West to make them feel young, vigorous, clean, and replenished again.

Patricia Nelson Limerick, *Something in the
Soil: Legacies and Reckonings in the New West*, 2000

The West is everybody's romantic home.

Wallace Stegner, *The Sound of Mountain
Water: The Changing American West*, 1980

William Kittredge (1996) says that the American West is an enormous empty and innocent stage waiting for a performance, and "we see the history of our performances everywhere . . . inscribed on the landscape (fences, roads, canals, power lines, city plans, bomb ranges)" (p. 97).[74] Moreover, the West is contained in the stories people tell about it.

Montana is both a performance and a place for performances, and it is hardly an innocent stage waiting for performances to happen. Montana is a place where people enact their own versions of the New West (Limerick 2000), their versions of being outdoors, of being in nature, of looking western (Dorst 1999), of looking for a place where "a river runs through it" (Maclean 1976). In these looks, poses, and theatrical performances, locals, neolocals, tourists, and old-timers reenact, re-present, and re-create multiple, gendered meanings of what the New West means to them. In these performances, as Kirshenblatt-Gimblett (1998:7) reminds us, people stage their tiny corners of the world as sites for performing culture, for performing Montana. Stories grow out of these performances. Kittredge (1996:164) says that we need new stories about performing Montana.

❖ RED LODGE, MONTANA

In 1994, my wife and I bought a little piece of land outside Red Lodge, Montana, population 1,875.[75] We got an acre with a cabin on the river called Rock Creek, and a big bluff of a rock outcropping behind the cabin. Indian paintbrush and lupine grow everywhere. In the summer, horses and deer graze in the valley above the road to our cabin. Off the big boulder under the big cottonwood tree, I catch rainbow and brook trout for breakfast. I fish; my wife quilts, hikes, and collects wildflowers. Last Christmas we took up cross-country skiing. I prefer winter fishing on Rock Creek. In the summer we go to auctions and yard sales and drive into town for groceries and to pick up items we need at the hardware store. The town has more restaurants per capita than any other town in Montana.

This is south-central Montana. Our little valley, nestled at the base of the Beartooth Mountains, is marked by lakes, snowcapped mountain peaks, alpine meadows, and sprawling ranches where the residents live in double-wide mobile homes. Early June brings fields of yellow sunflowers and raging, dark, angry rivers filled with melting snow and fallen trees from the upper mountain ranges.

Red Lodge is 4 miles from our cabin. It was primarily a mining town until the 1943 mine explosion that killed 74 miners. Hit hard by the Depression, even before the mines closed, looking for a way to stay alive, the town fathers pushed for a "high road" (the Hi-Road) that would connect Red Lodge to Cooke City and Silver Gate, the two little mining communities just outside the northeast entrance to Yellowstone National Park. It took a 1931 Act of Congress and 5 years of hard work to build the road over the mountain; the Beartooth Highway officially opened in 1936. Ever since, Red Lodge has been marketed as the eastern gateway to Yellowstone. That's what got us there in 1990.[76]

After reading Kittredge and studying Turner (1986a), Conquergood, (1998), Kirshenblatt-Gimblett (1998), and Bruner (1986, 1989, 1996), I have come to see our little part of Montana as a liminal place, Turner's no-person's-land, a place for new performances, new stories, a place betwixt and between the past and the future. When you are in Montana, you occupy this liminal place, a place that is constantly changing you.

Like good cultural, recreational, and entertainment tourists (Rothman 1998:23–24), we are learning how to perform Montana. We are learning to engage in the ritual performances that tourists and locals engage in when they are in and around Red Lodge, performances such as going to parades, shopping in the little craft and antique stores, buying things for the cabin, driving over the Beartooths to Yellowstone, driving to the ski slopes above town, eating out, having an espresso on the sidewalk in front of the Coffee Factory Roasters, having a fancy dinner at the Pollard (which is on the National Registry of Hotels), picking up our developed snapshots from Flash's Image Factory, buying quilting materials at Granny Hugs, volunteering in the local library (which is computerizing its entire collection), talking to the owner of the Village Shoppe, who at one time dated the niece of the former University of Illinois basketball coach.

❖   EXPERIENCE AND PERFORMANCES

We watch other people do what we are doing, separating the experience of being in Montana from its performances and representations, constructing culture and meaning as they go along (Bruner 1989:113). Three years ago, I overheard a man talking to the owner of the tackle shop in Big Timber. His BMW was still running out front, the driver's door open. He had on an Orvis fishing vest. He had driven with his family from Connecticut. "The kids saw that movie, *A River Runs Through It*. Where do we have to go to catch fish like they did in that movie? Can somebody around here give me fly-fishing lessons?" The owner said no on the lessons, but told the man to "go about 20 miles upriver, past Four-Mile Bridge. You can't miss it" (see also Dawson 1996:11).

Of course, the meanings of these Montana performance experiences are constantly changing. It is not appropriate to judge them in terms of their authenticity or originality. There is no original against which any given performance can be measured. There are only performances that seem to work and performances that don't. In any case, Montanans will always help you muddle through.

One perfect sunny, blue-skied Montana Sunday afternoon, I was fishing with a bobber and a worm off a big rock in a large pool near the headwaters of the Clark branch of the Yellowstone, just outside Cooke City. There were several other persons fishing the same area, and many were catching fish. I wasn't. My wife was reading a book, back in the shade at a picnic table near the path to the water. When I cast, I kept catching my line in the trees behind me, or the line would dribble down in front of me and the bobber would plop into the water. I was looking rather foolish.

The foolish feeling was compounded by the fact that I was fishing near a teenage boy, no more than 13 or 14 years old, who was having very good luck. He had a simple casting rod and was using a small woolly fly. He had tied a casting line, a tippet, to the end of his regular line, and he was getting good distance out over the water, especially in the shaded area near a big pine. He asked me if he could help me. I said sure, and within minutes he'd rigged me up with a setup like his, and I nearly caught a big trout with my next cast. This is what I mean. People in Montana help you muddle through these performances.

It is not possible to write an objective, authoritative, neutral account of performing Montana. Every account is personal and locally situated. In fact, people in Montana go to almost any length to respect personal differences. Kittredge (1996) is right: Montana is a place where "independence, minding your own business . . . and self-realization [are] regarded as prime virtues" (pp. 108–9).

Here are some of the ways Montana is performed.

Creating Local History

Every year, we try to observe part of Red Lodge's Festival of Nations celebration. This cultural performance has folk festival–like elements

(Kirshenblatt-Gimblett 1998:66). Participants stage performances that reenact and re-create rituals associated with Old World, European, folk and ethnic culture. Costumed in Old World style, the performers bring the Old World to the New World of Montana and Red Lodge. In staging their performances, in their dances, songs, music, and ethnic food, they keep this idealized Old World connection alive. For the parade down Broadway on the opening day of the festival, the sidewalk is crowded with tourists and locals who watch friends, neighbors, and family members proudly march by in proper ethnic costume. There is always a clear separation between doers, or performers (Red Lodge locals), and watchers, or audience members (tourists).

The 9-day ritual performance of the Festival of Nations reenacts the town's white European ethnic history. Each day of the festival is given a name—7 days are devoted to specific nationalities (Irish-English-Welsh, German, Scandinavian, Finnish, Italian, Slavic, Scottish), and the remaining 2 days are Montana Day and All Nations Day. At the beginning of the 20th century, men from the countries saluted in the festival came to Montana and became miners, ranchers, and shopkeepers. Later they married, and their wives taught school, cooked, had children, helped run little shops, and carried on native crafts from their home countries. Red Lodge tries to keep this history alive. The festival can be read as a democratic discourse of "pluralism, of unity in diversity" (Kirshenblatt-Gimblett 1998:77).

This multicultural festival, a large-scale performance event, is sponsored by the city. It draws performers from all over the United States. It has been written up in the *New York Times* and is recognized by the American Tour Bus Operators Association. Flags from more than 300 states and nations line Broadway and hang in the Red Lodge Civic Center, and the festival's organizers proudly announce each year how many nations from around the world are represented by that year's visitors.

Kirshenblatt-Gimblett (1998) observes that such large-scale festivals risk what might be termed the "'banality of difference,' whereby the proliferation of variation has the neutralizing effect of rendering difference (and conflict) inconsequential. This is the effect, by design, of the pageants of democracy so popular during the first decades of the [20th] century" (p. 77). Of course, this was and remains the intent of the organizers of such festivals; the original organizers were seeking an alternative to the ethnic hostilities embedded in the nativist ideologies of the post–World War I and II eras. A historian of the Red Lodge festival writes, "In the early days the festivities were presented by each select nationality. There was no desire on the part of any group to include those outside of its own culture. In fact, it often happened that if there were a crossing of the 'line,' at dances for instance, the contact would end in fist fights and brawls" (Hassen 2000:169).

National festivals like the Red Lodge Festival of Nations were popular across the United States during the first half of the 20th century (Kirshenblatt-Gimblett 1998:78). They staged idealized versions of "whiteness," versions that performed cultural difference. As in Red Lodge, they tended to defuse ethnic conflict while reinforcing the status quo and essentializing cultural traditions related to food, dance, song, music, and costume. Festivals such as the Festival of Nations encouraged assimilation to the norms of the New and the Old West, western versions of U.S. citizenship. These festivals celebrated pluralism and the ideologies of populism as integral features of the American way of life. They were not critical of democracy, and they were critical of capitalism only in their disdain for mine owners and bankers.

According to local history, the Red Lodge festival started shortly after World War II. Community leaders decided to build a civic center because they wanted a place where the townspeople could gather for community activities and for an annual summer music festival, where they could also hold arts and crafts exhibits and display flags and other cultural items related to each of the nations represented in the town. Thus was born the Festival of Nations, and Red Lodge was soon transformed into a "tourist town, a place that offered good scenery, fine fishing, the Hi-Road, the rodeo, cool summers" (Red Lodge Chamber of Commerce 1982:4). But the town had more to offer: "The inhabitants themselves were a resource" (p. 4). For 9 days every summer, Red Lodge puts its version of local ethnic culture on display, turning everyday people into performers of their respective ethnic heritages.

There are, then, festivals within the festival, and they constitute performance events in their own right (Kirshenblatt-Gimblett 1998:69). Each ethnic group has its own performance troupe, and the members train all year for their festival presentation. They take on tasks ranging from food preparation to the sewing of costumes, to choreography, musical arrangements, repertoires, and the teaching of dance steps to new groups of performers.

In the beginning, as they fashioned their performances, residents from each group had only their own white European ethnic history to go on, so they made it up as they went along. The festival allotted one day for each ethnic group, but all the groups would do pretty much the same things: a parade down Broadway with national flags from the country of origin, with participants in native costume, an afternoon performance of some sort (singing, storytelling, rug making, bagpipe playing, boccie games, dramatized folk legends), ethnic food at the Labor Temple (every day from 3:00 to 5:00 P.M.), and an evening of music and dance at the civic center. This is improvised ethnicity connected to the performance of made-up rituals handed down from one generation to the next (see also Hill 1997:245).

A couple of years ago, the ladies who run the Festival of Nations wanted to shorten it from 9 to 7 days. They were upset because there was usually not a big turnout for All Nations Day, so they proposed combining it with Montana Day and also putting the Scots in with the Irish, English, and Welsh. The Scots were firm in wanting their own day, however, and town merchants became angry at the prospect of losing business if the festival were shortened, so the proposal was dropped.

Performing Ethnic History

I like Finn Day. According to the little booklet I have that describes the Festival of Nations, in 1910 one-fourth of the population of Red Lodge was Finnish (Red Lodge Chamber of Commerce 1982). The town still even has an area known as Finn Town. On Finn Day, the all-male Finnish band plays marching songs. The women display their hooked rugs at the Festival Museum, just across the street from the Depot Gallery. Everybody who goes through the museum after the band plays gets a small paper plate filled with Finnish pastries and a cucumber sandwich on brown bread, served by women dressed in native Finnish costume (you can go back for seconds). Next to the food, in a corner of the museum, is a display of a Finnish kitchen circa 1910. There is a coal-burning stove, a wooden cupboard, a small kitchen table, a broom, and pots and pans hanging from a rack.

I also like Montana Day, especially the part that involves ranch women reading their stories about being Montana wives. A tent is set up over the dance pavilion in Lions Park, just next to the Depot Gallery, which is housed in a converted red train caboose. White plastic chairs are lined up in rows on the lawn. Loudspeakers are on each side of the stage. An old-fashioned Montana meal is served afterward: barbecued beef, baked beans, coleslaw, baked potatoes, Jell-o salad, brownies for dessert, coffee and iced tea for beverages.

Tall and short middle-aged, suntanned women take the stage. These are hardworking women, mothers, daughters, and grandmothers who live in the ranches in the Beartooth Valley, along the East Rosebud, Rock Creek, Willow Creek, and the Stillwater River south of Columbus, Absarokee, and Roscoe. Some have on cowboy boots, others wear Nike sneakers. They are dressed in blue jeans and decorated red, white, and blue cowboy shirts and skirts, and have red bandannas around their necks. They have short and long hair, ponytails and curls. They read cowboy poetry, tell short stories about hard winters and horses that freeze to death in snowbanks. Some sing songs. Country music plays quietly, and people come and go, some stopping and listening for a while. As these women perform, old ranchers in wide-brimmed cowboy hats close their eyes and tap their feet to the music. Young children run around through the crowd, and husbands proudly watch their wives read their poetry.

Reading the Montana Face

There are many Montana faces here. There is no single Montana face (Stegner 1980b:37, 198–99), few that strike the kinds of poses that Fiedler ([1949] 1971a:135, 1971b, 1971c, 1988), writing as an easterner in the 1940s, said were inarticulate and full of dumb pathos and self-sufficient stupidity. The faces I see have lived through harsh winters. Some are lined and wrinkled. The hands are strong, brown, callused, freckled. These faces and the stories behind them hide complicated emotions, yet they give off a gentle, weathered friendliness, a worldly, unself-conscious self-sufficiency.

Montana Day is about as close as many of the people in Red Lodge get to being cowboys, or to being near cowboys and cowgirls. This is about as close as they get to the Old West, to the West that exists in cowboy movies and in the national imagination. Oh, sure, you can still hear Patsy Cline, Hank Williams, and Dwight Yoakam on the jukeboxes at the Snag Bar and the Snow Creek Saloon, and tourists can sign up at Paintbrush Trails, Inc., for a trail ride or a scenic pack trip (the Paintbrush Trails ad shows a cowboy on a horse). In the summer, before Montana Days, the town does hold the Home of Champions Rodeo, which is part of the circuit of the Professional Rodeo Cowboys Association of America. At the rodeo, cowboys wrestle steers to the ground and Timber the rodeo clown shows off his pet chicken, who walks around on a leash.

Mountain Men and the Old West

The Red Lodge Mountain Man Rendezvous occurs every year just before the Festival of Nations ceremonies and just after the annual Summer Music Festival, which features classical musicians from Europe and all over the United States. A brochure distributed by the Red Lodge Rendezvous Committee describes the Rendezvous as follows:

> It is an historical re-enactment carried out by dedicated folks from all over the world. These lovers of America's history get together and create an old-time camp that re-creates the authentic costumes, sights, sounds, smells, flavors, events, and feelings of 160 years ago. Our "traders" have historically authentic goods, food, clothing, arms, flintlock guns and many other accoutrements of the Rocky Mountain fur trade era for sale. The Red Lodge Rendezvous is like stepping into a time-travel machine, to see Montana in 1940, the way it really was![77]

We went to the Mountain Man Rendezvous last summer. It was held out near the fair grounds, up past the airport landing strip. It was like an all-male costume show, men dressed up as mountain men, men in leather, men in loincloths, men as Indians, men as cavalry soldiers, as scouts, buffalo hunters, whiskey runners, mule skinners, ox drovers, and horse traders. It was Big Sky country, circa 1840 (see Guthrie 1947), just after the days of Lewis and Clark, mountain men and Indians living together in a little high-plains village, in an Edenic wilderness, in big tepees. There were campfires, men shooting old-fashioned guns, bartenders serving homemade sarsaparilla and old-fashioned root beer.[78] There was even a mountain man general store, where you could buy skins, baskets, bear-tooth necklaces, whiskey jars, and blankets. There were men making knives and men selling beads; there were men (and some women) selling clothes that could make you look like a mountain man.

Like the real mountain men Utley (1997) describes, these mountain men look-alikes were "garbed in greasy buckskin" and "imbibe[d] deeply of Indian technique, tools and weapons, costume, practice, and even thought and belief" (p. 14). They carried flintlock rifles. They warmed themselves with mackinaw blankets and wore shoulder belts to which they secured knives, tomahawks, pistols, powder horns, and shot pouches (see Utley 1997:14). To steal a line from Utley (1997), who quotes Washington Irving (1837] 1986:70), it would appear that "you cannot pay a free trapper [or mountain man] a greater compliment, than to persuade him you have mistaken him for an Indian brave; and in truth, the counterfeit is complete" (p. 14).

In addition to all the mountain men, there was a man dressed as a British trader working in front of a big white tepee (in another life he sold real estate). He claimed to be selling the kinds of beads that Indians liked to put on their warbonnets and headbands. Just as he finished making his sales pitch to us, the camp commander (a local banker in his other life) came marching by. He was accompanied by a bagpiper (Frank, a butcher) who would be playing on Scottish Day at the Festival of Nations.

Reenactment performances like the Mountain Man Rendezvous step outside time. Located away from established communities, in their own spaces, such spectacles function like living museums. They are sites for the display of objects, skills, crafts, and historical knowledge. They are also like theatrical exhibitions, performances where the performers perform the knowledge they create (Kirshenblatt-Gimblett 1998:3). Within these sites, each exhibit is like a diorama, or a period room, filled with objects and actors, with live displays. Each room comes alive as the performer performs his or her craft. Indeed, the display of humans in costume is central to this project (see Kirshenblatt-Gimblett 1998:4).

A mountain man in buckskin clothing works the forge in his tent, making a knife. Over a hot kettle of oil in the back of the tent, his wife, wearing a shawl and floor-length gingham dress, deep-fries authentic Indian fry bread. Their tent, one among many virtual worlds, is a site for manufacturing and performing historically accurate experiences. And as one wanders through the encampment, peering into tents, one becomes briefly a person who has stepped back in time, into an earlier historical moment (see Spindel 2000:110). I take pleasure in engaging this world to the fullest, forgetting that I have become yet another version of a cultural tourist. I get taken up in these cultural performances, thoroughly engaged by the ways in which these men and women perform their historical identities.

I forget that this is a masquerade, that these people are staging history, playing "Native," playing Other, and staging a particular version of whiteness, a version that says whites have control over how this period of the Old, now New, West is to be performed and represented. This whiteness is visible as a set of historical practices, strategic essentialisms, technologies, a spectacle in its own right (see King and

Springwood 2001:160; Prochaska 2001:173). These are white men and women claiming the right to name, present, and perform history.

These performances forge a bond between an imagined past and the present; indeed, these performers stand on both sides of history at the same time. In initiating, celebrating, and ultimately defending their version of the Mountain Man Rendezvous, today's participants repeat a familiar story about how the West was won (see also Hill 1997:237). That is, the camp signifies and performs conquest. There is a territorial politics at work here, a statement that says the white community owns this land, this place, and has the right to re-create on this land its version of the past, its version of how the West was won (see Hill 1997:236). So the camp and the performances that occur here represent an embodied political space, the white man's presence in the wilderness rewritten in the present.

More than presence is accomplished, however. The camp is a utopian site. It is a place that re-creates a particular version of community, a version that moves from the past to the present, a version that says, I prefer to sleep in tepees, sit on logs beside campfires, wear coonskin hats, sell beaver pelts and Hudson Bay blankets, and engage in tomahawk-throwing contests. By moving in and out of this space, the mountain men claim ownership of history, a history of whiteness and the West.

The camp is an economic spectacle, a small local economy where participants trade with one another and tourists buy authentic cultural objects. This is a New West consumer utopia; everything a mountain man (or woman) would want, or need, in order to be authentic is sold here. But in this postcolonial economic space, no mention is made of how mountain men economically exploited Native Americans. So in this mountain man festival, in this performance site, the ways in which "global capital flows rearticulate whiteness" (McLaren 1998b:67) remain invisible. And underneath it all, in the give-and-take that goes on in front of the tents and tepees, whiteness as a valued cultural commodity is privileged.

In staging this period of North American colonial (and now postcolonial) history, the festival's mountain men ignore many historical facts, including how the original mountain men, as trappers, virtually wiped out beavers as a native species in the Rocky Mountain West (see Utley 1997:99); how this act, in turn, changed the ecosystem of the region (see Chase 1986:12);[79] and how the Native Americans constantly resisted the encroachment of the mountain men (see Haines 1996a:36–59,

1996b:26, 60; Utley 1997:176). Thus a history of cultural and ecological destruction is repressed. Mountain men are presented as innocent of any violence. Participants in the festival are just having a good time, honoring a way of life that lasted for only approximately 15 years (from 1825 to 1840; see Utley 1997:79, 176). In this version of imperialist nostalgia (Rosaldo 1989:69), there is no hint of a conquest narrative (Prochaska 2001:164). Indeed, this invented set of performance narratives constitutes a social construction that implies an unbroken continuity with a sanitized past (Prochaska 2001:165).

Still, in taking on the identities of Native Americans, the festival's mountain men stage a ritual of racial difference (King and Springwood 2001:160). This is a ritual that presents history from one point of view, the view that it was the Manifest Destiny of whites to bring culture and civilization to Native Americans (Prochaska 2001:166). According to this view, the grateful Indians assimilated to white culture, and this can be seen by their economic and cultural presence at the Rendezvous. But Native Americans are present only as an absence. They can be seen in their trinkets, beads, arrows, headdresses, and tepees, and heard in the war chants that echo at the edge of camp in early evening.

Dead Indians

Fiedler (1988) argues that Montana as a white territory became psychologically possible only after the Native Americans—the Nez Percé, Blackfeet, Sioux, Assiniboine, Gros Ventre, Cheyenne, Chipewyan, Cree, and Crow—were killed, driven away, or confined to reservations. He asserts that the struggle to rid the West of the "Nobel Savage," or the "redskin," was integral to the myth of the Montana frontier as a wilderness (p. 745). Fiedler says that the Indian was Montana's Negro, an outcast living in an open-air ghetto (p. 752). With the passing of the Indian came trappers, mountain men, explorers, General Custer, Chief Joseph, and then ranchers and homesteaders. Indian sites were marked with names such as Dead Indian Pass.

Entering Red Lodge, you drive past a wooden statue of a Native American, a male Indian face sitting on a big stone. It was carved by a non–Native American. The history of Montana's relations with Native Americans is folded into mountain man festivals and events like Montana Days in Red Lodge. It is a history that simultaneously honors the dead Indian and denies the violent past that is so central to white supremacy.

Two summers ago, we drove over Dead Indian Pass, taking the Chief Joseph Highway back to Red Lodge from Yellowstone Park. Chief Joseph led the Nez Percé over this pass just months before Custer's last stand. At the top of the mountain there is a turnoff where you can stop and look back across the valley, 10,000 feet below. Although this place is called Dead Indian Pass, there is no mention of Chief Joseph on the little plaque at this viewing spot. Instead, there is a story about the ranch families who settled in Sun Light Basin in the Clark Fork river valley while fighting off the Indians—hence the name Dead Indian Pass. The whites, and not the Indians, are honored in popular memory.

Trout Fishing in Montana

I like to fish for trout. I grew up in a midwestern family, and I sometimes accompanied my father when he went fishing. Unlike in Norman Maclean's family, in my family there was a clear line between religion and fishing (see Maclean 1976:1). In fact, for a long time I connected fishing with harsh, dark childhood memories. My father and I would go out after he got home from work, ending up alongside some small muddy river or creek. Darkness, swarms of mosquitoes, and my father's heavy drinking went together. I'd be slapping away at mosquitoes and my father would be yelling at me to sit still. It was seldom a pleasant time, and if he caught a fish it would be a dirty catfish, or an ugly carp. He didn't let me fish.

So I gave up fishing and did not take it up again until Carl and Dee Dee Couch got us to visit them in 1989 at their cabin on the Boulder River, 30 miles south of Macloud, Montana. There I started to see what Maclean meant about fishing and religion. The Couches took this stuff pretty seriously. Carl even had wooden versions of trophy fish nailed up on a post in the screened-in porch off the kitchen of their cabin, with name, length, and date burned into the wood beneath each fish.

Still, it took me 3 years to learn how to catch a fish on Rock Creek. The first three summers we went out there, I swore there were no fish in the river. At that time I was fishing with a big red bobber on my line, a worm at the end. I used the bobber because it told me where my line was in the water. I used the worms because I could easily buy them at the True Value hardware store in town. I also used worms because I had no idea how to use a metal lure, and besides, I kept catching my lures on nearby trees and shrubs. Fly-fishing was a mysterious art to me. It was outside the limits of the image I was building of myself as a person who fished in Montana. I was happy to be known as a rod-and-reel, worm fisherman who used a red bobber.

I had a pretty simple fishing strategy. I would find a wide spot near the river, sit on a rock, pour a cup of coffee, light a cigarette (a habit I've since given up), throw my red bobber into the water, and wait for a fish to strike. I connected catching fish to smoking cigarettes, feeling that a fish would bite only if I had a cigarette in my mouth. I believed this because I caught a fish on the Yellowstone once while smoking a cigarette. For three summers I went through a lot of cigarettes without catching any fish. So I changed the color of my bobber. Still no fish.

One afternoon, I was on the Lake Fork branch of Rock Creek, about 300 yards upriver from the trailhead. Walking along the river, I came to a big boulder that sticks out into the water. The water runs around behind the boulder, forming a deep pool. I climbed up on the boulder, lit a cigarette, and started to prepare my line. I found myself without my trusty bobber, so I threw my line in with just a worm. I was smoking and sitting on top of the big rock when all of a sudden I felt a pull on my line, and I nearly fell off. I looked over the edge of the boulder and fed a little more line into the water, and the line pulled taut. I jumped off the rock onto the bank. I jerked my line, and a trout came out of the water. It flew over my head and landed on the bank behind me, flopping up and down on the ground, my hook still in its mouth.

In that instant I knew what Maclean (1976) means when he talks about "spots of time [and] fishermen who experience eternity compressed into a moment. No one can tell what a spot of time is until suddenly the whole world is a fish" (p. 44). Maclean adds, "and the fish is gone." Thankfully, my fish was still there. But I had compressed my entire consciousness into that single moment, landing that fish. I was breathing pretty heavily, excited, my first trout on Rock Creek! I put out my cigarette, knocked over my coffee cup, and inspected my prize. It was about 10 inches long, a brookie. I took out my red Swiss Army knife and cleaned it right there on a flat rock next to the river. (This was before fishermen were asked to stop cleaning fish by the rivers, because of the swirling trout disease.) I got right back at it, and in no I time had caught four more 8- to 10-inch brook trout. I cleaned them too, and then sealed them up in a plastic bag.

I walked on upriver and met my wife, who was returning from a hike. She took my picture near that big rock. There I am in my tan walking shorts, dark green fishing hat, blue fishing shirt, thong sandals on my feet, pole in one hand and four trout in a plastic bag in the other, the mountains in the background—a real outdoorsman. Huck Finn in Montana.

Later that same summer, we drove over the mountain and fished on the Soda Butte River, just outside the northeast entrance to Yellowstone Park. If you go down over the hill off the road and turn left, about 30 yards upstream a little sandbar extends out into the Soda Butte. Just behind the sandbar are three tall pine trees. At midday, they cast a big shadow across a deep pool in the river that was created when two big fallen trees floated down the river and jammed together on the sandbar.

My wife put a worm on her hook and cast her line into the water. A big cutthroat trout quickly took the worm. My wife yelled, "Get the net! Get the net!" I did, and we landed the 15-inch fish. I ran a stringer through its mouth and staked the cord to the bank, putting the fish back in the river. In 15 minutes we had eight cutthroat. It was like shooting fish in a barrel. Twice, a big cutthroat took a worm off my wife's line and slipped away. Time stood still. We were in a zone, in a groove; our entire existence was compressed into that spot on the Soda Butte.

We went back to the Soda Butte 2 years later with our son, Nate. The river had changed somewhat. Nate went to fish at the spot where his mother had lost that big cutthroat while she and I drove back into town. When we returned, Nate was coming up the hill toward the road. He had that big cut on a stringer and a smile a mile wide on his face. He had caught his mother's fish. We were quite angry—that fish belonged to his mother, and he should not have caught it! To this day, we talk about that fish that Nate took away from his mother on the banks of the Soda Butte, just outside the northeast entrance to Yellowstone.

These two experiences changed my fishing style. The red bobber disappeared. I now modeled myself after Carl: no-frills fishing, cast out into the dark pools, fish along the edges of the river under the little waterfalls, get down into the trees and shrubs that grow next to the water, look for little eddies of water behind big rocks. Go out after supper and look for the spots where the insects swarm and the trout feed in the cool evening waters. Keep it simple—a worm, the rod and reel, catch and release.

❖ PERFORMING MONTANA

There are many ways to perform Montana. Montana is a place where locals and tourists constantly commingle, where Orvis-outfitted fly fishermen from Connecticut connect with Huck Finn look-alike local kids who fish with worms and old bamboo poles. These Montana performances mix up many different things at the same time, different identities, different selves: cowboys, rodeos, classical music, antique hunters, skiers, mountain men, Finnish women who make rugs, ranchers' wives who write poetry, fishing for trout. Anybody can tell a story about doing or being one of these things.

But sometimes words fail. In its naturalness, Montana is a place that is stunning in its beauty, a world that defies words; Stegner (1980b) says simply that the "scenery is superlative" (p. 18). How do you create an image of the thousand shades and hues of brown and gold that shimmer at midday off the rocks and stones at the bottom of Rock Creek? How do you put a word to the color of the blinding light that comes off the water in the early morning? Words cannot adequately describe the strange-looking stone structures that appear in the river when the snow falls.

Being in nature is a major part of my Montana self. To perform Montana is to shed a little bit of my midwestern skin. These Montana performances teach my wife and me how first to see and then to love the mountains, the rivers, and the valleys; they teach us how to get outside ourselves and get back to a more basic way of life. We enact nature, we bring it to ourselves through the very act of bending down and smelling a wildflower or walking along the river. To borrow from Kittredge (1996), this contact with the "natural world is an experience that comes to us like a gift" (p. 108). So our corner of Montana is a sacred place, a hole in the sky and a house of sky, to use phrases from Kittredge (1992) and Doig (1978)—a place where wonderful things happen, and they happen when we perform them.

These are the kinds of things a minimalist, storytelling, performative social science makes visible. In these tellings the world comes alive. The ethnographer attempts to make these meanings available to the reader, hoping to show how this version of the sociological imagination engages some of the things that matter in everyday life.

9

Rock Creek History

There is nothing in nature that can't be taken as a sign of both mortality and invigoration. Cascading water equates loss followed by loss, a momentum of things falling in the direction of death, then life.... Everything in nature invites us constantly to be what we are. We are often like rivers: careless and forceful, timid and dangerous, lucid and muddied, eddying, gleaming, still.

Gretel Ehrlich, *The Solace of Open Spaces*, 1985

Our little corner of Montana is a sacred place.[80] Four miles from Red Lodge, our cabin sits beside the river, a house of sky or our hole in the sky (see Doig 1978; Kittredge 1992), a place where we perform Montana. Performing Montana allows us to bring a sacred sense of self into existence. By walking in the forest, smelling wildflowers, and hiking along the river, we create and enact a special relationship with the natural world (see Abram 1996:54; Merleau-Ponty 1962:317; Macnaghten and Urry 1998:1; Fine 1998:253; Scarce 1990:6). And all around us, the natural world enacts itself.

Rawlins (1994) expresses well our relationship with nature: "I could tell you about a place. . . . If you wakened there, you would hear a light wind, brushing downslope like a hand on a bare shoulder. . . . In the calm, a bird calls, is answered, calls again. The stream treads a staircase of boulders. At the corner of your eye, a doe and fawn step into the meadow and lower their heads" (p. 389). And "somewhere lawless animals cross boundaries without a blink" (p. 395).

I watch in wonder as a huge moose teaches her young calves how to jump over a dilapidated barbed-wire fence alongside the trout pool near the dam on the lower falls of Rock Creek. The moose and her young navigate this space shaped by humans, making it their own.

Nelson (1983) reminds me that while "moving through nature [one is] . . . never truly alone" (p. 14). It is midday. I am outside Silver Gate, Montana, knee-deep in the Soda Butte River, fishing for a huge brown trout. Having crossed the line into Yellowstone National Park, I am nervous. I do not have a park fishing permit. I turn around in reaction to a noise behind me. There on a sandy spit of land reaching out into the river stand four deer—a young buck, two smaller does, and a fawn. The deer stare at me, wide-eyed, as if I had walked into their backyard. I leave as quickly as possible. I brush against velvet-textured wild moss flowers. I look back as one of the does seems to spank the young fawn with a forehoof (see Senior 1997:335).

To paraphrase William Kittredge (1996:97), the "New West" is a not an innocent enormous stage waiting for new cultural performances.[81] Everywhere one looks it is possible to see the traces and histories of previous performances: campgrounds, ditches, logging roads, fencerows, hay fields, canals, bridges, bomb ranges, power lines, ski slopes, rodeo grounds, littered city streets, condo developments, petting zoos, theme parks, the graceful gates of national parks. These performances leave scars on the earth, and these scars become sites where nature and its meanings are contested—human-made nature in the natural world. Personal and collective stories grow out of these performances.[82]

Many critics now challenge the old western narratives, those gendered performances based on male stories about nature, frontier folklore, hunting, killing, Indians, settlers, mountain men, ski bums, drinking and driving, cattle drives, cowboy and cowgirl sexuality, the myth of the cowboy "as a kind of natural nobleman" (Abbey 1994:154), Wild West shows, and rodeos. They challenge the old depictions of the West through Hollywood movies (*Even Cowgirls Get the Blues*, *Unforgiven*) and old television shows about the imaginary West, from *Maverick* to *Bonanza* (see Stegner 1980a, 1980b:20; see also Rawlins

1994:393; Kittredge 1996:164; Blunt 1994; Bass 1996; Maclean 1976; Hasselstrom, Collier, and Curtis 1997a:xv, 1997b; Abbey 1984:xiv).

Since the beginning of the 20th century, Montana's rivers, mountains, forests, and national parks have been tourist sites, places "where life may often be seen copying art" (Stegner 1980b:20). These are places "about as far from life as we can make it" (Rawlins 1994:391), places where the imagination soars, where natural experiences in the wilderness are commodified; nature is bought and sold, given to you by a guide.

As Rawlins (1994) has observed, nature, "as we define it, is where we go on vacation. Wilderness is what our lives are not: noble, quiet, unhurried" (pp. 389–90). But there is no wilderness apart from our images of it (p. 394). A complex political economy, entrenched in the political history of the West itself, traverses this wild natural world. This is a history woven through the Great Depression, World War II, Roosevelt's Conservation Corps, mile-deep collapsing mine shafts, air and water pollution, huge dams across major rivers. This system of state-sponsored white patriarchal capitalism transformed the western landscape. The major industries—mining, lumber, ranching, and tourism—littered these magnificent natural spaces with tunnels, four-lane highways, dude ranches, tourist resorts, strip malls, Indian reservations, and trailer parks.

Of course, as Stegner (1980b:12–14) reminds us, there is no quintessential West. The West exists only as a multiplicity of conflicting symbols, distorted pictures, plundered sites, and romantic myths. These myths privilege some experiences over others. We need new stories based on new and different ways of performing Montana.[83] We need narratives that embed the self in storied histories of sacred spaces and local places. Such tellings chart the outlines of an epistemology that stresses the sacredness of human life and its relationship to nature (see Christians 1998:3). Here are some of mine. I call them "Rock Creek Stories" or "Performing Montana, Part II."

❖   ROCK CREEK STORIES

A photo sat on my grandfather's dresser in his south-facing small bedroom in the 100-year-old Iowa farmhouse he shared with my grandmother, my brother, and me. I have searched in vain for that photograph, a picture of Grandpa in Yellowstone Park in the 1930s, wearing a white shirt, tie, and gray fedora, with his Lincoln roadster parked next to his campsite. A big grin lights his face. I do not know who took the picture. He never told me. I know it was not Grandma. She never went to the park with him.[84] Grandpa is holding a string of brown trout, maybe 20 of them. He told me stories about this trip to Yellowstone, how the fish were there for the catching. He promised me that one day we would make a trip to Yellowstone together. We never did.[85] The photograph has been lost, but I seek today to place myself in it.

I have come to mountain waters late in my life, for I am a child of the prairie (see Stegner 1980b:41). Growing up, I knew only flatlands, fields of green corn that stretched to the edge of the pale-blue, pink, and orange skies on hot July nights. I knew only prairie waters, the muddy Iowa and Mississippi Rivers in springtime. When river floods came, creeks backed up over their borders. Bridges washed out. You had to drive 10 miles south and 3 miles east before you could find a road not covered with water that would take you safely north into Iowa City.

My family took no delight in these muddy waters. The river's sounds were the sounds of destruction, the muddy water working its defiant way across the flat Iowa farmlands and into our basements. It washed out fences and bridges. It muddied and mangled culverts and floodgates. It littered ditches with silt, broken cornstalks, fence posts, jagged-edged field tiles, old bed frames and tires, drowned pigs and rabbits.

So it was pure delight in June of that first summer in 1995 when I stepped outside our Montana cabin and looked upward, "where the land lifted in peaks and plunged in canyons" and the air was "full of pine and spruce smells" (Stegner 1980b:42). I realized that from our little place beside the river, if I climbed the point of rocks behind the cabin, I could practically reach out and touch the five shades of blue of the "improbable indigo sky" (Stegner 1980b:42). At ground level, I could smell the sage still wet with early-morning dew. I could watch teardrops of moisture run off the petals of the Indian paintbrush. Like Stegner, in that moment I gave myself to this Montana place. I closed my eyes and dreamed myself into my grandfather's photo. I'd found Yellowstone Park right here alongside Rock Creek (see Schullery 1997:19).

I walked to the river and felt its cold spray hit my face. I heard the river thunder over the little falls past the waterwheel upstream. I watched it run smooth and gold, then shimmer green and brown as it moved over and around half-submerged boulders and rocks. I looked downriver, where it smoothed out like a silver ribbon before turning the bend under the bridge, racing past fallen trees, to yet another set of falls.

When I returned in early spring the next year, the river had turned dark and angry. It ran full force, carrying fallen trees along its course. I watched kayakers with helmets carom from side to side on the white-capped raging current. In a blink of an eye, they shot past our cabin. Then I understood just how strong this river is. I felt proud to stand on a stretch of Rock Creek, before it combined again with the West Fork, to race across the valley and empty first into the Clarks Fork of the Yellowstone River, and finally into the Yellowstone outside Laurel, 60 miles north. When I studied maps later, I saw how the Yellowstone empties into the Missouri, and the Missouri into the Mississippi, just as my little childhood farm creek flowed first into the Iowa River and then into the Mississippi, 60 miles away. Rock Creek brought me back to my childhood.

Beside a river such as Rock Creek, it is impossible ever to feel tired or old (see Stegner 1980a:146, 1980b:42). The river is pure energy, a constant, ceaseless renewal of force. I feel its chill on my skin. I listen to its movements, its roar when it comes over the falls 100 yards upstream, the "symphony of smaller sounds, hiss and splash and gurgle, the small talk of the side currents, the whisper of blown and scattered spray" (Stegner 1980b:42).

Like the Ohio River for Wendell Berry (1981:53), Rock Creek is always there for me. It is impossible to escape its thunder and hush. When I am inside the cabin, my consciousness is always folded into the sounds of the river outside. In order to hear each other speak over the sounds of Rock Creek, my wife and I have to yell, even if we are only one room apart.

In its natural presence, the river sets the stage for Montana performances. From morning to night, squirrels come to drink and jabber. Birds land on the rocks in midstream. In the coolness of the evening, brook trout jump. Small logs float by. Wild berries fall in the water, and the river continues its roar.

❖ ALICIA'S HORSES

To reach the six cabins that sit along our stretch of Rock Creek, you have to cross a narrow wooden bridge made of railroad ties. The bridge is about 4 miles south of Red Lodge, off of Highway 212, which runs over the Beartooth Mountains into Yellowstone Park (Graetz 1997). Once you cross the bridge, you take a dirt road that meanders past all of the cabins. The cabins are small, single-story affairs; most look like log cabins on the outside, except ours, which has wood siding painted soft forest green. The James cabin is the most elaborate. It has a loft, a floor-to-ceiling rock fireplace, and a small deck that extends out over the river.

Every cabin owner has a piece of the dirt road, so to speak. To get to our cabin, we have to drive past three other cabins. The road helps to create a sense of community. We all feel like neighbors. We wave at each other as we come and go over the bridge. In the winter, the Jameses, our neighbors to the east, keep the road free of snow, and we do the same when we come for Christmas. This little country lane eventually forms a half circle, crossing another bridge about a mile upstream.

The Sun Dance estate is upriver, past these six cabins. Indeed, our country lane runs through Sun Dance and out again, across a bridge onto Highway 212. Sun Dance is a large, extravagant five-acre site.[86] It languished on the real estate market for more than a year with an asking price of $975,000. The two-story, lodge-style main house on the estate includes five bedrooms, a wall of picture windows overlooking the river, a swimming pool, and a great hall. At the end of the estate is a spacious four-bedroom guest house, and next to the main house is a two-story caretaker's cottage. The property curves along the river, through the forest, for almost a quarter of a mile. Several dark, deep trout pools hide along the banks of the river within the estate property, and in the evening hours I used to fish in these shadows for pan-sized brook and rainbow trout.

Last spring, a recently divorced woman from Las Vegas named Alicia bought Sun Dance.[87] She paid cash—somebody said she brought the money in a suitcase. She wired the perimeter of the property with motion detectors, alarm bells, and flood lights and installed an electronic security gate. Alicia moved in with a friend named Jake, her teenage daughter and son, a Toyota Land Cruiser, a silver Porsche, a gold-plated Lamborghini, two gold Rolls-Royces, three motorcycles, an 18-foot speedboat, four German shepherds, and five horses. Jake, a crack marksman and self-proclaimed wild animal sportsman, brought with him 16 stuffed lion and tiger heads that now hang from the walls of the great room. The locals grumbled that such tasteless, garish displays of wealth are to be expected of people from Las Vegas, with their dirty drug money, guns, and need for high security.

On the curve of the river across from Sun Dance sits another large property that is owned by Bob, a retired police officer from San Diego who trains seeing-eye dogs. Splitting the river into two streams, a densely forested peninsula partially separates the two properties. This stretch of land extends 200 yards downstream and is owned by Jim, an architect from Butte who likes to build things. Ten years, ago Jim built the waterwheel connected to the covered wooden bridge that crosses the river.

Shortly after Alicia moved in, she had two log footbridges built across Rock Creek. The bridges provided access from her property to Jim's peninsula. She stretched an electrified fence across the river and put up a sign warning, "This is an electric fence." Soon Alicia's horses were walking across the bridges to the peninsula, stomping around, eating Jim's grass, and fouling the area with manure. The horses also attracted the attention of Bob's seeing-eye dogs, and that interfered with the dogs' training. Bob called Jim, who called Alicia and told her, "Those horses have to go." Alicia agreed to keep her horses off the peninsula.

In order to bring hay in for the horses, the men who worked for Alicia began using the road that runs past the six cabins. No one had ever used the road for access to Sun Dance before. In fact, everybody in the neighborhood thought the road stopped at Jim's cabin. But suddenly truck tracks could be followed from the bridge all the way past the six cabins, up to and into the Sun Dance property. The tires of the trucks crushed wildflowers and the knee-high prairie grass that had once nearly covered the old road. The Sun Dance people were also using the old road as a trail for their horses. Clumps of horse manure appeared alongside the Indian paintbrush growing in the road.

Folks started complaining. "Why don't they use their own bridge?!" "They are wrecking our bridge!" Skip James, the retired doctor whose cabin is next to ours, suggested that we all start driving through Alicia's property, "We need to go up to her and ask for the keys to her back gate. We can form a caravan of cars and pickups and drive from one bridge to the next. We can go in shifts." "I'll help organize the project," I said.

The protest project never got off the ground, but Alicia's people eventually stopped using the community bridge so much. All seemed well and good until Frank, the horseshoer who lives next to Jim, began to see horse manure in the river. He came over to me one afternoon while I was fishing off the big rock near our cabin. He pointed to clumps of stained straw and debris along the edge of the river, and then he pointed upstream. "They are cleaning out the horse barn and throwing the straw and manure in the river. Smell it?" "Dammit. Good Grief," I said. "Who do those people think they are anyway? What can we do?" I asked.

Frank, who speaks very little and wears a big black cowboy hat, replied, "We can stop 'em from ridin' their horses up this way if you agree to put a 'No Trespassing' sign on the old Pear property. That way they won't have anyplace to ride the horses, 'cause they are shut off from up above by them rocks." I agreed. Frank continued, "Maybe you can talk to somebody in town about them throwing manure in the river. Go to the courthouse." I said we would.

So we did. At the courthouse, they sent us to the office of the county commissioner, Dan Farley. Dan said, "Oh, you folks live down river from those Sun Dance people. I heard about them, Bob Nichols has been in complaining about their horses bothering his dogs. What are they doing now?"

My wife began, "They seem to be cleaning out the horse stalls and throwing the straw and manure in the river."

"Have you seen them do this?" Farley asked.

"No," I said, "but there is manure and straw in the river, and it was not there before."

"How do you know it is not coming from someplace farther upstream?"

"I don't," I said, "but it started appearing after they moved in with their five horses. Seems pretty clear to me."

"What do you think happens on the ranches in this valley?" he asked. "Don't you suppose their manure gets into the river too? There is nothing we can do about it. There were 35 new families who moved into this valley last year, and 10 of them have horses. Am I supposed to go out and check on each one of them? I can't do that. But it is illegal to pollute a Montana river. Maybe you'll have some luck with the Montana Water Commission. Here is their telephone number."

Not hopeful, we left the commissioner's office and returned to our cabin. I put in a call to the water people. As we drove back to the cabin, I recalled Edward Abbey's (1994) complaints about cattle and the West: "The whole American West stinks of cattle. Along every flowing stream, around every seep and spring and water hole and well, you'll find acres and acres of what range management specialists call sacrifice areas. . . . Places where the earth is . . . denuded of forage—except maybe for some cacti . . . or maybe a few mutilated trees" (p. 150; see also Stuebner 1999:8). Abbey's solution to the cattle problem also came to mind: "I suggest that, in order to improve the range, we open a hunting season on cattle" (p. 153). Maybe we could shoot Ashley's horses. But that seemed too cruel. Maybe she could just move, or board her horses on a ranch, as Frank proposed.

Alicia had turned her stretch of Rock Creek into one of the sacrifice areas that Abbey describes. She had workers trim back all the underbrush near the river, so that now previously dark and shaded areas were open to partial, and in some places full, sun. This gave her horses free access to the entire riverbank, and within weeks they had crushed and destroyed all of the ground-level vegetation beneath the trees next to the water. The riverbank started to crumble, and the once crystal-clear water was clouded by mud. In front of each of the new footbridges, Alicia's workers had placed boulders and large rocks in the river. These new rocks altered the flow of the water and disturbed the old trout pools that had been hidden in the shade. Horse manure appeared on the edges of the river, transforming the banks into a breeding ground for mosquitoes and flies. These flies competed with the mayfly hatches that had always danced and dived on the surface of the water in the early evening.

Trout fishing went to hell. Every time I crossed over into Alicia's property, a horse came up to me. If I got near the water, a horse stuck its head over my shoulder, and flies and mosquitoes swarmed around my head. My old trout pools had disappeared. Gone were the days when I could throw a line in the water and pull out a brook trout for breakfast.

Two summers earlier, I had made this part of the river a sacred place. At that time, the guest house on the Sun Dance estate had been rented to a family from Portland. The family included two teenagers, Mark and Leigh, and a big sheep dog named Rufus. I taught Mark and Leigh how to catch brook trout in the stream. Rufus and I became friends. Often I'd catch a trout and it would jump out of the river with a force that would cause my fishing line to become caught on a tree limb extending out over the water. When that happened, Rufus would jump up on my shoulders and try to take a bite out of the trout as it dangled back and forth in the air over my head. In the process, Rufus would get trout blood smeared on his face and dirt on my shirt. My warm memories of fishing this pristine stretch of Rock Creek with Mark, Leigh, and Rufus have been ruined by the presence of Alicia and her horses.

It took us two days to get through to the Water Commission people. The man I spoke with was anxious for details but slow to act. "When did this pollution start?" he asked. "Can anyone else confirm what you have seen? We will be in that area next week. I'll see what I can do. We sure appreciate your calling, but unless we see someone in the act, we can't do much."

I gave him Bob's name and phone number. Two days later, we left for the summer. In early September I got an e-mail note from Skip James. He said:

Trying to deal with the people who bought the Sun Dance property isn't going anywhere. The Montana Water Control people in Helena tell me that they cannot enforce any change other than in court, and that eyewitness or photographic proof would be required. Talking with the owners is pointless, because the man Alicia lives with is a nut. (He has 130 mounted specimens of animals he has slaughtered, including a full-sized hippo.) . . . The fact that they have five horses on a place unfit for one is not relevant so long as the animals are well-fed and not mistreated. The horse urine and excrement filters into Rock Creek, but a specific source can't be proven: too many horses along the creek upstream. . . . There isn't much we can do other than prevent them from riding across our property. With your permission, I will plant a "No Trespassing" sign at the foot of the trail they use to get up the hill. . . . if we refuse to permit crossing our property, they'll have to use the YBRA bridge. Won't change the horse problem, but we won't have to look at it. . . . everyone is angry. Sic transit gloria mundi: So passes away the glory of the world. See you at Christmas. Skip.

When we returned at Christmastime, I walked up the lane to Alicia's electrified fence and looked through the fence at her horses. They seemed undernourished to me. They looked too thin. But maybe I wanted to see that. These were sad lonesome horses with nowhere to go. They were fenced in by a partially frozen river on one side and a rock cliff on the other. There were mounds of steaming manure and straw along the banks of the river.

On Christmas day, we walked up the canyon, past Alicia's estate. Inside the great hall somebody was playing Christmas music. The sound of Frank Sinatra singing "White Christmas" came from the outside speakers located on the deck around the sunken swimming pool. Near her bridge, in a snowbank next to the river, between two pine trees, loomed a large, elk-sized animal. It seemed poised in mid-step, immobile. At first I thought it was a frozen, dead, bloated horse. The next morning the animal still stood there in the same bizarre position.

That afternoon, my wife met with a seamstress in town, Mrs. Smith, to talk about finishing a quilting project. When my wife told Mrs. Smith where we live, the seamstress said she knew Alicia. In fact, she was making living room curtains for her, but things had gotten complicated: Alicia had to pick out new fabric because Jake did not like the wild-animal pattern she had first selected.

My wife told Mrs. Smith about the animal we had seen near the river. Mrs. Smith said that Jake had stuffed a bull elk and placed it next to the river. He wanted people to think they had elk on their property. Somehow this all seemed fitting. A stuffed bull elk at one end of the estate, starving live horses on the other. Artificial nature, preserved wildlife, the hunter's bounty on display for the world to see—no pollution here.

I fantasized that Jake would kill and stuff the five starving horses on the back end of the property. Maybe Edward Abbey had gotten to me. Jake and I would locate the horses near the river, next to the rock cliffs, even beside one of the trout pools where I used to fish with Rufus. I could go and sit on a rock and pretend that a stuffed horse was nuzzling my neck. I'd have my little spot of pure nature all to myself, no real horses to bother me. Maybe Jake was onto something.

In looking back at my grandfather's photo, I imagine he would take delight in my having found my place along a river that runs into the Yellowstone. So it is with his imagined regret that I share something sad about this little piece of Rock Creek history. This something perhaps reveals more about me and my relationship to Grandpa, and to the natural world, than it does to Rock Creek, Montana, or even the West, for that matter. To trace the history of a river, or "a raindrop, as John Muir would have done, is also to trace the history of the soul" (Ehrlich 1988:72). When Rufus left, he took a little bit of the soul of Rock Creek with him. Alicia and her horses have made the river a less sacred place. In turn, our performances, our efforts to enact narratives of the self, become less sacred as well.

10

Cowboys and Indians

In the 1950s my brother, Mark, and I spent our summers, until we were young teenagers, with our grandparents on their farm south of Iowa City, Iowa.[88] Saturday nights were special. Grandpa loved "cowboy and Indian" movies, and so did I. Every Saturday, Grandma fixed an early supper, and after supper, Grandpa and I, wearing going-to-town clothes, drove to Iowa City to catch a double feature at the Strand Theater. There we watched westerns starring John Wayne, Glenn Ford, Henry Fonda, or Jimmy Stewart. Soft summer nights in cool darkness, nighttime dreams of cowboys, Indians, the cavalry, six-guns, stagecoaches, saloon girls and schoolmarms, and a little blond boy running after a lonely rider on a horse. "Shane! Shane! Shane, come back!" I still remember the names of the movies: *Stagecoach, Broken Arrow, Colt 45, She Wore a Yellow Ribbon, Winchester '73, High Noon, The Naked Spur, The Far Country, Bend of the River,* and *Shane,* the only film I ever watched with my father. We'd leave home by 6:00 and often not get back until after 11:00.

I wanted to be a cowboy when I grew up. So did Mark. On Saturday mornings, while Grandma made hot doughnuts for us in the new deep-fat fryer in her big country kitchen, we watched "cowboy and Indian" television shows: *The Lone Ranger, Red Rider and Little Beaver, The Roy Rogers Show, Hopalong Cassidy.* Mark and I had cowboy outfits—wide-brimmed hats, leather vests, chaps, and spurs, along with toy pistols and holsters. Grandpa bought us a horse. I have a photograph of Mark and me in our cowboy outfits on the back of sway-backed Sonny, who was deaf in his right ear. We'd ride Sonny around and around the corral, waving at Grandpa and Grandma. When I was in fourth grade, I was Squanto in the Thanksgiving play about the pilgrims.

A blue-wind-swept Montana night, a red sun setting over the Beartooth Mountains. It's hot inside the crowded Red Lodge Civic Auditorium. Montana Night, a special part of this year's Festival of Nations, is about to begin.[89] The Montana Tune Smiths softly play their new song, "Montana Miners Story."[90] Tall, slender, blue-eyed Miss Rodeo Montana waves and smiles at the audience.

Everyone sings the "Festival of Nations Anthem." A tall cowboy walks to the podium. The mistress of ceremonies asks the audience to "please give a friendly Montana hello to Bill Greenough of the famous rodeo-riding Greenough family."[91] Bill removes his cowboy hat and, in a swooping gesture, waves to the crowd. The audience stands and cheers.

I can still hear Waylon Jennings in the back of my mind. I remember all those times I listened to Waylon and Willie Nelson sing "Whiskey River." I remember drinking myself to sleep. Country music floats through these memories. I used to think of my myself as an "angel flying too close to the ground," to steal a line from Willie. My heroes were cowboys in those days, and it seems they are even tonight. Like them, I am "sadly in search of myself, one step in back of my slow movin' dreams." A midwesterner in a small Montana town, dreaming about the West, cowboys and Indians, whiskey rivers. So for years I turned off the country music, fearful that its soulful sounds would take me back to those drunken nights. Tonight, here in Red Lodge, on Montana Night, I come face-to-face with those suppressed, painful memories. I thought I had left that past behind me.

The lights dim. The mistress of ceremonies asks the audience to "give a big Red Lodge welcome to Crow Indian Chief Heywood Big Day and his family, who are visitors tonight from the Crow Reservation near Pryor." In full tribal regalia, Chief Big Day walks to the center of the stage. I flash back to those "cowboy and Indian" television shows of my childhood. The chief looks like a television Indian. Maybe he is another version of "Kaw-Liga," the wooden Indian in the Hank Williams song—the sad Indian who never smiled at the little Indian maiden next door.

But Heywood Big Day is no wooden Indian. He stands in a circle of white light in the middle of the darkened auditorium.[92] He extends his arms skyward, as if praying. Turning slowly, he bends at the waist four times, first to the north, then to the east, then to the south, and finally to the west. A "real" live Indian in Red Lodge. Sherman Alexie (1993:18) says that "Indians make the best cowboys."[93]

As if on cue, Bill Greenough, this evening's version of Roy Rogers and the Lone Ranger, walks to the center of the gym. Chief Big Day turns and smiles. He speaks to the audience:

Hello. My family used to come to Red Lodge during your ceremonies. We would come to the rodeo. We rode down Broadway with you and your family. Then they stopped asking us. It is good to be back. My family joins me tonight.

The chief, now acting like the Lone Ranger's Tonto, beckons to his family. In full Native American ceremonial regalia, his wife and daughter solemnly walk across the gym and stand behind him. His four young grandsons, all wearing Los Angeles Lakers basketball jerseys, follow their mother to the center of the gym. Their blue-and-gold shirts have Shaquille O'Neal's face on the front and his number, 34, on the back.

Seven Crow Indians stand in a row in the center of the Red Lodge Civic Auditorium. In the 50 years since the Festival of Nations began, Indians have never shared this stage. Cowboys and Indians together again.

Bill extends his hand to Chief Heywood Big Day. "Welcome to the Festival of Nations! You are First Nation! You were here before us! Thank you for coming back. I remember when we rode together in the rodeo." Then, as if remembering a line from Red Rider or the Lone Ranger, Bill says to tonight's Tonto, "Please entertain us."

The chief demurs, "There will be no square dancing tonight! We are First Nation. We will do a war dance." And seven Indians, four dressed in L.A. Lakers jerseys, do a war dance across the gym floor.

For a brief moment, all who are present bear witness to a colorful montage. Everything is mixed up at the same time: race, ethnicity, the NBA, Shaquille O'Neal and the Lakers, rap and hip-hop, Miss Rodeo Montana, Crow Indians on reservations, war dances, cowboys, country music, dead miners. The crowd of more than 800 stands as one, applauding Chief Big Day and his family, chanting, "First Nation, First Nation." I can hear that old Paul Revere and the Raiders song: "They took the whole Cherokee Nation / Put us on this reservation."[94]

A postmodern racial performance right here in Red Lodge. All that's missing is Lyle Lovett singing "If I Had a Boat"; these lines from the song run through my mind:

The mystery masked man was smart

He got himself a Tonto

'Cause Tonto did the dirty work for free

But Tonto he was smarter

And one day said kemo sabe

Kiss my ass I bought a boat

I'm going out to sea.

I wonder if Heywood Big Day will tell Bill to "shove off."

I wonder how the chief got here tonight. Four years earlier, a controversy raged in Red Lodge about the Redskin mascot used by the high school's athletic teams (see Beaumont 1997). The Lady Redskins stopped using the name, and the boys' teams started calling themselves the Red Lodge Pride. Semiotic warfare right here in this little mountain Montana village. Last week, I asked one of the people who had been an anti-Redskin advocate about Chief Big Day's performance. She told me she thought it was hypocritical. "It was an insult. The people of Red Lodge drove the Crow Indians away."

We take a cab to the airport in Billings. The young driver says he is a Crow Indian from "the rez." He tells us family stories as we make our way through the snow-packed city streets. "My father was an alcoholic. A drunken Indian like in the movies. I never see him." In early May of 1981, I spent a morning on Hennepin Avenue in Minneapolis drinking with a group of Chippewa Indians. Four drunken days later, I entered a treatment center in a Minneapolis suburb. Indians, drunk and sober, have been a part of my recovery ever since. And so it was that night in the Red Lodge Civic Auditorium.

I think back now to those childhood days with Grandpa and Grandma. I did not know then that my father was an alcoholic. I just knew he drank a great deal. During our long summers on that Iowa farm, I dreamed my way out of a painful family situation, away from those fights Mother and Dad had all the time. I dreamed my way into cowboy heaven, into a small, snug safe space that I found on Saturday nights when Grandpa and I drove to Iowa City. I would sit in the passenger seat, my arm out the window, the soft warm summer breeze blowing through my hair, my face level with the green fields of corn that flashed by. We'd drive through those tunnels of green. We'd drive, like Dorothy in *The Wizard of Oz,* straight into another world, where I imagined life was better.

In front of the big and little silver screens, with Dale and Roy, John and Jimmy, Red Rider and Little Beaver, I became a boy-man, a warrior of sorts, a brave man, a cowboy, a rancher, a man of property who fought Indians. On Friday nights we listened to *Gunsmoke* on the big Philco radio next to Grandpa's desk in his corner of the kitchen. I loved Matt and Miss Kitty and Festus, and I loved knowing that there could be justice out on the prairie. You just might have to kill drunks, rowdies, crooks, and Indians to get it.

Now on this blue August night, which is turning cold, I dream myself past those childhood reveries. Here in Red Lodge I come face-to-face with real Indians and cowboys. I wonder how I could have been so naive, how *we* could have been so naive. Indians are people too; they are not put here to perform for us, to entertain us. But those movies I watched as a child with my grandfather created a discourse that exists to this day, for we only know Native Americans in their relationship to our whiteness (see Shoemaker 1997). We were never shown how to take them on their own terms—on any terms, for that matter.

And that is why these lines from Lyle Lovett's song are so important to me today:

> If I had a boat
>
> I'd go out on the ocean
>
> And if I had a pony
>
> I'd ride him on my boat
>
> And we could all together
>
> Go out on the ocean
>
> Me upon my pony on my boat.

I'd ask Tonto and his wife if they wanted to come with me. They could choose to come or stay. They both could ride upon my pony on my boat. They could have the boat and the pony.

These thoughts ran through my mind that night when I walked away from the Civic Auditorium in Red Lodge, Montana.

❖ REFLEXIVE AFTERWORD

Kathy Charmaz and Laurel Richardson have suggested that I write a writing-story about the process of writing "Cowboys and Indians."[95] Here I offer a not-so-innocent account of my experience with this mixed-genre writing form (see Richardson 2000b:931). A writing-story is a narrative or story about the contexts, experiences, and emotions that shape the writing process. Writing-stories situate texts within other parts of the writer's writing life. Writing-stories reveal the influence of "disciplinary constraints, academic debates, . . . familial ties, and personal history. . . . They can evoke deeper parts of the Self [and] heal wounds" (Richardson 2000b:931–32). Writing-stories are about the writer's taking risks and putting him- or herself on the line.

In writing "Cowboys and Indians," I was influenced by symbolic interactionism. The process of writing was a process of self-construction and then reconstruction based on ongoing conversations with myself and with memories from my past. I reconstructed these memories through interior dialogue. I attempted to make sense of the present by writing through these memories. The writing had consequences; a meaningful reality was created out of this interpretive process.

I wanted a story that would connect to the interactionist tradition of writing about race and ethnicity in American society (Denzin 2001e). I wanted this story to be autoethnographic, to connect to my childhood and the movies about the West that I watched with my grandfather. I wanted to show how my childhood and family experiences continue to shape what I write about today. At another level, this meta-analysis, as imagined by Charmaz and Richardson, would discuss the discursive practices, tropes, and rhetorical strategies that I employed in the essay, including the use of dualisms (men/women, grandparents/grandchildren, country/town), particular terms and images (Tonto, Greek gods, drunken Indians), and hierarchies (cowboys/Indians), as well as references to gender (Miss Montana) and to alcoholism and recovery.

There is an additional need for these stories. They locate the narrative within an interpretive framework that helps guide the reader in terms of the expectations and criteria he or she brings to the text. The writing-story establishes a contract between reader and writer. This contract covers the criteria I have outlined in Chapter 5: literary and aesthetic value, interpretive sufficiency, representational and authentic adequacy, showing rather than not telling, exhibiting an ethic of care, inviting moral dialogue, and engendering resistance. A willing reader accepts these terms; a skeptic may not. In either case, these criteria are the grounds on which the text should be judged. Other criteria should be suspended, including those that reflect positivist and more traditional scholarly concerns and preoccupations.[96]

❖ A WRITING-STORY

In "Cowboys and Indians," I intend a writing form that moves from interpretation to praxis. "Cowboys and Indians" is part of a larger performance text project that deals with Native Americans and negative racial imagery (Denzin 2002d; see also Chapter 11). As I have argued in Chapters 1 and 5 and in the introduction to Part II, I seek an autoethnographic writing form that illuminates liminal, epiphanic moments connected to instances of racial and social injustice. This performance-based writing should not parade its theoretical underpinnings. Still, as I have argued previously, it should be saturated in theory, deeply embedded in the principles of critical race theory, critical pedagogy, performance ethnography, and symbolic interactionism (Richardson 2000b:926–29, 2002a:878–80; Ladson-Billings 2000; Conquergood 1998; Madison 1999; Denzin 1992, 2001e).

In March 2001, as I was writing "Cowboys and Indians," debate raged on the University of Illinois campus about Chief Illiniwek (see Ebert 2001).[97] This official mascot and symbol of the university was created in 1926. The dancing Chief has been a presence at university athletic events ever since (see Spindel 2000; King and Springwood 2001; Crue 2002). In February 2000, the North Central Association of Colleges and Schools stated in its accreditation report, "There are inconsistencies between exemplary diversity policies and practices and the University's policies regarding the Chief."

I had gone to Red Lodge for a vacation, to escape to the mountains and leave racial politics and Chief Illiniwek behind. But as I sat in the Red Lodge Civic Auditorium on Montana Night in August 2000 and watched the performance of Chief Heywood Big Day, I was thrown back inside the very situation I thought I had left. Here a live version of Chief Illiniwek unfolded before me!

I attempted to write the two stories as one, a crisscrossing performance tale of negative images of Native Americans in two community contexts, Red Lodge, Montana, and Urbana, Illinois. But the story got out of hand. There was too much material. I decided to narrow the focus to just the memories and feelings I had that night in the Civic Auditorium in Red Lodge. I had made notes the next day on the memories and the images I experienced that night, including memories of going to cowboy movies with my grandfather. But the story would not write itself until I returned to the music of Hank Williams, Willie Nelson, and Waylon Jennings. That music brought all the memories together: summers on my grandparents' farm, my father's drinking, my own drinking, listening to Willie sing while I got drunk, media images of Native Americans, painting my skin red and brown and playing Squanto in my grade school Thanksgiving play.

Seeing Tonto as the embodiment of all Indians, I awakened from a fitful sleep. As if in a dream, Waylon singing in the background, the story poured out of me. The discourses that circulate through the story came, it seems now, from my unconscious. As a young man I was not consciously aware of how those movies provided symbolic escape from the world of family alcoholism. I had never made the connection between Native Americans, drunk and sober, and these slices of family history. Tonto emerged from my childhood memories as a stand-in for all Native Americans. That night, Chief Big Day stood in for Tonto. But here was a Tonto with a family—a wife, a daughter, grandchildren—a Tonto with a history. This was a Tonto from Lyle Lovett's song, a Tonto who would not play second fiddle to the Lone Ranger.

The cowboy movies of my childhood divided the world into dualisms: cowboys and Indians, men and women, children and adults, country and city, West and non-West. In writing my story I fell into these tropes. They write themselves over and over again in my story. Indeed, gender inscriptions carry out the work of the cowboy/Indian split and reproduce the white/nonwhite gender racialization that I wish to deconstruct (see Nagel 2001).

I attempt to undo these splits and dualisms in the moment when Chief Big Day's grandsons appear in L.A. Lakers basketball jerseys. In that postmodern space everything slides together. All dichotomies dissolve into a single blurring performance—the spectacle of seven Native Americans doing a war dance for a predominantly white audience.

In giving Tonto a life in the figure of Chief Big Day, I rescue myself from my past. Tonto and I now circulate through the lines of the Lovett song. I'm no longer a boy-man. To rework a line from Bob Dylan, for just that moment I become the Chief, I become Tonto, and stand inside his shoes, and I see what a drag it is to see the Lone Ranger. I should call my story "Indians and Cowboys" or "Tonto and the Lone Ranger."

"What if?" Mary Weems (2002:123) asks in "Brotha Wearing a Mask and a White Earring":

If the Lone Ranger

had been a brotha

him and Tonto woulda

hooked up

kicked butt

and took the long way

Home.

What if?

11

Redskins and Chiefs

If we do a census of the population in our collective imagination, imaginary Indians are one of the largest demographic groups. They dance, they drum; they go on the warpath; they are always young men who wear trailing feather bonnets. Symbolic servants, they serve as mascots, metaphors. We rely on these images to anchor us to the land and verify our account of our own past. But these Indians exist only in our imaginations.

—Carol Spindel, *Dancing at Halftime: Sports and the Controversy Over American Indian Mascots,* 2000

❖ PROLOGUE

"Redskins and Chiefs" is intended as a coperformance text, a three-act play of sorts. It enacts a critical cultural politics concerning the use of Native American representations by white communities and institutions.[98] There are multiple speaking parts, and a given participant may speak for more than one voice. The play may be performed in parts or whole, depending on the amount of available time, the purpose, and the audience. In any case, audience members are obliged to assume speaking parts in the performance.

❖ ACT 1

Scene 1: Chief Illiniwek Day Hearings

Narrator: It took me days to put these few words together. *April 14, 2000:* Chief Illiniwek Day Hearings in Follenger Auditorium, Urbana, Illinois. The auditorium is packed, filled with pro– and anti–Chief Illiniwek partisans, Native Americans, students of color, white male and female faculty members, housewives, alumni in blue and orange University of Illinois jerseys with the Chief's image on the front and back. The Chief looks like this:

A judge sits on the stage. He is taking testimony, 50 pro speakers and 50 con speakers. It's called a dialogue.

Voice 1:   My name is called. I stand and walk down the aisle, approaching the stage. Speaking directly into the microphone, I look at the judge and read my prepared remarks. My hands tremble, my voice cracks.

> I am honored to be part of these proceedings. I am honored to be a faculty member at this great university. I cringe when I see the image of Chief Illiniwek appear on the television screen, or in the pages of the daily newspaper, or on a package of meat sold by Agricultural Sales. Native Americans say this image is offensive to them. The symbol arouses great conflict. Can't we find a way out of this situation? Let us follow a higher moral principle. It is no longer appropriate for one social group to use the imagery of another racial group for political, cultural, or entertainment purposes. We must select a new school mascot.
>
> I walk back to my seat and smile at Cyd Crue, a sociology graduate student and leader of the anti-Chief coalition.
>
> I leave the auditorium. Outside, Native Americans have erected a huge white tepee with white river birch lodge poles. A table with brochures is in front of the tepee. A Native American drummer drums, and Cyd's adopted son, Wayne, a Shoshone Indian, walks by and gives me a high five.

Chief Illiniwek

Scene 2: Red Lodge, Montana

Narrator: My mind drifts back to Red Lodge, Montana. When you drive into Red Lodge you can't miss the Indians. As Highway 210 curves into town, you drive by two large statues. The first is a huge, life-size metal statue of Plenty Coups, chief of the Crow Indians, mounted on a horse. The statue sits in front of the Red Lodge Tourist Welcome Center.

Voice 2: First Red Lodge Resident:

That statue is so crazy! Who are

they trying to fool?

Voice 3: Document in Red Lodge Tourist Center:

Plenty Coups—Chief of the Crows

Circa 1848–March 4, 1932

The Buffalo are gone and freedom denied him, the Indian was visited by two equally hideous strangers—famine and tuberculosis. He could cope with neither. His pride broken, he felt himself an outcast, a beggar in his own country. It was now that Plenty Coups became the real leader of his people. . . . Red Lodge was a place of worship, food, and protection for the Crow people when it was theirs. Please respect and love it.

Narrator: A block past the statue of Plenty Coups, just east of the Carnegie Library, there is a 40-foot wooden carving of a male Indian face.

Chief Plenty Coups

Voice 4:   Just when you start to think, "This is a town that honors its Native American heritage" you hear this voice:

Voice 5:   **Second Red Lodge Resident:** That totem pole is an insult!

Voice 6:   Maybe the voice is wrong. Indeed, according to one version of local history, Red Lodge takes its name from the red clay that was used to cover the tepees of the Crow Indians [Lampi 1998:8]. And you read in *Go Red Lodge Magazine* that the neon sign above the Red Lodge Café—a sign in the shape of a tepee, with Indians waving tomahawks and running in a circle—won a national award in 1965. And the weekly newspaper, the *Carbon County News*, lists the scores of the high school basketball games. The boys' team, the Red Lodge Redskins, won, but the Lady Redskins lost.

Scene 3: Memorial Stadium, Champaign, Illinois

Narrator: Halftime, any October Saturday afternoon, Memorial Stadium, University of Illinois:

The Marching Illini step out onto the bright green astroturf. The band calls this medley the "Three-in-One." They march down the field to 'The Pride of the Illini March.' . . . Then the band changes direction and begins to play 'March of the Illini,' standing so their bodies spell out ILLINI. Chief Illiniwek, who has been hiding among the band members, emerges and dances down the field to what the band calls "an Indian-flavored march melody." BOOM-boom-boom-boom-BOOM-boom-boom-boom.

"Chieeeef! Chieeeef!" yell the fans. . . . The chief, a university student dressed in beaded buckskin and a trailing turkey feather headdress performs a vigorous, rhythmic dance that ends in acrobatic leaps. Legs split wide, he vaults into the air and touches his toes, fringe flying. The crowd cheers. Then he strides to the Illinois side of the field, raises his arms wide, folds them down, one over the other, lifts his chin as high as it will possibly go, and stands facing the fans. [Spindel 2000:11–12]

Voice 7:   The situation clarifies. Red Lodge residents are just like the pro-Chief fans in Urbana. They believe that they are honoring Native Americans.

Scene 4: Red Lodge, Montana

Narrator: The lights dim. The mistress of ceremonies asks the audience to "give a big Red Lodge welcome to Crow Indian Chief Heywood Big Day and his family, who are visitors tonight from the Crow Reservation near Pryor."

So here is the irony. It seems that wherever I go there are Indians, real and imitated, being honored by white people, and where this happens there is controversy.

Voice 8:   Lyle Lovett, like Sherman Alexie [1993], imagines the Lone Ranger and Tonto fighting. In Alexie's version they fist-fight in heaven. In Lovett's version, in his song "If I Had a Boat," Tonto buys a boat and tells the Lone Ranger to kiss off. The Alexie and Lovett tellings challenge the "Huck Finn" myth about cowboys and Indians.[99] Tonto refuses to be the white man's trusty sidekick.

Narrator: So here's another version of this story; it is about the Crow Indians and their place in Red Lodge history.[100] This is also a story about where I work, a story about Native Americans on the campus of the University of Illinois, a story about Chief Illiniwek, a constructed Native American who functions as the official mascot for the Fighting Illini, the university's athletic teams. This is not a story I wanted to tell.[101]

❖ ACT 2

Scene 1: Red Lodge, Montana

Narrator: I asked one of the anti-Redskin advocates in Red Lodge about Chief Big Day and his performance at the festival.

Voice 1:   **First Red Lodge Resident:** This performance is hypocritical, an insult. This is a lie. The people of Red

Lodge drove the Crow Indians away. They stole their land. They destroyed a culture. This is a sham! It is an embarrassment. Indians are a taboo topic in this town. Everybody knows that. Talk on this has been silenced. This is pure public relations!

Voice 9:   **Carbon County Historical Society:** In October of 1909, the Red Lodge city fathers asked the Crow Indian Agent if some of the tribe would attend the Carbon County Fair. . . . The agent replied that Red Lodge could have the Indians. . . . It was agreed the Indians would be allowed no whiskey [Zupan and Owens 2000:6].

Reporter 1:   Chief Plenty Coups and about 200 squaws, bucks and papooses traveled to Red Lodge in carriages, wagons and on horseback. The trip, via Pryor and Joliet, took two days. . . .

Reporter 2:   The Indians rode in the relay races, performed sham battles and war dances, and were pronounced "excellent" by the Red Lodge citizens.

Reporter 3:   In full regalia they were quartered at the fairgrounds, just north of town. . . . In later years, the Crow Indians would visit the Red Lodge Rodeo in July. . . .

Reporter 4:   They participated in Indian relay and running games, adding a great deal of color to the celebration.

Voice 9:   It was a great mistake when the rodeo committee decided not to invite the Indians anymore, as they added so much flavor to the celebration.

Scene 2: Red Lodge Cafe

Voice 10:   **Local Dignitary:** We stopped inviting them because they got drunk, and they'd never show up on time [August 2000].

Voice 11:   **Carbon County Historical Society:** Now the Indian is seldom seen in Red Lodge. . . . Even when they do visit, it is hard to recognize them as Indian. Gone are the days when one could see the men in their tall black hats and braids, accompanied by their squaws wearing their colorful blankets, head scarves, and buckskin leggings [Zupan and Owens 2000:6].

Voice 10:   **Local Dignitary:** We've found a way to get them here now, so we think they will be back to the Festival next year. Before, you could never count on them [August 2000].

Scene 3: Red Lodge High School

Voice 5:   **Second Red Lodge Resident:** What a lie! They just want a cowboy and Indian show for the Yellowstone tourists!

Scene 4: Historical Society

Voice 12:   **Carbon County Historical Society:** The Indian is being assimilated into the white man's society, losing much of his color identity and culture [Zupan and Owens 2000:6].

Voice 13:   **Second Local Dignitary:** In retrospect, it is easy to develop a strong empathy with the plight of the American Indian. . . . Now there are rumblings to do away with the reservation and completely absorb the Indian into the white man's society. In a few decades, any semblance of an Indian culture would completely disappear, genocide at its worst [Zupan and Owens 2000:6]!

Voice 14: Lyle Lovett:

> But Tonto he was smarter
>
> And one day said kemo sabe
>
> Kiss my ass I bought a boat
>
> I'm going out to sea.

Scene 5: Civic Auditorium

Voice 15:   **Chief Heywood Big Day:** Now why did you stop inviting us?

Scene 6: Red Lodge High School

Voice 16:   **Fourth Red Lodge Resident, a Mother and School Board Member:**

> Redskins, that name, that's what started our protest.
>
> My daughter was a cheerleader. They traveled to the reservation schools.
>
> She said, "Mother, I can't sing those
>
> chants for the Redskins. It is an embarrassment for
>
> the school, for me. We are not going to use this term in
>
> our chants."
>
> So three of us on the school board
>
> called for a vote to retire the symbol. You should've
>
> heard the uproar. They called us racists.
>
> They said, How can you do this? We are honoring
>
> the Crow Indians with our name.

Voice 17:   *Carbon County News,* **Reporter Number 1:** Last spring the school board agreed to let the student body make the decision about a name change. A student poll was taken, revealing that the majority of students wanted to keep the Redskin name. The students did, however, express their willingness to invite Native Americans in to address the student body about their feelings on the issue. As yet, no such arrangements have been made [Beaumont 1997].

Voice 18: Parent Number 1:

Asking the students to vote

is like asking

your child to make

the major decisions

in your family.

What do they know?

Children cannot

make this decision.

It needs

to be made by the adults.

Voice 19: School Board Member Number 2:

Redskins! It's the same as

using any ethnic slur.

Voice 20: Fourth Red Lodge Resident, a Mother and School Board Member:

The Booster Club this year

is

making a special effort

to not include the word

REDSKIN

on any of its promotional

material, including

buttons and

pins.

We're trying to

teach tolerance

and respect.

We need to take a

leadership

role in this.

I'm calling

for a vote by the

board.

Voice 21: School Board Member Number 3:

I'm against the name

change.

We've got

a lot more important

things to

worry about.

Scene 7: Crow Reservation

Voice 22: Crow Indian Mother:

How would you like it

if we

called you

Krauts?

You call us

Redskins

squaws,

whores.

The reservation is

not

our nation.

Scene 8: Champaign, Illinois; Red Lodge, Montana

Voice 23:   University of Illinois Board of Trustees Member: I
believe it is not only appropriate but it is expected that we
show respect and honor to those who came before
us. . . . The vast majority of the people of Illinois think that
Chief Illiniwek is that respectful honor [March 8, 2001].

Voice 24: Red Lodge Community Member Number 1:

Historically, the name Red Lodge Redskins

was

selected to honor

the Crow Indians.

It was never

intended

to be

a racial

slur.

The students

of

Red Lodge

have treated their

mascot with

dignity.

According to the Indian Treaty

of 1868, Carbon County Territory

was included within the Crow Reservation.

It was not until 1882 that the Crow Reservation was

thrown open to mining and settlement.

Voice 25: Leslie Fiedler:

Montana

as a white territory

became psychologically possible

only after the Native Americans,

the Nez Percé, Blackfeet, Sioux, Assiniboine, Gros Ventre,
Cheyenne, Chipewyan, Cree, and Crow,

were killed, driven away, or

placed on reservations.

The struggle

to rid the West of the Noble Savage

and the "redskin" is

integral to the myth of the

Montana frontier

as a wilderness.

The Indian was Montana's

Negro, an outcast

living in an

open-air ghetto. [Fiedler 1988:745, 752; see also Fiedler 1971a, 1971b, 1971c]

Voice 26: The *Daily Illini:* A Lesson in History

October 30, 1926:

Chief Illiniwek created by

Ray Dvorak, assistant director of bands.

Performed by university student

Lester Leutwiler.

1943: Only female performer, as Princess Illiniwek.

1975: First sign of protest, "A Challenge to the Chief" excerpt in Illio yearbook.

1989: U.S. Senator Paul Simon signs petition to retire Chief.

1990: Charlene Teeters protests Chief to Board of Trustees.

1990: Board of Trustees votes 7–1–1 to make Chief official university symbol.

1997: Release of Jay Rosenstein film *In Whose Honor,* a documentary on the Chief's history.

1998, March 9: University of Illinois Faculty Senate passes resolution calling for the Board to retire the Chief immediately.

2000: North Central Association of Colleges and Schools, 10-year accreditation report: "There are inconsistencies between exemplary diversity policies and practices and the University's policies regarding the Chief."

2000, February 15: Board of Trustees announces renewal of Chief dialogue.

2000, March 30: Board of Trustees appoints Judge Garippo to preside over special intake session.

2000, April 14: Speakers from both sides share views at special intake session.

2001, March 7: Board suggests desire for compromise on Chief.

2001, March 16: Board votes 8–1 against removal of Chief.

2001, May 20: Anti-Chief packets mailed to prospective student athlete recruits.

2001, May 23: Board asks Trustee Plummer to determine if a room exists for compromise.

2002, January 27: Chief protester arrested at women's basketball game.

2002, March 13: Trustee Plummer presents report on Chief to Board.

2002, March 25: Chief's use as a mascot protested on Madison campus of University of Wisconsin.

2002, May 1: UIUC undergraduates vote on and pass a motion to retire the Chief.

Voice 27: Chief Illiniwek, 75th Pictorial History:

Earlier Days: After protesters objected to the Chief representation, the university chose to limit public appearances. Previously, the Chief represented the university at a variety of educational and humanitarian functions.

The Dance: The Chief's dance, like his authentic Plains Indian costume, is carefully passed down to each successive performer. The first students to depict the Chief were trained in traditional dance steps by Native Americans.

Voice 28: Red Lodge Community Member Number 2:

I noticed in a recent issue of your paper

that the political correctnoids have

found our town

and are attacking

the high school's

Redskin

mascot.

The people who are pushing

this little

guilt agenda

are likely a

handful of people

with

no life of their own.

I have immense respect for

Native Americans. . . .

My guess is that a true

Crow warrior

would not spend

time agonizing over a white

man who called his tribe

the Redskins.

He'd most likely laugh and

think,

"How could they possibly

live up to

the name?"

Voice 29: Proud Graduate Who Takes Pride in Redskin Name:

Well, it's time to get my two-bits'

worth in.

Forty-six or so

years ago, I

had the privilege of

being on the first "Redskins"

football team.

The school had

to come up with a

new name

after the school went from Carbon

County High School to

Red Lodge High School.

The change from

Carbon County "Coyotes"

to Red Lodge

"Redskins" was definitely

done without

ethnic slurs

in mind.

Think of where

Red Lodge

got its name,

the color of

Crow Lodges.

Think of where Red Lodge is

located,

on a former Crow Reservation.

What could be more fitting than "Redskins?"

Voice 30:   **University of Illinois Board of Trustee Member:**   The Chief is an important symbol of the Urbana campus, for which I have great pride. . . . The Chief is a tangible and dignified tradition. . . . I believe the value of this tradition far outweighs any objections that have been raised. . . .

Voice 31:   **University of Illinois Alumnus:**   We live in the state of Illinois, named for the Illini tribe. . . . It was inescapable that the state would celebrate an Illini chief. . . . He is the single most positive public image of Indians in Illinois. . . .

Voice 32:   **University of Illinois Anthropology Department Faculty Member:**   The Illini were primarily farmers. . . . the men did not wear warbonnets, it is inaccurate to dress the university's mascot in the military regalia of a Sioux warrior. . . . the young man portraying the Chief has not earned the right to wear Lakota Sioux military regalia [Farnell 1998].

Voice 33: Native American Woman:

How would you like it

if we

called you

Krauts?

Voice 34:   University of Illinois Alumnus: In recent years, however, Illiniwek has been under attack from a small, self-righteous coalition that wants to wipe him from the University's history.

Voice 35:   *News-Gazette:*   Nine hundred miles from here, a 13-year-old American Indian boy follows the Chief Illiniwek debate with great interest. . . . Wayne Crue was born on a Shoshone-Bannock reservation and spent several years in the Champaign school system before deciding that pro-Chief rhetoric was contributing to an intolerable environment—including pupils calling him a "savage" [Wood 2001:A1].

Voice 36:   Michel Foucault: The problem is not changing people's consciousness—or what's in their heads—but the political, economic, institutional regime of the production of truth" [Foucault 1980b:133].

❖   ACT 3

Scene 1: Champaign, Illinois

Voice 37:   University of Illinois Chancellor (letter, September 16, 1999): In October 1997, several complaints about the label used for packaging of products by the University Meat Salesroom were brought to the attention of the campus administration. Subsequently, Associate Chancellor Jones asked Dr. Smith to send us a copy of this label in order that it could be reviewed. Dr. Smith provided Bill Jones with a sample of the label that indeed reflected an inappropriate use of the Chief Illiniwek image. Chancellor Jones wrote to Dr. Smith asking him to stop the use of the label. . . . I have received another complaint from yet a different source about this label and I am very disappointed to learn that the directive to change the label sent in 1997 has yet to be implemented.

Scene 2: University of Illinois Chancellor's Office

Chief Illiniwek Logo: Guidelines for Commercial Use, 4/91:

Voice 38:   **Vice Chancellor Jones:** Merchandise displaying the University of Illinois Chief Illiniwek logo must be dignified and not engender disrespect for the symbol. . . . any use of the Chief Illiniwek that does not fit clearly into the approved uses below must be submitted to the University for individual and specific approval. Representations:

Allowable are: Exact reproductions of the Chief Illiniwek logo. **Prohibited** are: Any alterations of the logo; any use of the logo in connection with a commercial product or words or pictures not specifically approved by the university. **Specifically prohibited** are: underwear, including boxer shorts, toilet paper and toilet seats. **Generally allowable** are: bags, bedroom accessories, belt buckles, buttons, calendars, floor coverings, Christmas accessories, timepieces, toilet goods (colognes, cosmetics), stadium seats, stuffed animals, sleepwear, socks, tie tacks.

Scene 3: *Daily Illini,* Op-Ed Page, March 7, 2001

Voice 39:   **Roger Ebert:** "Noble Spirit More Than Just a Mascot"

MILD ITALIAN SAUSAGE

INGREDIENTS   PORK. WATER. SALT. SUGAR   AND FLAVORINGS

U.S.
INSPECTED
AND PASSED BY
DEPARTMENT OF
AGRICULTURE
EST. 6962

University of Illinois
1503 S. Maryland, Urbana, IL 61801

KEEP REFRIGERATED   NET WT. _1.56_ LBS.

Meat Packaging Label

We live in the state of Illinois, named for the Illini tribe of Native Americans. It was inescapable that the state university would celebrate an Illini chief. Chief Illiniwek, for nearly a century the symbol of the University of Illinois, was until recently seen as a positive image of American Indians.

The Chief never was a "mascot." . . . He did not do back flips or high-five the fans. He dressed in authentic ceremonial garb and did a traditional dance at the halftimes of Illinois football games, materializing from the ranks of the marching band and then disappearing again. He . . . seemed like the embodiment of a noble spirit.

A case could be made that he was the single most positive public image of Indians in Illinois. . . . Many Indians shared in the affection for Illiniwek. . . . In recent years, however, Illiniwek has been under attack from a small, self-righteous coalition that wants to wipe him from the University's history. Again on Wednesday, the . . . Board of Trustees will consider the question of whether Illiniwek should continue as the university's image, or be banished—to be replaced, no doubt, by an inane character of no race, gender or species.

It would be a shame if that happened. . . . When the trustees vote, I hope they will recognize the simple truth, which is that Chief Illiniwek is a positive, not a negative symbol.

Scene 4: _Daily Illini,_ Op-Ed Page, March 20, 2001

Voice 40: Roger Ebert: "New Thoughts on the Chief"

Chief Illiniwek has been supported, for now, by the University of Illinois Board of Trustees, but I believe the handwriting is on the wall. The Chief cannot continue in his current manifestation. There is too much passion and pain on both sides. . . . The arguments for the Chief are familiar; I wrote an op-ed piece a week ago defending him. . . . I read the torrent of words, pro and con, inspired by the Trustees' public hearing on March 7, and I realize it is time to think again.

The Chief goes back to my childhood. . . . as an adult he remained for me a link to something that was good and true. . . . But in recent days Corinthians has haunted me: "When I was a child I spoke as a child, I understood as a child, I thought as a child; but when I became a man, I put my childish things away."

I must listen again to what Native Americans are saying, and they are saying they feel wounded and dismayed by this depiction of their culture. If that is how they feel, then I must respect them. . . . It is time to move on. . . . What if the University committed itself to becoming a leader in Native American studies. . . . It is time for both sides to reason together, to investigate whether the Chief can become a focus for us to come together, instead of drawing us apart.

Scene 5: University of Illinois
Board of Trustees Meeting, March 13, 2002

Voice 41: Trustee Roger Plummer: Two alternatives are presented for
                                        the Board's consideration:

> **Retain the Chief**, arrest, and reverse the slow marginalization that has occurred over the last several years. . . . retain the dance, Fighting Illini, the graphic image and the Three-in-One. . . .
>
> **Retire the Chief**, including the dance, by a date certain, with a transition plan. Discontinue use of chief graphic. . . .
>
> It is abundantly clear there is no compromise available. The positions staked out on all sides of the Chief issue make the development of a solution acceptable to dedicated and determined pro- and anti-Chief groups virtually impossible. . . . If the Trustees decide to keep the

Chief they need to work to reverse the marginalization of the Chief, whose appearances have been limited in the last few years. Trustees should strengthen support for the symbol by making it less offensive.... The current state of the Chief is an unstable one, and the turmoil created by the chief issue will not abate without significant change. We must acknowledge in some meaningful way the importance of Native Americans in the state of Illinois.

If the Board decides to retire the Chief, they need to do so by a certain date, through a transition plan, and possibly a celebration, and discontinue use of the Chief graphic. Retiring the Chief would not have to include retiring the name "Fighting Illini."

Voice 42:   **Professor Stephen Kaufman, Critic of the Chief:**   The report is thoughtful, skillful, and very well-presented. I do not agree with the conclusion that the "Fighting Illini" is a separate issue from that of the Chief.

Voice 43:   **Mike Drish, President, Students for Chief Illiniwek:**   I like his take-action approach.

Voice 44:   **Roger Huddleston, Leader of Pro-Chief Groups**: Plummer is steering the Chief agenda in at least one approved direction, the "Illini" and "Fighting Illini" should stay no matter what happens to the Chief.

Voice 45:   **Susan Shown Harjo, Executive Director, Morning Star Institute** (a national American Indians rights organization): This report marginalizes native voices. Wednesday's meeting was a whitewash. I was shocked at the rudeness of the trustees. While I was making my presentation, most of them were talking to each other.

Voice 46:   **Fred Cash, a Former Performer of the Chief:**   Plummer presented his report exquisitely well, and gave a very, very fair assessment: there's no point in compromise.... A lot of people will be leaving before the Chief does, including, hopefully, Kaufman and Chancellor Nancy Cantor.

Trustee Roger Plummer

Scene 6: E-Mail Message to University Faculty, April 19, 2002

Voice 47: Professor Stephen Kaufman:

Dear Colleagues and supporters: In the past five years many of you have written letters, spoken at meetings, and educated students about the problem posed by Chief Illiniwek. Trustee Plummer's recent report acknowledges many of the points you have helped us to make. The Board of Trustees is poised to act... The trustees and the administrators who are trying to enact change need your support. . . . Please write a brief message . . . explaining why you feel that Chief Illiniwek contradicts the university's educational mission and undermines the efforts the campus is making to become more diverse and inclusive. . . .

Sincerely,

Fred Hoxie, Swanlund Professor of History

Stephen Kaufman, Professor of Cell & Structural Biology

Debbie Reese (Nambe Pueblo), Ph.D., Department of Anthropology

Carol Spindel, Unit One/English/African Studies; author, *Dancing at Halftime*

* * *

Voice 48: Cyd Crue:

White Racism/Redface Minstrels

What's at Stake in the Chief Debate?

❖ The American Indian of the past is more real than the Indian of the present.
❖ The Euro-American perspective determines who and what is an authentic Native American representation.
❖ This perspective is neocolonial, masked behind a cultural altruism that treats all criticism as an instance of political correctness.
❖ The neocolonial perspective speaks for the greater good, the majority, what is true and correct.
❖ The Native American has become more symbolic than real, symbolic of whiteness in relation to the redskin, the noble savage.
❖ The practice of redface that structures the Chief's performances perpetuates 19th-century racist ideologies.

* * *

Narrator: Here at the end I seek a way out of this story, which seems to have no exit. Everywhere I turn, from Champaign to Red Lodge, it seems there are representations of Native Americans constructed by whites. These representations replay two versions of white male patriarchal history. The Chief is represented by young white men in redface entertaining other whites, in the football or basketball arena. In contrast, would-be "mountain men"—that is, nearly naked men in Native American costume—act out wilderness and male fantasies about Manifest Destiny, about masculinity, nature, God, and man.

Elizabeth Cook-Lynn (1996) says she that can't read the work of Wallace Stegner because of his misunderstanding and dismissal of Native American indigenousness "and his belief in the theory that

American Indians are 'vanishing'" (p. 32). Indeed, Stegner's history of the West, like Red Lodge's history of the Crow Indians, is a history written through the experiences of white Americans—first-, second-, third-, and fourth-generation European immigrants—a history that begins with the movement that located Native Americans on reservations, out of sight and out of mind. Thus Stegner has created a literature and a history of the West that has no place for and does not need Native Americans. And in this, Cook-Lynn observes, Stegner's experiences "are those of a vast portion of the American public" (p. 29). Stegner's West and his stories have become part of our collective unconscious. In our unconscious fantasies, isolated from their own past and their own history, Native Americans live as mascots, symbols of a symbolic past that never existed.

The hearings and protests surrounding Redskins and Chiefs in Red Lodge and Champaign-Urbana forcefully inform white Americans of a sad truth:

Voice of Elizabeth Cook-Lynn (1996:33):

> They have to come face to face with the
>
> loathsome idea
>
> that their invasion of the New World
>
> was never a movement of moral
>
> courage at all;
>
> rather it was a pseudoreligious
>
> and corrupt socioeconomic movement for
>
> the possession of resources.
>
> It may be that the Plains Indians are
>
> not "done," as assumed by
>
> Stegner's fiction;
>
> rather, they continue to multiply
>
> and prosper.

Cook-Lynn asks that these historical narratives and performances be contested. They support a cultural nationalism and a view of nation building that is racist and self-serving. There are four problems with these narratives.

Voices of Native Americans:

Voice 1:   These narratives allow whites to interpret day-to-day Indian/white relationships through an imagined native response to history and historical events [Cook-Lynn 1996:36].

Voice 2:   This supportive mythology writes the end of Plains Indians and their history, and excludes them from a place in this history.

Voice 3:   This fiction deprives Plains Indians of a valid claim to tribal lands.

Voice 4:   This mythology makes the claim of nativeness of all European immigrants to this land more valid because . . . indigenous populations [did] not last long, and if they somehow survive their own ridiculousness, they will do so as degenerates of history, defeated and outrageous [Cook-Lynn 1996:34–35].

Last Voice:

The immigrant/colonist grandchild

who remains

tied historically and culturally

to the purist's notion

of the making of America

as a morality play may,

unfortunately,

continue to exert

the greatest influence

on the taking of action in this country's

political, social, and academic life

that is inappropriate for the twenty-first century. . . .

the results of such

colonialistic imaginations

are

disastrous not only to Indians,

but perhaps, to all the world. . . .

I weep for Stegner. (Cook-Lynn 1996:34, 38, 39)

As do I.

12

Searching for Yellowstone

I am now ready for the Yellowstone Park, and look forward to the trip with intense pleasure.

—General William E. Strong, *A Trip to the Yellowstone National Park in July, August, and September, 1875,* 1876

Native American writer Elizabeth Cook-Lynn (1996) says that she can no longer read the work of Wallace Stegner, the founding father of contemporary literature about the American West.[102] But today I read Stegner because his autobiographical novels and his family history help me find my way back to my father, my grandfather, and my mother (see Stegner 1943, 1962, 1979, 1992b).[103] Dreaming my way into a midcentury landscape, I seek to understand my family's white middle-class version of the American dream. Yellowstone Park is as good a place as any to start.

In 1932, about the same time the father in Stegner's autobiographical novel *The Big Rock Candy Mountain* (1943:356) was taking a shortcut through Yellowstone Park on a bootleg whiskey run to Cody, Wyoming, my grandfather was fishing for browns and rainbow trout in the Firehole River near Old Faithful Lodge. I have a picture of Grandpa smiling, standing beside a Lincoln roadster, wearing a white shirt, tie, and gray fedora, proudly pointing to a string of more than 20 trout. Today I search for that spot in Yellowstone where Grandpa caught those trout, wondering if he and Stegner's own father may have been in the same place at the same time.[104]

Stegner's father was a salesman, as was Grandpa, and my father. Grandpa made his money during the Depression. He invented a mechanical device that was something like a slide rule or today's hand calculator. Used properly, it allowed users to compute sums, fractions, decibels, and ratios instantly. The slender bronze-colored metal device was made in the shape of a monkey suspended in midair in a metal cage; the monkey wore a red hat. The user moved the monkey's arms and feet back and forth and up and down across a sliding metric in a certain way, and the monkey's hands indicated the answer. When a person divided 30 by 2, for instance, the monkey's hands pointed to the number 15. Grandpa talked small-town store owners into buying franchise rights to his calculating monkey. For $10,000, a store owner could have the sales rights to an entire county. Grandpa then showed the owners how they could use trading stamps that would give customers discounts on purchases at their stores, if they bought the monkey. Grandpa printed and sold these stamps. In his Lincoln roadster, Grandpa toured the Midwest, the West, and the South, selling this system. He got rich and retired to the farm at the age of 40, taking hundreds of boxes of monkeys with him. One version of family legend holds that he was chased out of Kansas City by the Mob, the same Mob that helped Truman gain the White House in 1945.

My father sold hardware, John Deere tractors and plows, Farm Bureau life and car insurance, Ramblers, Dodges, Pontiacs, used cars of all kinds, sunken treasure from pirate ships, antiques and collectibles, and fake-brass doorknobs. He could sell anything. During my junior year in high school, my class read Arthur Miller's *Death of a Salesman*. I saw too many parallels between Dad and Willy Loman. Like one of Willy's sons, I was ashamed to have a father who was a salesman. My girlfriend at the time, whose father was a physician, said I had nothing to be ashamed of. I cried anyway, reading Willy Loman's disgrace and death as if they were my father's. My father never got rich. When I was 16, he sold me a $5,000 life insurance policy. The premium has stayed the same for 45 years, $44.80 payable June 1 and November 1. Every time I write out the check, I think of that night when he sold me the policy, telling me that this sale helped him make his quota for that month, might even qualify him for a 10-day company fishing trip to Canada and a Hudson Bay wool blanket.

My father was a devout conservative, a Reagan-Bush Republican. Over his desk hung a photo of him and George Bush (the elder) shaking hands. Across the top, Bush had written, "Thanks to my good friend Ken Denzin." My father believed in the American dream, the Horatio Alger myth, a welfare-free nation, capitalism, hard work, handcrafted bookcases, dark-blue serge suits, gray sweaters, home-cooked meals, community theater, and, when he attained sobriety, kindness, generosity, and fierce loyalty to family.

When he died he left a few clothes, three broken Timex watches, two pocketknives, and a woodworking shop full of hand-oiled tools—awls, files, screwdrivers, little planes, saws, drills and drill bits, levels, hammers, pliers. I gathered them up and took them home. I bought a sheet of pegboard and some hooks. I hung the pegboard on the wall in my basement shop and neatly arranged the awls, hammers, and screwdrivers. It looks like a display in a museum, my father's legacy, three wooden boxes and a handful of tools. We spread his ashes on the Mississippi River.

In *The Big Rock Candy Mountain,* Stegner's (1943) narrator says that his father, Bo Mason, "was born with the itch in his bones. . . . He was always telling stories of men who had gone over the hills to some new place . . . made their pile, got to be big men" (p. 83). By the time I was 8 years old, we had moved 10 times. The next sales job was always going to be the best. Like Bo Mason, he was looking for somewhere, "if you knew where to find it, some place where money could be made like drawing money from a well, some Big Rock Candy Mountain where life was effortless and rich" (p. 83). Also like Bo, "he hadn't found it in Chicago or Milwaukee or Terre Haute or the Wisconsin woods or Dakota" (p. 83). The family in Stegner's story lived in "twelve houses at least in the first four years in Salt Lake" (374). Stegner's (1943:461) narrator quotes the lyrics of a popular Depression-era song:

On the Big Rock Candy Mountain

Where the cops have wooden legs,

And the handouts grow on bushes,

And the hens lay soft-boiled eggs,

Where the bulldogs all have rubber teeth

And the cinder dicks are blind—

I'm a-gonna go

Where there ain't any snow,

Where the rain don't fall

And the wind don't blow

On the Big Rock Candy Mountain.

He quotes the song further: "Where the bluebird sings to the lemonade springs" (p. 461; in 1992, Stegner used this line as the title of a collection of essays). When Bo Mason died, the narrator tells us, the sum total of his possessions were "one dented silver mug. . . . One pair of worn shoes, one worn suit, a dozen spotted neckties, a third interest in a worthless mine" (p. 556).

The Big Rock Candy Mountain was always just around the corner, and my father, like the father in Stegner's novel, never seemed to have the nerve or the resolve to get there. Perhaps it was the fear of really getting to the top of the mountain, or maybe it was pride, or restlessness, or an arrogance born of knowing he had a natural talent, even though it was never fully realized. To paraphrase Stegner's (1943) description of Bo Mason, my father was haunted off and on throughout his life by the dream of quick money, but he was never quite unscrupulous enough to make his dream come true. He was a gambler of sorts, but not quite gambler enough. He had "a kind of dull Dutch caution"; he was the kind of gambler who "gambles with one hand and holds back a stake with the other" (p. 437). My father was self-centered, stubborn, an egotist dependent on women, stern voiced, and quick to anger; he had 2 years of college, a childhood of poverty and illness, three wives, and three divorces.

My grandfather, a stern Irish Protestant married to an equally stern Scottish Methodist, did not have these characteristics. He realized his version of the American dream by following the Protestant Ethic. He lead a life of sobriety and temperance. Grandpa had no self-doubt. He always exhibited self-control. He believed in having clear-cut goals and a positive attitude.

Men like Miller's Willy Loman, my father, and Stegner's Bo Mason are victims of the post–World War II version of the American dream: Work hard, listen to your government, save your money, and you will succeed; do your own thinking, but keep it defined in narrow terms, good versus evil. Men like my grandfather escaped this version of the dream. They learned how to get to the top of the Big Rock Candy Mountain, no dull Dutch caution in them, no self-doubt, no crippling addiction—always self-controlled and good-humored, never showing anger except to family.

Grandpa left Yellowstone with a pocketful of memories and one photograph. The father in Stegner's novel drove through the park and made a bundle on the whiskey he sold to bootleggers in Cody. Memories of these two men come together in my mind; they are opposites, each seeking something in this sacred site called Yellowstone.

By the time he had that photo taken, Grandpa was a man of leisure, a man of wealth. In those days such men were tourists, travelers to places of natural wonder, places like Yellowstone (see Shaffer 2001: 286–87; Pomeroy 1957:223–24; Dorst 1999:72; Rothman 1998: 147–48). Male tourists in those days wore suits, white shirts, and gray fedoras and drove Lincoln roadsters. Grandpa fit this model to a tee. Old Faithful became the place where he performed his version of this identity. For him, that picture represented in a timeless way what his version of the American dream had allowed him to become, a tourist from the Midwest, a man of means occupying a position of authority in nature (Dorst 1999:72).

The father in Stegner's novel, like mine, never had time to be a tourist. There are no photographs of Dad in a park. For him, parks like Yellowstone were places to drive through on the way to somewhere else, somewhere money could be made. The exception was when he won a trip from the Farm Bureau Life Insurance Company; selling a million dollars in premiums bought him 10 days in a Canadian fishing camp with a group of salesmen who were strangers to one another. But there are no photos from that trip, just a story or two and a faded Hudson Bay blanket. "Peanuts," he said to me, "one day we'll go to

Canada on a fishing trip, catch walleyes and pike." But we never went. And then, on another day, Grandpa said, "One day we'll go to Yellowstone, and I'll take you to Old Faithful." And we never went.

As a child and a young man, I grew up with these two stories. Somehow they were sandwiched between and around that photograph of Grandpa and his trout. When Grandpa died and we took his belongings from the nursing home, I got the Yellowstone picture. I feel like Terry Tempest Williams (2000), who also grew up with a picture hanging over her head. My question is hers: "What do I make of this legacy, of this picture?" (p. 6).

Williams (2000) writes of her picture:

> As a child I grew up with Hieronymus Bosch's painting . . . El jardin de las delicias . . . hanging over my head. My grandmother had thumbtacked the wings of Paradise and Hell to the bulletin board over the bed where I slept. The prints were . . . part of the Metropolitan Museum of Art's series of discussions designed for home education. . . . Whenever my siblings and I stayed overnight, we fell asleep in the "grandchildren's room" beneath Truth and Evil. (Pp. 5–6)

Whenever I stayed overnight with my grandparents, I fell asleep in the bedroom that had Grandpa's Yellowstone picture sitting on the dresser. I awakened each morning to the picture of Grandpa and his fish. I have followed that picture into the heart of Yellowstone Park, to the inn at Old Faithful. I have walked along the banks of the Madison and Firehole Rivers, where he surely fished. I have stood, as he surely did, with other tourists and waited for Old Faithful to erupt skyward. I have hiked past Upper Geyser Basin to the campground at Fountain Paint Pot and wondered whether Grandpa camped here. I have driven to West Thumb, Grant Village, and Geyser Basin, looking for his footprints.

Paul Schullery (1997) writes:

> We say that Yellowstone National Park was established on March 1,
> 1872, but in fact we have never stopped establishing Yellow-
> stone. . . .
>   . . . Our continuing . . . search for Yellowstone is . . . a search
> for ourselves. (pp. 2–3, 261–62)

Like Schullery, I search Yellowstone Park for meanings, for answers,
and I find them in my reflections in the clear evening waters of the
Yellowstone River itself. Rod and reel in hand, gray-haired, in baggy
khaki shorts and faded blue shirt, with Birkenstocks on my feet, I stand
at the water's edge. I stand not in the image of my father or my grandfather. I have become someone else, a 61-year-old college professor
who writes stories about who he might have been.

The meaning of the picture is now evident: My grandfather's smile
was an invitation to come to this site. Like others of his generation, he
searched for meaning in his life. He was drawn to and found
Yellowstone, and in this site he felt fulfilled and complete in a way that
he never felt anywhere else. This is why he wanted to take me to
Yellowstone, so I could experience this feeling for myself, so I could
find myself in the fast-running waters of this river.

And finding myself I am. I use this river as a bridge between two
landscapes: the plains of the Midwest and the mountains of Montana and
Wyoming. And on this bridge I look in two directions at the same time. I
see two reflections: my father on one side, my grandfather on the other.
And in this moment, as these two reflections come together, I see myself
more clearly than ever before. There has always been too much of my
father in me for me to have become someone like my grandfather: a man
who would wear a suit into the park. And there has been too much of my
grandfather in me for me to be like my father, a restless man of get-rich-
quick schemes who would race through the park to get somewhere else.

But I'm always pulled in both directions at the same time. Their
memories flow through me as I stand and look into this river. I suppose, then, this is why I read Stegner; reading him helps me continue
my search for Yellowstone, "the everlasting stream" (Harrington 2002).

And my mother? When Grandpa was staying at Old Faithful Lodge and fishing for trout, Mother and Grandmother were visiting Aunt Elizabeth in her summer home in the Berkeley Hills above Oakland, California. Grandma did not like to travel with Grandpa, so they took separate vacations. She did not like his line of work, and she did not like the women he met on the road. So she and Mother never went to Yellowstone. I do not know who took Grandpa's picture.

PART III

Pedagogy, Politics, and Ethics

13

Critical Performance Pedagogy

My abhorrence of neoliberalism helps to explain my legitimate anger when I speak of the injustices to which the ragpickers among humanity are condemned. It also explains my total lack of interest in any pretension of impartiality. I am not impartial, or objective. . . . [This] does not prevent me from holding always a rigorously ethical position.

—Paolo Freire, *Pedagogy of Freedom: Ethics, Democracy, and Civic Courage*, 1998

It started before the terrorist attacks of September 11, 2001; nowadays, to paraphrase C. Wright Mills (1959:3), men, women, and children everywhere feel that their private lives are a series of traps. They feel a loss of control over what is important, including family, loved ones, sanity itself. The dividing line between private troubles and public issues has slipped away. People feel caught up in a swirl of world events, from the Middle East to Afghanistan and Iraq. These events and their histories seem out of control. Life in the private sphere has become a public nightmare.

We live in dark and bitter times. Democratic public life is under siege. A culture of fear has spread around the world. In the United States, reactionaries and neoliberals have all but overtaken the language and politics of daily life, locating Americans in a permanent, open-ended war against faceless, nameless terrorists. We are poised on the brink of yet another war. Preemptive strikes, assassinations, and regime changes have become part of our new Bush-led foreign policy. Patriotism has become the national watchword.

The economy is slumping, and unemployment is at a record high. Crony capitalism reigns. Conservative politicians tied to global capitalism advocate free markets defined by the languages of commercialism and commodified social relations (Giroux 2003:2). Neoliberals contend that what is good for the economy is good for democracy. The gap between rich and poor widens. Social injustices extending from "class oppression to racial violence to the ongoing destruction of public life and the environment" (Giroux 2003:2) have become commonplace. The ideological relationship between capitalism and neoliberal democracy must be broken.

We live in a new garrison state. Since September 11, 2001, America's public spaces have become increasingly militarized. Armed guards and openly visible security cameras are everywhere now, at airports and pedestrian malls, outside hospitals and schools, even on college campuses. President Bush has authorized war tribunals and detention camps for suspected terrorists. Civil liberties are disappearing. Racial profiling operates behind the guise of protecting national security. A five-level civil-defense alarm system is in place.

Public education and civic, participatory social science are in jeopardy. Academics and pacifists critical of the war on terrorism are branded traitors. More and more restraints are being applied to qualitative, interpretive research, as conservative federal administrators redefine what constitutes acceptable inquiry (Lincoln and Cannella 2002; Shavelson and Towne 2002). Right-wing politicians stifle criticism while implementing a "resurgent racism . . . [involving] punitive attacks on the poor, urban youth, and people of color" (Giroux 2000a:132).

These are the troubled spaces that radical performance ethnography must enter. A several-sided thesis, grounded in the seventh moment of inquiry, has organized my arguments in this book. The interpretive methods, democratic politics, and feminist, communitarian ethics of performance (auto)ethnography offer progressives a series of tools for countering reactionary political discourse. At stake is an "insurgent cultural politics" (Giroux 2000a:127) that challenges neofascist state apparatuses.[105] This cultural politics encourages a critical race consciousness that flourishes within the free and open spaces of a "vibrant democratic public culture and society" (Giroux 2000a:127). But more is involved, for performance ethnography is more than a tool of liberation. It is a way of being moral and political in the world. Performance ethnography is moral discourse. In the discursive spaces of performativity there is no distance between the performance and the politics that the performance enacts. The two are intertwined, each nourishing the other, opposite sides of the same coin, one and the same thing.

Within the spaces of this new performative cultural politics a radical democratic imagination redefines the concept of civic participation and public citizenship.[106] This imagination turns the personal into the political. Struggle, resistance, and dialogue are key features of its pedagogy. The rights of democratic citizenship are extended to all segments of public and private life, from the political to the economic, from the cultural to the personal. This pedagogy seeks to regulate market and economic relations in the name of social justice and environmental causes.

A genuine democracy requires hope, dissent, and criticism. Performance (auto)ethnography is a strategic means to these political ends. This project celebrates the ethnographer as a public intellectual who produces and engages in meaningful cultural criticism. Like McLaren's (1997a:151) postmodern flaneur, the performance ethnographer critically inspects everyday urban life under late capitalism. Through resistance texts, the performance ethnographer offers moral tales that help men and women endure and prevail in the frightening environment of this new century. It is our obligation to future generations—we must make our voices heard. When we do so, we speak and perform as critical autoethnographers.

Performance (auto)ethnography is the future of ethnography, and ethnography's future is the seventh moment. In the seventh moment, the dividing line between autoethnography and ethnography disappears. The reflexive ethnographer becomes the guiding presence in the ethnographic text. In the seventh moment, critical social science comes of age and becomes a force to be reckoned with in the political and cultural arenas.

It remains, then, to return to the beginning, to take up again the task of offering a critical framework for reading performance ethnography's place in a progressive discourse that advances a pedagogy of freedom and hope in this new century. It is not enough just to do ethnography or qualitative inquiry. Of course we seek to understand the world, but we demand a performative politics that leads the way to radical social change.

Throughout this volume, I have attempted to join several discourses, including critical pedagogy, cultural studies, the performative turn in (auto)ethnography, critical race theory, and radical democratic theory. I revisit these topics in this chapter and in Chapter 14, outlining the many possible futures that lie in front of performance ethnography and cultural studies. Building on arguments I have made in earlier work (Denzin 1997, 2000b, 2001d), I propose a civic, publicly responsible autoethnography that addresses the central issues of self, race, gender, class, society, and democracy.

I begin by addressing pedagogies of hope and the sociological and ethnographic imaginations. I then turn to the topic of the ethnographer and cultural studies, reviewing several models of critical ethnography (Willis and Trondman 2000; McLaren 1997; Kincheloe and McLaren 2000; Carspecken 1996, 1999). I next examine critical performance pedagogy, politics, and critical race theory, and conclude with a brief discussion of the practices of a performative cultural politics (Parker 1998; Parker et al. 1998; Ladson-Billings 2000).

❖ THE CRITICAL IMAGINATION AND PEDAGOGIES OF HOPE

The need for a civic, participatory social science—a critical ethnography that moves back and forth among biography, history, and politics—has never been greater. Such a performative discourse, grounded in the sociological and ethnographic imagination (Mills 1959; Willis 2000), can help individuals to grasp how the fascist structures of the neoliberal world order, the new global empire, relate to one another. These discourses help to locate this new form of fascism within recent world history, including its previous European and American formations during and after World War II.

Following C. Wright Mills (1959:7), the critical ethnographer seeks to identify the varieties of men, women, and children that prevail in this current historical moment, including war widows and orphans, Afghan tribal lords, filthy-rich CEOs, homeless persons, Texas politicians, Palestinian refugees, militant Islamics, right-wing Christians, white supremacists, skinheads, bisexuals, transgendered persons, gays and lesbians, African American feminists, Latinos, First Nations persons, and "twice-hyphenated" Americans (from Asian-American-Japanese to Hispanic-American-Bolivians). The ethnographer connects these varieties of personhood to the experiences of racism, violence, oppression, and injustice. The critical imagination moves dramatically back and forth between the personal troubles experienced under global, terrorist capitalism and public responses to this capitalism and these private troubles.

Today, however, as Bauman (1999:4) and Giroux (2001b:4) have observed, the connections between the public and the private are being dismantled. This means that in neoliberal societies such as the United States it is becoming increasingly more difficult, except under the most superficial of conditions, to translate private troubles into public issues. Indeed, today public issues trump private troubles. For example, there was a wide-scale social response to the loss of lives after the attacks of 9/11, from newspaper stories to the outpouring of financial aid. But this humane response was quickly enveloped in patriotic flag-waving and the display of the American flag on automobiles, on homes, and in schoolrooms across the country. The loss of lives was used as an excuse for gearing up the American war machine.

When there is a disconnect between the public and the private, notions of the good society and the public good are eroded or turned into political capital. The pursuit of private satisfaction and the consumption of consumer goods become ends as well as goals for the good life. Human tragedies fall by the wayside.

The critical imagination is radically democratic, pedagogical, and interventionist. To build on arguments made by Freire (1998:91), this imagination dialogically inserts itself into the world, provoking conflict, curiosity, criticism, and reflection. It advocates a "rigorous 'ethical grounding' in a commitment to combat 'racial, sexual and class discrimination'" (Aronowitz 1998:12). It aspires to radical social change in such areas as "economics, human relations, property, the right to employment, to land, to education, and to health" (Freire 1998:99). Its ethics challenge the ethics of the marketplace; it seeks utopian transformations committed to radical democratic ideals.

These ideals embrace a democratic-socialist-feminist agenda. This agenda queers straight heterosexual democracy (Butler 1997). It is always relational, temporary, and historically specific. It is founded on its own conditions of hope and impossibility (Fraser 1993; McLaren 1997b:250, 279; Laclau 1990). This agenda asserts capitalism's fundamental incompatibility with democracy while thinking its way into a model of critical citizenship that attempts to unthink whiteness and the cultural logics of white supremacy (McLaren 1997b:237, 259; West 1993b; Roediger 2002). It seeks a revolutionary multiculturalism that is grounded in relentless resistance to the structures of neoliberalism. It critiques the ways in which the media are used to manufacture consent (Chomsky 1996). It sets as its goal transformations of global capital, so that individuals may begin to "truly live as liberated subjects of history" (McLaren 1997b:290).

A Moral Crisis

Indigenous discourse thickens the argument, for the central tensions in the world today go beyond the crises in capitalism and neoliberalism's version of democracy. The central crisis, as defined by American Indian pedagogy, is spiritual, "rooted in the increasingly virulent relationship between human beings and the rest of nature" (Grande 2000:354). Smith (1999), writing as an indigenous Maori woman from New Zealand, discusses the concept of spirituality within indigenous discourse, giving added meaning to the crisis at hand:

> The essence of a person has a genealogy which could be traced back to an earth parent. . . . A human person does not stand alone, but shares with other animate . . . beings relationships based on a shared "essence" of life . . . [including] the significance of place, of land, of landscape, of other things in the universe. . . . Concepts of spirituality which Christianity attempted to destroy, and then to appropriate, and then to claim, are critical sites of resistance for indigenous peoples. The value, attitudes, concepts and language embedded in beliefs about spirituality represent . . . the clearest contrast and mark of difference between indigenous peoples and the West. It is one of the few parts of ourselves which the West cannot decipher, cannot understand and cannot control . . . yet. (P. 74)

A respectful, radical performance pedagogy must honor these views of spirituality. It works to construct a vision of the person and ecology or the environment that is compatible with these principles. This pedagogy demands a politics of hope, of loving, of caring nonviolence grounded in inclusive moral and spiritual terms (see also West 1993b).

Performance (Auto)ethnography as a Pedagogy of Freedom

Within this framework, to extend Freire (1998) and elaborate Glass (2001:17), performance autoethnography contributes to a conception of education and democracy as pedagogies of freedom. As praxis, performance ethnography is a way of acting on the world in order to change it. Dialogic performances, enacting a performance-centered ethic, provide materials for critical reflection on radical democratic educational practices. In so doing, performance ethnography enacts a theory of selfhood and being. This is an ethical, relational, and moral theory. The purpose of "the particular type of relationality we call research ought to be enhancing . . . moral agency" (Christians 2002:409; see also Lincoln 1995:287), moral discernment, critical consciousness, and a radical politics of resistance.

As Freire (1998), Marx ([1888] 1983), Mead (1938), Dewey ([1922] 1930), and Glass (2001) have observed, praxis is a defining feature of human life and a "necessary condition of freedom" (Glass 2001:16). Human nature is expressed through intentional, meaningful conduct that is anchored in historically specific situations. The desire for freedom is basic. People make history and culture through their performative acts, and these acts enable the "realization of freedom" (Glass 2001:16), the opening up of choices, often in the face of oppression and resistance. Freedom is never given. Race, class, and gender oppressions limit human agency and the freedom that individuals have to act in given ways. Freedom is always contingent—contingent on a pledge to struggle and resist, and contingent on individuals' willingness to accept the consequences of their actions. The practice of democratic freedom requires a condition of permanent struggle, the promise to transform the world in the name of freedom itself.

A position of militant nonviolence is paramount. The struggle for freedom and for democracy must honor human life. As Glass (2001) writes, the "certitude of death demands that those who take life possess a level of certitude . . . that is perhaps beyond reach, especially in the case of death on the scale of war" (p. 23). Violence is not justified. A commitment to nonviolence structures struggles of liberation, and these struggles always occur within contested terrains. In turn, the permanent struggle for freedom and liberation gives to "all equally the power to seek self-determined hopes and dreams" (p. 23). Performance ethnography performs these struggles and becomes, in the process, the practice of freedom itself.

Indeed, performance ethnography enters the service of freedom by showing how, in concrete situations, persons produce history and culture, "even as history and culture produce them" (Glass 2001:17). Performance texts provide the grounds for liberation practice by opening up concrete situations that are being transformed through acts of resistance. In this way, performance ethnography advances the causes of liberation.

Hope, Pedagogy, and the Critical Imagination

As an interventionist ideology, the critical imagination is hopeful of change. It seeks and promotes an ideology of hope that challenges and confronts hopelessness (Freire [1992] 1999:8). It understands that hope, like freedom, is an "ontological need" (Freire [1992] 1999:8). Hope is the desire to dream, the desire to change, the desire to improve human existence. As Freire ([1992] 1999) says, hopelessness is "but hope that has lost its bearings" (p. 8).

Hope is ethical. Hope is moral. Hope is peaceful and nonviolent. Hope seeks the truth of life's sufferings. Hope gives meaning to the struggles to change the world. Hope is grounded in concrete performative practices, in struggles and interventions that espouse the sacred values of love, care, community, trust, and well-being (Freire [1992] 1999:9). Hope, as a form of pedagogy, confronts and interrogates cynicism, the belief that change is not possible or is too costly. Hope works from rage to love. It articulates a progressive politics that rejects "conservative, neoliberal postmodernity" (Freire [1992] 1999:10). Hope rejects terrorism. Hope rejects the claim that peace must come at the cost of war.

The critical democratic imagination is pedagogical in four ways. First, as a form of instruction, it helps persons think critically, historically, and sociologically. Second, as critical pedagogy, it exposes the pedagogies of oppression that produce and reproduce oppression and injustice (see Freire 2001:54). Third, it contributes to an ethical self-consciousness that is critical and reflexive. It gives people a language and a set of pedagogical practices that turn oppression into freedom, despair into hope, hatred into love, doubt into trust. Fourth, in turn, this self-consciousness shapes a critical racial self-awareness. This awareness contributes to utopian dreams of racial equality and racial justice.

For persons who have previously lost their way in this complex world, using this imagination is akin to being "suddenly awakened in a house with which they had only supposed themselves to be familiar" (Mills 1959:8). They now feel that they can provide themselves with critical understandings that undermine and challenge "older decisions that once appeared sound" (Mills 1959:8). Their critical imagination enlivened, such persons "acquire a new way of thinking. . . . in a world by their reflection and their sensibility, they realize the cultural meaning of the social sciences" (Mills 1959:8). They realize how to make and perform changes in their own lives, to become active agents in shaping the history that shapes them.

Recall Madison's (1998) account of the service workers who led a strike at the University of North Carolina (see Chapters 1 and 4). The performance of their stories empowered these women and helped them experience a kind of dignity that had previously been denied them. This form of political theater redresses past misdeeds while criticizing specific institutional patterns of discrimination. In so doing, it maps pathways of praxis that help create a progressive citizenship. The critical, ethnographic imagination becomes the vehicle for helping persons realize a politics of possibility.

❖ A PERFORMATIVE CULTURAL STUDIES

Following Conquergood (1998), Pollock (1998a), Madison (1998), and Giroux (2000a:127), I have attempted to retheorize the grounds of cultural studies, redefining the political and the cultural in performative and pedagogical terms. On this point Diawara (1996) is instructive, arguing that the new black public sphere "needs both an economic base for young people and definitions and discussions of the culture it is producing daily" (p. 306). Diawara suggests that these discussions will take place from within a cultural studies model that uses performance "as a mode of interpolating people in the black cultural sphere, positioning the people of the black good life society as its 'ideal readers'" (p. 306). For Diawara the cultural is always performative and pedagogical, and hence always political, and too frequently racist and sexist. The performative practices that enact pedagogy are the very practices that bring meaning and power into play. They shape the "performative character ... of identity" (p. 302) as it is socially constructed.

History is the unwritten word in Diawara's argument. Today the cultures of millennial capitalism and neoliberalism hover like dark shadows over the pedagogical and performative features of a progressive cultural studies. It is culture in these forms that cultural studies resists. To repeat, Americans live under the Orwellian structures of a government whose motto seems to be "Perpetual war brings perpetual peace." This self-same government brings new meanings to fascism. In fashioning free-market, state-supported millennial capitalism, neoliberalism makes the corporate marketplace primary (Comaroff and Comaroff 2001:7). It encourages consumption by redefining citizens as consumers and equating freedom with the choice to consume.

The concepts of multiple democratic public spheres, civic space, citizenship, and democratic discourse disappear in the pedagogical practices and spaces of millennial capitalism. In these deregulated corporate spaces a dismantling of the structures of public education, welfare, housing, and affirmative action occurs. Corporate and (ad)venture capitalists define the new public morality. They know no shame. This is a racist Darwinian morality, celebrating the survival of the fittest. It refuses any commitment to the values of environmentalism, social justice, nonviolence, grassroots democracy, feminism, affirmative action, and the rights of First Nations persons.

These are the situations a performative cultural studies confronts. People in Diawara's new black public sphere face almost insurmountable odds as they attempt to fashion democratic ideologies and identities in these racist spaces.

Of course, culture and power are experienced in the pedagogical performances that occur in these spaces. Viewed thus, culture *is* public pedagogy, a set of recurring interpretive practices that connect ethics, power, and politics (Giroux 2000b:25). Obviously, cultural performances cannot be separated from power, politics, or identity. In cultural performances, identities are forged and felt, agency is negotiated, citizenship rights are enacted, and the ideologies surrounding nation, civic culture, race, class, gender, and sexual orientation are confronted.

Power and culture are opposite sides of the same coin. The conditions under which they are joined and connected are constantly changing. Power (like culture) is always local, contextual, and performative, linking ideologies, representations, identities, meanings, texts, and contexts to "existing social formations [and] specific relations of power" (Giroux 2000b:169).

Pedagogy-as-performance is central "to the theory and practice of . . . radical cultural politics" (Giroux 2000b:158–59). The performative side of culture shows how the pedagogical is always political. That is, through their performances persons represent, disrupt, interpret, "engage and transform . . . the ideological and material circumstances that shape their lives" (Giroux 2000b:166).

Radical cultural critique and radical social change occur at the intersection of the pedagogical, the performative, and the political. Repression occurs in the same sites. In the spring, summer, and fall of 2002 and continuing into 2003, the Bush administration placed the United States in a permanent state of war against terrorism. Many on the left were critical, fearing the rapid development of a neofascist state. Supporters of the administration argued that Bush's critics were being unpatriotic; they said that in a time of war, it is every citizen's duty to support the president. When those in power attempt to shut down the performances of those who question their power, they are engaging in power politics. Through these articulations, they are attempting to govern public culture, to set the terms around which discourse on war, peace, and terrorism will occur.

Critique and criticism begin in those places "where people actually live their lives . . . where meaning is produced . . . and contested" (Giroux 2000b:170; see also Sterne 1999:262). These meanings are filtered through the systems of representation that are produced by the media. Cultural criticism treats these texts as forms of public pedagogy. They shape and give meaning to lived experience within specific historical moments. The ethnographer works back and forth between the contexts and situations of lived experience and the representations of those experiences. The critical ethnographer criticizes the pedagogical structures of capitalism, using radical pedagogy to undermine the very authority of capitalism's central ideological arguments.

In an article published in late autumn 2002, Rorty addresses Washington's appetite for war against Iraq:

On some days Washington tells us that we need to go after Iraq for reasons that were present before 9/11, and are quite independent of that event. On others we are told that the plan to depose Saddam Hussein is part of "the war on terrorism" that began on 9/11. This rapid alteration produces a blur. This blur helps conceal the fact that neither of the two arguments for attacking Iraq has been laid out in terms that would justify the sort of resolution (the equivalent of a War Powers Act . . .) that a spineless Congress was, as of this writing, about to pass. (P. 11)

Critically interrogating the Bush administration's arguments, Rorty exposes the contradictions in its ideological position. This unraveling of official pedagogy creates the space for protest that connects the personal and the political in acts of resistance.

New York Times columnist Maureen Dowd (2002) wrote this commentary on political discourse in Washington just after the House and Senate voted to give the president war powers in Iraq:

This has always been the place where people say the opposite of what they mean. But last week the Capital soared to ominous new Orwellian heights. . . . Mr. Bush said he needed Congressional support to win at the U.N., but he wants to fail at the U.N. so he can install his own MacArthur as viceroy of Iraq. . . . The Democrats were desperate to put the war behind them, so they put it front of them. . . . Senator Hillary Rodham Clinton voted to let the president use force in Iraq because she didn't want the president to use force in Iraq. . . . The C.I.A. says Saddam will use his nasty weapons against us only if he thinks he has nothing to lose. So the White House leaks its plans about the occupation of Iraq, leaving Saddam nothing to lose.

Extending Tyler (1986), Diawara (1996), and Conquergood (1998), I have suggested that the discourses of postmodern (auto)ethnography provide a framework against which all other forms of writing about the politics of the popular under the regimes of global capitalism are judged (Denzin 1997:167; see also Tyler 1986:122). Within this model, a performative, pedagogical cultural studies becomes autoethnographic. The autoethnographer becomes a version of McLaren's (1997a) reflexive flaneur/flaneuse and Kincheloe's (2001) critical *bricoleur*, the "primordial ethnographer" who lives "within postmodern, postorganized, late capitalist culture" (McLaren 1997:144) and functions as a critical theorist, an urban ethnographer, an ethnographic agent, a Marxist social theorist (see McLaren, 1997a:164, 167, 2001:121–22).

Listen to McLaren (1997a):

Thursday, May 9, 1996, Florianopolis, Brazil   Each time I give a speech here I realize how partial my knowledge is compared to the students or the workers. Today during my visit with Father Wilson, I was reminded of the terrible beauty among the people in the *favela*. . . . Father Wilson made me a wonderful fish stew. The tires of his car have recently been slashed, the windows broken. . . . Father Wilson is not popular with the *favela* drug dealers. (P. 172)

The radical performance (auto)ethnographer functions as a cultural critic, a version of the modern antihero, who, as Spender (1984) describes, "reflect[s] an extreme external situation through his own extremity." The performance ethnographer's autoethnography is like the antihero's story, which "becomes diagnosis, not just of himself, but of a phase of history" (p. ix). Because the critical autoethnographer is a reflexive flaneur/flaneuse or *bricoleur*, his or her conduct is justified; the story he or she tells is no longer just one individual's case history or life story. Within the context of history, the autoethnography becomes the "dial of the instrument that records the effects of a particular stage of civilization upon a civilized individual" (Spender 1984:ix). The autoethnography is both dial and instrument.

The autoethnographer functions as a universal singular, a single instance of a more universal social experience. As Sartre (1981) describes the universal singular, this subject is "summed up and for this reason universalized by his epoch, he resumes it by reproducing himself in it as a singularity" (p. ix). Every person is like every other person, but like no other person. The autoethnographer inscribes the experiences of a historical moment, universalizing these experiences in their singular effects on a particular life.

Using a critical imagination, the autoethnographer is theoretically informed in poststructural and postmodern ways. He or she has a commitment to connect critical ethnography to issues surrounding cultural policy, cultural politics, and procedural policy work (Willis and Trondman 2000:10–11). The commitment, as McLaren (1997a) argues, is to a theory of praxis that is purposeful, "guided by critical reflection and a commitment to revolutionary praxis" (p. 170). This commitment involves a rejection of the historical and cultural logics and narratives that exclude those who have previously been marginalized. This is a reflexive, performative ethnography. It privileges multiple subject positions, questions its own authority, and doubts those narratives that privilege one set of historical processes and sequences over another (p. 168).

❖ A REFLEXIVE CRITIQUE OF
REFLEXIVE CRITICAL ETHNOGRAPHY

Bourdieu and Wacquant (1992), Carspecken (1996), Kincheloe and McLaren (2000), Foley (2002), Willis (2000), Willis and Trondman (2000), Burawoy (1998, 2000), and Visweswaran (1994) all speak favorably of a global, reflexive, critical ethnography. The concept of reflexivity is critical to this discourse. Foley (2002), Marcus (1998), and Tedlock (2000) distinguish at least three types of reflexive ethnography. The first is a confessional reflexivity. The writer refuses to make a distinction between self and other, creating the space for autoethnography, for feminist, racial, indigenous, and borderland standpoint theories and inquiries (Foley 2002:475).

The second type of reflexivity is theoretical. It is associated with the work of Bourdieu and Wacquant (1992) and, to a lesser degree, that of Burawoy and Willis, all of whom advocate an epistemologically reflexive sociology and ethnography grounded in everyday cultural practices. The sociologist works back and forth between field experience and theory, cultivating a theoretical reflexivity that produces a detached, objective authoritative account of the world being studied (Foley 2002:476). This form of reflexivity questions the value of autoethnography, suggesting that it is shallow textuality (Foley 2002:475).

Burawoy (2000:28) wants an extended, reflexive case method that takes observers into the field for long periods of time, across multiple sites. In the process, ethnographers learn how move back and forth between macro and micro processes while developing theory grounded in the data. Willis and Trondman (2000), influenced by Bourdieu, call for a "theoretically informed methodology for ethnography" (TIME). Also grounded in ethnographic data, this reflexive approach insists on recording lived experience while bringing that experience into a "productive but unfussy relation to 'theory.' . . . the criterion for relevance is maximum power in relation to the data for purposes of illumination" (p. 12). Such illuminations produce "aha" experiences and become the catalyst for "self-reflexivity and self-examination" (p. 14). The researcher maintains a self-reflexivity that emphasizes history and biography while producing objective ethnographic accounts that are as rigorous as possible (Willis 2000:113, 116).

Carspecken (1996) offers an elegant model for critical ethnography that deploys a critical, reflexive epistemology involving the collection of monologic data, dialogic data generation, the discovery of systems relations, and using systems relations to explain findings. In Carspecken's model, truth is judged in terms of a set of regulative rules, including normative and intersubjective referenced claims that a statement must meet in order to be judged truthful.

Visweswaran (1994) anticipates a third type of reflexivity that complicates this picture by unsettling the notion of an objective, reflexive ethnographer. She criticizes the reflexive, normative ethnographic approach that presumes an observer and a subject with stable identities. She contrasts this stance with deconstructive ethnography, where the observer refuses to presume a stable identity for self or other. If Carspecken's reflexive ethnography questions its own authority, Visweswaran's deconstructive ethnography "forfeits its authority" (Kincheloe and McLaren 2000:301). Deconstructive reflexivity is postmodern, confessional, critical, and intertextual.

Foley (2002) can be read as extending Visweswaran. He calls himself a reflexive, realist, critical ethnographer. Unlike Carspecken, Foley has little interest in developing a foundational scientific method for his ethnography. He states: "I am much more interested in expanding the notion of cultural critique by tapping into the genres of autobiography, new journalism, travel writing and fiction. Appropriating epistemologies and textual practices from these genres will help us create more public, useful ethnographic storytelling forms" (p. 486).

Still, Foley is contained within a scientific frame. He states that his science would "still subscribe to extensive, systematic fieldwork. It would speak from a historically situated standpoint" (p. 486). This science "would be highly reflexive. . . . I continue to use a quasi-scientific abductive epistemology, or what Paul Willis now calls an 'ethnographic imagination.' . . . But I am also trying to tap into introspection and emotion the way that autoethnographers and ethnic and indigenous scholars are" (p. 487). He is doing so because this "eclectic approach helps produce realist narratives that are much more accessible. . . . I feel a great need to communicate with ordinary people" (p. 487).

It is not enough to want to communicate with ordinary people. That is no longer an option. The critical performance ethnographer is committed to producing and performing texts that are grounded in and co-constructed in the politically and personally problematic worlds of everyday life. This ethnographer does not use words like *data*, or *abduction*, or *objectivity*. These words carry the traces of science, objectivism, and knowledge produced for disciplines, not everyday people. Bourdieu's theoretical reflexivity coupled with Willis's ethnographic imagination may produce detached accounts that satisfy the social theorist, but such accounts have little place in the pedagogical practices of performance ethnography.

McLaren's postmodern ethnographer does not fall into these linguistic traps. His critical, reflexive ethnographer is thoroughly embedded in the world of praxis and acts as an agent of change. His ethnographer holds to a radical pedagogy, a militant utopian vision that is missing from the larger group of scientifically oriented, contemporary, reflexive, critical ethnographers. McLaren's ethnography and pedagogy are the kinds that cultural studies needs today.

❖ CRITICAL PERFORMANCE PEDAGOGY

A commitment to critical performance pedagogy and critical race theory gives cultural studies a valuable lever for militant, utopian cultural criticism. In his book *Impure Acts* (2000a), Giroux calls for a practical, performative view of pedagogy, politics, and cultural studies. He seeks an interdisciplinary project that would enable theorists and educators to form a progressive alliance "connected to a broader notion of cultural politics designed to further racial, economic, and political democracy" (p. 128). This project anchors itself in the worlds of pain and lived experience and is accountable to these worlds. It enacts an ethic of respect. It rejects the traditional denial by the West and Western scholars of respect, humanity, self-determination, citizenship, and human rights to indigenous peoples (Smith 1999:120).

Critical Race Theory

Such a project engages a militant utopianism, a provisional Marxism without guarantees, a cultural studies that is anticipatory, interventionist, and provisional. It does not back away from the contemporary world in its multiple global versions, including the West, the Third World, the moral, political, and geographic spaces occupied by First Nations and Fourth World persons, persons in marginal, or liminal, positions (Ladson-Billings 2000:263). Rather, it strategically engages this world in those liminal spaces where lives are bent and changed by the repressive structures of the new conservatism. This project pays particular attention to the dramatic increases around the world in domestic violence, rape, child abuse, and violence directed toward persons of color (Comaroff and Comaroff 2001:1–2; Grossberg 2001; Finley forthcoming).

Extending critical legal theory, critical race theory theorizes life in these liminal spaces, offering "pragmatic strategies for material and social transformation" (Ladson-Billings 2000:264). Critical race theory assumes that racism and white supremacy are the norms in U.S. society. Critical race scholars use performative, storytelling autoethnographic methods to uncover the ways in which racism operates in daily life. Critical race theory challenges those neoliberals who argue that civil rights have been attained for persons of color. It also challenges those who argue that the civil rights crusade is a long, slow struggle (Ladson-Billings 2000:264). Critical race theorists argue that the problem of racism requires radical social change, and that neoliberalism and liberalism lack the mechanisms and imaginations to achieve such change (Ladson-Billings 2000:264). Critical race theorists contend that whites have been the main beneficiaries of civil rights legislation.

Strategically, critical race theory examines the ways in which race is performed, including the cultural logics and performative acts that inscribe and create whiteness and nonwhiteness (McLaren 1997b:278; Roediger 2002:17). In an age of globalization and diasporic, postnational identities, the color line should no longer be an issue, but, sadly, it is (McLaren 1997b:278).

Participatory, Performance Action Inquiry

Drawing on the complex traditions embedded in participatory action research (Kemmis and McTaggart 2000; Fine et al. 2003) as well as the critical turn in feminist discourse and the growing literature for and by indigenous peoples (Smith 1999), critical performance pedagogy implements a commitment to participation and performance *with*, not *for*, community members. Amplifying the work of Fine et al. (2003: 176–77), this project builds on local knowledge and experience developed at the bottom of social hierarchies. Following Smith's (1999) lead, participatory, performance work honors and respects local knowledge, customs, and practices and incorporates those values and beliefs into participatory, performance action inquiry (Fine et al. 2003:176).

Work in this participatory, activist performance tradition gives back to the community, "creating a legacy of inquiry, a process of change, and material resources to enable transformations in social practices"

(Fine et al. 2003:177). Through performance and participation, the scholar develops a "participatory mode of consciousness" (Bishop 1998:208) and understanding. This helps shape the participant-driven nature of this form of inquiry and folds the researcher as performer into the narrative and moral accountability structures of the group.

This project works outward from the university and its classrooms, treating the spaces of the academy as critical public spheres, as sites of resistance and empowerment (Giroux 2000a:134). Critical pedagogy resists the increasing commercialization and commodification of higher education. It contests the penetration of neoliberal values into research parks, classrooms, and the curriculum. It is critical of institutional review boards that pass ever-more restrictive judgments on human subject research.

A commitment to critical pedagogy in the classroom can be an empowering, dialogic experience. The instructional spaces become sacred spaces. In them, students take risks and speak from the heart, using their own experiences as tools for forging critical race consciousness. The critical discourse created in this public sphere is then taken into other classrooms, into other pedagogical spaces, where a militant utopianism is imagined and experienced.

As a performative practice, this project interrogates and criticizes those cultural narratives that make victims responsible for the cultural and interpersonal violence they experience, thus blaming and revictimizing them. But performance narratives do more than celebrate the lives and struggles of persons who have lived through violence and abuse. They must always be directed back to the structures that shape and produce the violence in question. Pedagogically, the performative is political and focused on power. Performances are located within their historical moment, with attention given to the play of power and ideology. The performative becomes a way of critiquing the political, a way of analyzing how culture operates pedagogically to produce and reproduce victims.

Pedagogically, and ideologically, the performative becomes an act of doing (Giroux 2000a:135), a dialogic way of being in the world, a way of grounding performances in the concrete situations of the present. The performative becomes a way of interrogating how "objects, discourses, and practices construct possibilities for and constraints on citizenship" (Nelson and Gaonkar 1996:7; quoted in Giroux 2000a:134). This stance connects the biographical and the personal to the pedagogical and the performative. It casts the cultural critic in the identity of a critical citizen, a person who collaborates with others in participatory action projects that enact militant democratic visions of public life, community, and moral responsibility (Giroux 2000a:141). This public intellectual practices critical performance pedagogy. As a concerned citizen, working with others, he or she takes positions on the critical issues of the day, understanding that there can be no genuine democracy without genuine opposition and criticism (Giroux 2000a:136; see also Bourdieu 1999:8).

In turn, radical democratic pedagogy requires citizens and citizen-scholars who are committed to taking risks, persons who are willing to act in situations where the outcomes cannot be predicted in advance. In such situations, a politics of new possibilities can be imagined and made to happen. Yet in these pedagogical spaces there are no leaders and followers; there are only coparticipants, persons working together to develop new lines of action, new stories, new narratives in a collaborative effort (Bishop 1998:207).

Consider the following excerpts from the Susan Finley's poem "Dream Child" (2000:433–34). This poem is drawn from Finley's larger life-history, arts-based research project on homeless youth. In this participatory, performance action project, Finley followed the practice of representing her understandings of homeless street life in stories and poems that she would share with participants, including performances in public venues, such as at schools and at meetings with street youth or with the parents of missing children. The poem features snippets of interviews, descriptions of living situations, and a shorter, embedded poem titled "Is This My Life?" Written by a female traveler, "Is This My Life?" expresses the experiences of a young homeless woman. In these lines, Finley-as-poet and the young traveler forge a new narrative.

Hey, que pasa? I just got out of jail here in Austin

Wrote a poem while I was in jail and decided to mail you a copy.

A young girl writes a sad poem.

Is This My Life?

"Once in a while I awaken, asking myself 'what am I doing?' . . .

Have the streets really become my home . . .

Spare change, leftovers, or just anything . . .

Alcohol's treating me good. Smile. . . . It's good for you too."

Smile . . .

Bright morning light sneaks through slatted boards nailed loosely over glassless window frames forming streaked patterns on stained dark floors. Stretches feline

= into sun's warmth . . .

Propped on one elbow she reaches for a bottle: "Alcohol's treating me good. Smile. It's good for you too."

❖ CONCLUSION

Performing ethnography politically means putting the critical socio-logical imagination to work. This work involves pedagogies of hope and freedom. A performative cultural studies reflexively enacts these pedagogies. These practices require a performance ethics, the topic of my concluding chapter.

14

Performance Ethics

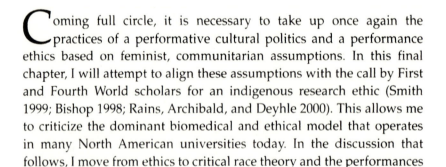

Coming full circle, it is necessary to take up once again the practices of a performative cultural politics and a performance ethics based on feminist, communitarian assumptions. In this final chapter, I will attempt to align these assumptions with the call by First and Fourth World scholars for an indigenous research ethic (Smith 1999; Bishop 1998; Rains, Archibald, and Deyhle 2000). This allows me to criticize the dominant biomedical and ethical model that operates in many North American universities today. In the discussion that follows, I move from ethics to critical race theory and the performances of race under local neoliberalism. I end with a racial performance and a brief discussion of the politics of resistance in the seventh moment of inquiry.

❖ CULTURAL POLITICS AND AN
   INDIGENOUS RESEARCH ETHIC

We have much to learn from indigenous scholars about how radical democratic practices can be made to work. Maori scholars Linda Tuhiwai Smith (1999) and Russell Bishop (1998) are committed to a set of moral and pedagogical imperatives and, as Smith expresses it, "to acts of reclaiming, reformulating, and reconstituting indigenous cultures and languages . . . to the struggle to become self-determining" (p. 142). Such acts lead to a research program that is committed to the pursuit of social justice. In turn, a specific approach to inquiry is required. In his discussion of a Maori approach to creating knowledge, Bishop (1998) observes that researchers in Kaupapa Maori contexts are

> repositioned in such a way as to no longer need to seek to *give voice to others*, to *empower* others, to *emancipate* others, to refer to others as *subjugated* voices, but rather to listen and participate . . . in a process that facilitates the development in people as a sense of themselves as agentic and of having an authoritative voice. . . . An indigenous Kaupapa Maori approach to research . . . challenges colonial and neo-colonial discourses that inscribe "otherness." (Pp. 207–8)

This participatory mode of knowing privileges subjectivity, personal knowledge, and the specialized knowledges of oppressed groups. It uses concrete experience as a criterion of meaning and truth. It encourages a participatory mode of consciousness that locates the researcher within Maori-defined spaces in the group. The researcher is led by the members of the community and does not presume to be a leader, or to have any power that he or she can relinquish (Bishop 1998:205).

As a way of honoring the group's sacred spaces, the researcher gives the group a gift. In laying down this gift, the researcher rejects the ideology of empowerment. There is no assumption that the researcher is giving the group power. Rather, the laying down of the gift is an offering, a pure giving. And in this act, the researcher refuses any claim to anything the group might give him or her in return. If the group picks up the gift, then a shared reciprocal relationship can be created (Bishop 1998:207). The relationship that follows is built on understandings involving shared Maori beliefs and cultural practices. In turn, the research is evaluated according to Maori-based criteria, not criteria imported from the international literature, including Western positivist and postpositivist epistemologies, as well as certain versions of critical pedagogy that think in terms of grand narratives and "binaries" or "dialectical linear progressions" (Bishop 1998:209, 211).

Like Freire's revolutionary pedagogy, West's prophetic pragmatism, and Collins's Afrocentric feminist moral ethic, the Maori moral position values dialogue as a method for assessing knowledge claims. The Maori culture also privileges storytelling, listening, voice, and personal performance narratives (Collins 1990:208–12). This moral pedagogy rests on an ethic of care, love, and personal accountability that honors individual uniqueness and emotionality in dialogue (Collins 1990:215–17). This is a performative, pedagogical ethic grounded in the ritual, sacred spaces of family, community, and everyday moral life (Bishop 1998:203). It is not imposed by some external, bureaucratic agency.

Within the Kaupapa Maori community, this ethic sets out specific guidelines for respecting and protecting the rights, interests, and sensitivities of the people being studied (Smith 1999:119). These guidelines ask that Maori researchers make themselves present, that they meet face-to-face with the members of the community they are studying. In these encounters, the Maori scholars listen, show respect, and share knowledge while behaving in a cautious, gentle, and humble manner, thus displaying many of the personal qualities that the Maori value (Smith 1999:120). These ethical codes are the same protocols that govern the relations the Maori have with one another and their environment. Through such shows of respect, "the place of everyone and everything in the universe is kept in balance and harmony" (Smith 1999:120). Among the Maori, respect is a principle that is felt as it is performed, experienced, and "expressed through all aspects of social conduct" (Smith 1999:120).

In the Maori context, the concept of "person" applies to a being who has a series of rights and responsibilities that are basic to the group. These obligations include a commitment to warm, respectful interpersonal interactions as well as respect for actions that create and preserve group solidarity. There is also a commitment to a shared responsibility for one another, which extends to corporate responsibility for the protection of group property, including the knowledge, language, and customs of the group (Bishop 1998:204). In this context, as Bishop (1998:204) notes, group achievement often takes the form of group, not individual, performance.

This view of performance parallels the commitment within certain forms of "red pedagogy" to the performative as a way of being, a way of knowing, a way of expressing moral ties to the community (Graveline 2000:361; Grande 2000:356). Fyre Jean Graveline (2000:363), a Metis woman, speaks:

As Metis woman, scholar, activist, teacher, healer

I enact First Voice as pedagogy and methodology

Observing my own lived experience as an Educator

Sharing meanings with Others . . .

My Voice is Heard

in concert with Students and Community Participants . . .

I asked: What pedagogical practices

Enacted through my Model-In-Use

contribute to what kinds of transformational learning?

For whom?

The Performative as a Site of Resistance

Because it expresses and embodies moral ties to the community, the performative view of meaning serves to legitimate indigenous worldviews. Meaning and resistance are embodied in the act of performance itself. The performative is political, the site of resistance. At this critical level, the performative provides the context for resistance to neoliberal and neoconservative attacks on the legitimacy of the worldview in question. Indigenous discourses such as those of the Maori are constantly under assault. Neoliberals and neoconservatives deny indigenous cultures any legitimacy and blame the members of these cultures for the problems that they experience. Liberals encourage assimilation and melting-pot views of race and ethnic relations. As Bishop (1998) notes, radical, emancipatory theorists "claim that they have the formula for emancipation of Maori as oppressed and marginalized people" (p. 212).

Bishop, Collins, and Smith all remind us that these positions presume that persons inside an indigenous culture are incapable of solving their own problems. Neoconservatives and postpositivists want to control the criteria that outsiders use to evaluate indigenous experience, and these criteria usually involve statistics and outcome measures that record the appalling conditions in the culture (Bishop 1998:212). Liberals rewrite school curricula, and "radical emancipationists argue that Maori cultural practices do not conform to their perspectives of how emancipatory projects should develop" (Bishop 1998:212). Under the guise of objectivity and neutrality, neoconservatives deny indigenous cultures' rights to self-determination. Multicultural curriculum revisionists rewrite the cultures' narratives to fit a hegemonic liberal discourse. And some radical theorists think that only they and their theories can lead such cultures into freedom, as if members of these cultures suffer from an indigenous version of false consciousness (Bishop 1998:213).

Each of these political positions undermines the integrity of indigenous cultures and these cultures' commitments to the performative as a way of being, a way of knowing, and a way of being political. The performative is where the soul of the culture resides. The performative haunts the liminal spaces of the culture. In their sacred and secular performances, the members of indigenous cultures honor one another and their cultures. In attacking the performative, the critics attack these cultures.[107] Smith (1999) states the issue clearly: "The struggle for the validity of indigenous knowledges may no longer be over the *recognition* that indigenous people have ways of knowing the world which are unique, but over proving the authenticity of, and control over, our own forms of knowledge" (p. 104).[108]

Resisting Colonialism

In response to the continuing pressures of colonialism and colonization, Smith (1999:142–62) outlines some 25 different indigenous projects, including those that create, name, restore, democratize, reclaim, protect, remember, and celebrate lost histories and cultural practices.[109] These indigenous projects embody a pedagogy of hope and freedom. They turn the pedagogies of oppression and colonization into pedagogies of liberation. They are not purely utopian, for they map concrete performances that can lead to positive social transformations. They embody ways of resisting the process of colonization.

Smith's moral agenda privileges four interpretive research processes. The first, *decolonization*, reclaims indigenous cultural practices and reworks these practices at the political, social, spiritual, and psychological levels. *Healing*, the second process, also involves physical, spiritual, psychological, social, and restorative elements. The third process, *transformation*, focuses on changes that move back and forth among psychological, social, political, economic, and collective levels. *Mobilization*, at the local, national, regional, and global levels, is the fourth basic process. It speaks to collective efforts to change Maori society.

These four complex, interdependent processes address issues of cultural survival and collective self-determination. In each instance, they work to decolonize Western methods and forms of inquiry and to empower indigenous peoples. These are the states of "being through which indigenous communities are moving" (Smith 1999:116). These states involve spiritual and social practices. They are pedagogies of healing, pedagogies of recovery, material practices that materially and spiritually benefit indigenous peoples.

A Moral Code

In turn, these processes require a set of moral and ethical research protocols. Fitted to the indigenous (and nonindigenous) perspective, these are moral matters. They are shaped by the feminist, communitarian principles of sharing, reciprocity, relationality, community, and neighborliness discussed in previous chapters (Lincoln 1995:287). They embody a dialogic ethic of love and faith grounded in compassion (Bracci and Christians 2002:13; West 1993b). Accordingly, the purpose of research is not the production of new knowledge per se. Rather, the purposes are pedagogical, political, moral, and ethical, involving the enhancement of moral agency, the production of moral discernment, a commitment to praxis, justice, an ethic of resistance, and a performative pedagogy that resists oppression (Christians 2002:409).

A code embodying these principles interrupts the practice of research, resists the idea of research being something that white men do to indigenous peoples. Further, unlike the Belmont principles (see below), which are not content driven, this code is anchored in a culture and its way of life. Unlike the Belmont principles, it connects its moral model to a set of political and ethical actions that will increase well-being in the indigenous culture. The code refuses to turn indigenous peoples into subjects who are the natural objects of white inquiry (Smith 1999:118). These principles argue that Western legal definitions of ethical codes privilege the utilitarian model of the individual as someone who has rights distinct from the rights of the larger group, "for example the right of an individual to give his or her own knowledge, or the right to give informed consent. . . . community and indigenous rights or views in this area are generally not . . . respected" (Smith 1999:118).

Bishop's (1998) and Smith's (1999:116–19) ethical and moral models call into question the more generic, utilitarian, biomedical Western model of ethical inquiry (see Christians 2000). A brief review of the biomedical model will serve to clarify the power of the indigenous position.

❖ THE BIOMEDICAL MODEL OF ETHICS AND THE BELMONT PRINCIPLES

As Gunsalus (2002) has observed, the rules governing human subject research are rooted in scandal: the Tuskegee Syphilis Study (American Association of University Professors, 1981), the Willowbrook Hepatitis Experiment, Project Camelot in the 1960s, and a series of events in the 1970s, including Milgram's deceptions of experimental subjects, Laud Humphreys's covert research on homosexuals, and the complicity of social scientists with military initiatives in Vietnam (Christians 2000:141). As Christians (2000) notes, concern for research ethics during the 1980s and 1990s, support from foundations, the development of professional codes of ethics, and extensions of the institutional review board (IRB) apparatus "are credited by their advocates with curbing outrageous abuses" (p. 141). However, these efforts have been framed, from the 1960s forward, in terms of a biomedical model of research. As implemented, this model involves institutional review boards, informed consent forms, value-neutral conceptions of the human subject, and utilitarian theories of risk and benefits.[110]

Today, the institutional protection of human subjects has expanded far beyond these original impulses, and Gunsalus (2002) asserts that this has led many to fear that there may be a growing "harm to academic freedom and scholars' First Amendment rights if the authority of IRBs is interpreted too broadly or becomes too intrusive." Puglisi (2001) demurs, arguing that these regulations "are extremely flexible and should present no impediment to well-designed behavioral and social science research" (p. 1). This, however, is not the case.

At issue are five elements: the terms *human subjects, human subject research, harm,* and *ethical conduct,* and the institutional apparatus of the IRB itself, including its local makeup and membership. These five elements, in turn, are embedded in six larger institutional and cultural formations, or social arenas and social worlds: universities and colleges; the federal government and its regulatory agencies; professional associations such as the American Association of University Professors (AAUP); disciplinary associations such as the American Sociological Association, the American Historical Association, and the American Anthropological Association; individual researchers; and human subjects.

As currently constituted, IRBs tend to privilege medical and experimental science membership. This leads IRBs to use highly restrictive biomedical definitions of *research, human subject, harm,* and *ethics*. It also leads to the uncritical implementation of federal guidelines, although the current Bush administration has "allowed the charter of the National Human Research Protections Advisory Committee, which had been studying these issues, to expire" (Gunsalus 2002).

Professional associations such as the AAUP act as watchdogs over the abuse of federal guidelines. Many disciplinary associations do the same while also overseeing the conduct of their own members. Individual researchers have to work through local IRBs, but their human subjects seldom have recourse to appeal procedures. However, as Smith and Bishop note, some Fourth World peoples are actively taking inquiry into their own hands and developing their own conceptions of human subject, researcher, research, ethics, harm, and community review apparatuses.[111]

Models of Critical, Interpretive Inquiry

The IRB framework assumes that one model of research fits all forms of inquiry, but that is not the case. This model requires that researchers fill out forms concerning subjects' informed consent, the risks and benefits of the research for subjects, confidentiality, and voluntary participation. The model also presumes a static, monolithic view of the human subject. Performance autoethnography, for example, falls outside this model, as do many forms of participatory action research, reflexive ethnography, and qualitative research involving testimonios, life stories, life-history inquiry, personal narrative inquiry, performance autobiography, conversation analysis, and ethnodrama. In all of these cases, subjects and researchers develop collaborative, public, pedagogical relationships. The walls between subjects and observers are deliberately broken down. Confidentiality disappears, for there is nothing to hide or protect. Participation is entirely voluntary, hence there is no need for subjects to sign forms indicating that their consent is "informed." The activities that makes up the research are participatory; that is, they are performative, collaborative, and action and praxis based. Hence participants are not asked to submit to specific procedures or treatment conditions. Instead, acting together, researchers and subjects work to produce change in the world.

The IRB model presumes a complex ethical framework (see below) that is problematic. This leads to a peculiar conception of harm, for why would collaborative researchers bring harm to those they study? In short, the Belmont principles (see below) need to be recast in light of contemporary understandings of participatory, performance autoethnography and empowerment inquiry.

The Professional Associations and Societies

In 1998, numerous professional associations, including the American Historical Association, the Oral History Association, the Organization of American Historians, and the American Anthropological Association, started communicating with one another and with more than 700 institutional review boards to encourage the IRBs to take account of the standards of practice relevant to the research in their specific disciplines (AAUP 2001:56). Concerns among the members of the professional societies involved the biomedical definition of research applied by the IRBs and the corresponding definitions of *harm, beneficence, respect, justice,* and *informed consent*. The problems start with how *research* is defined in Title 45, Part 46, of the U.S. Code of Federal Regulations. According to the regulations, research is

> any activity designed to test an hypothesis, permit conclusions to be drawn, and thereby to develop or contribute to generalizable knowledge expressed in theories, principles, and statements of relationships. Research is described in a formal protocol that sets forth an objective and a set of procedures designed to reach that objective.

This definition turns human beings into research subjects who may be exposed to harm because of the protocols that implement the research design.

The model works outward from the Belmont Report (the 1978 report of the U.S. National Commission for the Protection of Human Subjects in Biomedical and Behavioral Research) and its ethical principles (see Christians 2000; Lincoln and Tierney 2002; Lincoln and

Cannella 2002; Pritchard 2002: AAUP 2001, 2002). The current version of these rules, the 1991 regulations and their revisions, are also known as the "Common Rule" (AAUP 2001:55, 2002). The Common Rule describes the procedures of review that are used by more than 17 different federal agencies. It is often presumed that this single regulatory framework will fit all styles and forms of research, but, as Pritchard (2002:8) notes (see below), this is not always the case. In principle, the Common Rule is implemented through informed consent.

The Belmont Report sets forth three basic ethical principles: respect for persons, beneficence, and justice. Respect involves treating persons as autonomous agents and protecting them from harm, as well as protecting persons who exhibit diminished autonomy. Respect implies the subject's voluntary participation in the research project. The principle of beneficence asks that the research maximize benefits to the subject, and the collectivity, while minimizing harm. Typically, harm has been determined through the application of the Common Rule, which requires that harm or risk to the subject not exceed what is "ordinarily encountered in daily life" (AAUP 2001:56). This rules asks that members of society accept the fact that long-term benefits may result from research that harms certain subjects or places them at risk. Justice, the third ethical principle, requires that researchers treat persons equally; particular groups should not be disadvantaged in terms of being selected as subjects or in terms of being able to benefit from the research.

The three principles of respect, beneficence, and justice are implemented through disciplinary codes of ethics and through a set of procedures administered by IRBs that follow the Common Rule. The principle of respect is implemented through the obtainment of subjects' *informed consent* (passive versus active). Informed consent involves at least three issues: ensuring that subjects are adequately informed about the research, although deception may be allowed; ensuring that the information is presented in an easily understood fashion, which may also include seeking third-party permission; and ensuring that consent is voluntarily given.[112]

The principle of beneficence is applied through a complex set of procedures designed to assess the *risks and benefits* to the subjects of participation in the research. The term *risks* refers to potential harm to subjects, and *benefits* refers to potential positive value to the subjects' health or welfare. If an IRB determines that subjects in a given research project are at risk, it then asks whether the risks are minimal or can be minimized and whether the risks are warranted (Pritchard 2002:8). Under this risk-benefit model, risk is measured in terms of the probability of benefits, and benefits are contrasted with harms, rather than risks. There are multiple forms of harm—psychological, physical, legal, social, economic, cultural—and corresponding benefits. Risks and benefits must be assessed at the individual, family, and societal levels. Risks must be exceeded by benefits, although risks at the individual level may be justified if the benefits serve a larger cause. Although not specified in the Belmont Report, the codes of ethics developed by many scholarly professional associations also insist on "safeguards to protect people's identities and those of the research locations" (Christians 2000:139).

The principle of justice is expressed in the assurance that the procedures used in the *selection* of research subjects are fair. Special populations should not be unduly burdened by being required to participate in research projects. In addition, the benefits of research should not be unfairly distributed throughout a subject population or made available only to those who can afford them.[113]

Internal Criticisms of the Model

This model, with the apparatus of the institutional review board and the Common Rule, has been subjected to considerable criticism. The arguments of most critics center on the four key terms and their definitions: *human subject, human subject research, harm,* and *ethical conduct.*

First, I want to address the issue of science and ethics. As Christians (2000) notes, the Common Rule principles "reiterate the basic themes of value-neutral experimentalism—individual autonomy, maximum benefits and minimal risks, and ethical ends exterior to scientific means" (p. 140). These principles "dominate the codes of ethics: informed consent, protection of privacy, and nondeception" (p. 140). These rules do not conceptualize research in participatory or collaborative formats. Christians observes that, in reality, IRBs protect institutions and not individuals. The guidelines do not prevent other ethical violations, including plagiarism, falsification or fabrication of data, and violations of confidentiality.

As Pritchard (2002:8–9) notes, there is room for ethical conflict as well. The three principles contained in the Common Rule rest on three different ethical traditions: respect, from Kant; beneficence, from Mill and the utilitarians; and justice, as a distributive idea, from Aristotle. These ethical traditions are not compatible; they rest on different moral, ontological, and political assumptions, different understandings of what is right and just and respectful. The Kantian principle of respect may contradict the utilitarian principle of beneficence, for instance.

Respect, beneficence, and *justice* are all problematic terms. Surely there is more to respect than informed consent, more than simply getting people to agree to be participants in a study. Respect involves caring for another, honoring that person and treating him or her with dignity. Obtaining a person's signature on an informed consent form is not the same as demonstrating true respect.

Beneficence, including risks and benefits, cannot be quantified, nor can we attach a clear meaning to *acceptable risk* or clearly define what benefits may serve a larger cause. Smith (1999) and Bishop (1998), for instance, argue that the collectivity must determine the costs and benefits of the group's participating in research. Further, individuals may not have the right, as individuals, to allow particular forms of research to be done if the research results are likely to affect the greater social whole. A cost-benefit model of society and inquiry does injustice to the empowering, participatory model of research that many Fourth World peoples are now advocating.

Justice extends beyond fair selection procedures or the fair distribution of the benefits of research across a population. Justice involves principles of care, love, kindness, fairness, and commitment to shared responsibility, to honesty, truth, balance, and harmony. Taken out of their Western utilitarian framework, respect, beneficence, and justice must be seen as principles that are felt as they are performed—that is, they can serve as performative guidelines to a moral way of being in the world with others. As currently applied by IRBs, however, they serve as cold, calculated devices that may turn persons against one another.

And now to address research. Pritchard (2002) contends that the model's concept of research does not deal adequately with procedural changes in research projects, with unforeseen contingencies that lead to changes in the purposes and intents of studies. Often researchers cannot maintain their subjects' anonymity, nor is this always even desirable; for example, participatory action inquiry presumes full community participation in a research project.

The staffing of IRBs presents another level of difficulty. IRBs are often understaffed, and many include members who either reject or are uninformed about the newer, critical qualitative research tradition.

Many IRBs have not instituted suitable appeal procedures or methods for expediting the identification of research that should be exempted from IRB review.

Recent summaries by the American Association of University Professors (2001, 2002) raise additional reservations about IRBs that center on the following issues.

Research and Human Subjects

- ❖ Failure on the part of IRBs to be aware of new interpretive and qualitative developments in the social sciences, including participant observation, ethnography, autoethnography, and oral history research
- ❖ Application by IRBs of a concept of research and science that privileges the biomedical model and not the model of trust, negotiation, and respect that must be established in ethnographic or historical inquiry, where research is not *on* but rather *with* other human beings
- ❖ IRBs' event-based rather than process-based conception of research and the consent process

Ethics

- ❖ Failure on the part of IRBs to see human beings as social creatures located in complex historical, political, and cultural spaces
- ❖ Infringements on academic freedom by IRBs in not allowing certain types of inquiry to go forward
- ❖ IRBs' inappropriate applications of the Common Rule in assessing potential harm to subjects
- ❖ IRBs' overly restrictive applications of the informed consent rule

IRBs as Institutional Structures

- ❖ IRBs' failure to have adequate appeals systems in place
- ❖ IRBs' failure to recognize the need to include members who understand the newer interpretive paradigms

Academic Freedom

- ❖ IRBs' infringements on researchers' First Amendment rights and academic freedom

❖ IRBs' policing of inquiry in the humanities, including oral history research
❖ IRBs' policing and obstruction of research seminars and dissertation projects
❖ IRBs' constraints on critical inquiry, including historical or journalistic work that contributes to the public knowledge of the past while incriminating or passing negative judgment on persons and institutions
❖ IRBs' failure to consider or incorporate existing forms of regulation into the Common Rule, including laws concerning libel, copyright, and intellectual property rights
❖ IRBs' general extension of their powers across disciplines, creating negative effects on researchers' choices concerning what they will or will not study
❖ IRBs' vastly different applications of the Common Rule across campus communities

The AAUP has also noted the following as important areas that are not addressed by IRB reviews:

❖ The conduct of research with indigenous peoples (see below)
❖ The regulation of researchers' unorthodox or problematic conduct in the field (e.g., sexual relations with subjects)
❖ Relations between IRBs and ethical codes involving universal human rights
❖ Disciplinary codes of ethics and new codes of ethics and moral perspectives coming from feminist, queer, and racialized standpoint epistemologies
❖ Appeal mechanisms for human subjects who need to grieve and who seek some form of restorative justice as a result of harm they have experienced as research subjects
❖ Fourth World discourses and alternative views of research, science, and human beings

Disciplining and Constraining Ethical Conduct

The consequence of these restrictions, as Lincoln and Tierney (2002) and Lincoln and Cannella (2002) observe, is a disciplining of qualitative inquiry that extends from granting agencies to the policing of qualitative research seminars and even the conduct of qualitative dissertations.

In some cases, lines of critical inquiry have not been funded and have not gone forward because of the criticisms of local IRBs. Pressures from the right discredit critical interpretive inquiry. From the federal level to the local level, a trend seems to be emerging. In too many instances, there seems to be a move in IRBs' purposes away from protecting human subjects and toward increased monitoring and censuring of projects that are critical of the right and its politics.

Lincoln and Tierney (2002) observe that these policing activities have at least five important implications for critical social justice inquiry. First, the widespread rejection of alternative forms of research means that qualitative inquiry will be heard less and less in federal and state policy forums. Second, it appears that qualitative researchers are being deliberately excluded from the national dialogue. Consequently, third, young researchers trained in the critical tradition are not being listened to. Fourth, the definition of research has not changed to fit newer models of inquiry. Fifth, in rejecting qualitative inquiry, traditional researchers are endorsing a more distanced form of research that is compatible with existing stereotypes concerning persons of color.

Christians (2000) summarizes the poverty of this model. It rests on a cognitive model that privileges rational solutions to ethical dilemmas (the rationalist fallacy), and it presumes that humanity is a single subject (the distributive fallacy). It presents the scientist as an objective, neutral observer. Private citizens are coerced into participating in so-called scientific projects in the name of some distant public good. The rights-, justice-, and acts-based system ignores the dialogic nature of human interaction. The model creates the conditions for deception, for the invasion of private spaces, for the duping of subjects, and for challenges to subjects' moral worth and dignity. Christians calls for its replacement with an ethics based on the values of a feminist communitarianism, an ethic of empowerment, a care-based, dialogic ethic of hope, love, and solidarity.

This is an evolving, emerging ethical framework that serves as a powerful antidote to the deception-based, utilitarian IRB system. It presumes a community that is ontologically and axiologically prior to the person. This community has common moral values, and research is rooted in a concept of care, of shared governance, of neighborliness, of love, kindness, and the moral good. Accounts of social life should display these values and should be based on interpretive sufficiency. They should have sufficient depth to allow the reader to form a critical understanding about the world studied. These texts should exhibit an absence of racial, class, and gender stereotyping. They should generate social criticism and lead to resistance, empowerment, and social action, to positive change in the social world

❖ AN INDIGENOUS FEMINIST, COMMUNITARIAN ETHIC

Against this background, indigenous peoples debate codes of ethics and issues of intellectual and cultural property rights. In this politicized space, as Smith (1999) observes, "indigenous codes of ethics are being promulgated . . . as a sheer act of survival" (p. 119). Thus the charters of various indigenous peoples include statements that refer to collective, not individual, human rights. These rights include control and ownership of the community's cultural property, its health and knowledge systems, its rituals and customs, the culture's basic gene pool, rights and rules for self-determination, and an insistence on who the first beneficiaries of indigenous knowledge will be.

These charters call upon governments and states to develop policies that will ensure these social goods, including the rights of indigenous peoples to protect their cultures' new knowledge and its dissemination. These charters embed codes of ethics within this larger perspective. They spell out specifically how researchers are to protect and respect the rights and interests of indigenous peoples, using the same protocols that regulate daily moral life in these cultures. In these ways, Smith's arguments open the space for a parallel discourse concerning a feminist, communitarian moral ethic.

In the feminist, communitarian model, participants have a coequal say in how research should be conducted, what should be studied, which methods should be used, which findings are valid and acceptable, how the findings are to be implemented, and how the consequences of such actions are to be assessed. Spaces for disagreement are recognized at the same time discourse aims for mutual understanding and for the honoring of moral commitments.

A sacred, existential epistemology places humans in a noncompetitive, nonhierarchical relationship to the earth, to nature, and to the larger world. This sacred epistemology stresses the values of empowerment, shared governance, care, solidarity, love, community, covenant, morally involved observers, and civic transformation. This ethical epistemology recovers the moral values that were excluded by the rational, Enlightenment science project. This sacred epistemology is based on a philosophical anthropology that declares that "all humans are worthy of dignity and sacred status without exception for class or ethnicity" (Christians 1995:129). A universal human ethic that stresses the sacredness of life, human dignity, truth telling, and nonviolence derives from this position (Christians 1997:12–15). This ethic is based on locally experienced, culturally prescribed protonorms (Christians 1995:129). These primal norms provide a defensible "conception of good rooted in universal human solidarity" (Christians 1995:129; see also Christians 1997, 1998). This sacred epistemology recognizes and interrogates the ways in which race, class, and gender operate as important systems of oppression in the world today.

Thus Smith, Bishop, and Christians outline a radical ethical path for the future. In so doing, they transcend the Belmont principles, which focus almost exclusively on the problems associated with betrayal, deception, and harm. They call for a collaborative social science research model that makes the researcher responsible not to a removed discipline (or institution), but to those he or she studies. This model stresses personal accountability, caring, the value of individual expressiveness, the capacity for empathy, and the sharing of emotionality (Collins 1990:216). This model implements collaborative, participatory, performative inquiry. It forcefully aligns the ethics of research with a politics of the oppressed, with a politics of resistance, hope, and freedom.

This model directs scholars to take up moral projects that decolonize, honor, and reclaim indigenous cultural practices. Such work produces spiritual, social, and psychological healing. Healing, in turn, leads to multiple forms of transformation at the personal and social levels. These transformations shape processes of mobilization and collective action. These actions help persons realize a radical politics of possibility.

❖   A RED PEDAGOGY

I want to end this book on another racial performance. On November 8, 2002, Chief Illiniwek returned to Champaign-Urbana, Illinois.[114] A full-page ad that ran in that day's the *News Gazette* is headlined "Evidence Demands a Verdict!" The text of the ad offers several arguments for why the University of Illinois should keep the Chief as its symbol: He represents an honorable tradition; he is a symbol of our great university and its intercollegiate athletic teams; he (and the teams) are loved by the people of Illinois; he is a link to a great past; he is an intangible spirit, filled with qualities "to which a person of any background can aspire: goodness, strength, bravery, truthfulness, courage, and dignity."

The ad goes on to state that, as a result of limits put on the Chief's appearances, this great symbol has been marginalized over the years. His logo has disappeared from university stationery, and he performs at halftime only during select athletic events. Citing a controversial poll conducted by *Sports Illustrated*, the ad argues that Native Americans endorse the Chief, and that 81% of Native Americans support the use of Indian nicknames for sporting teams.

The ad argues that the Chief's attire is authentic, that his costume was sewn by a member of the Oglala Sioux, although less is known about the style of dress of the Illini tribes because they came from an earlier culture. The text asserts that the Chief's dance is historically accurate, that it is similar to Native American "fancy dancing" and has evolved over the years. The original dance was based on Lester Leutwiler's Eagle Scout studies of Native American customs. Although opponents of the dance say it is sacrilegious, the ad asserts that today, at Native American gatherings and "powwows," Native Americans and non-Natives dance side by side. This evidence clearly disputes the claim of sacrilege.

The ad then asks why minority groups oppose the Chief. It answers its own question by stating that the Chief has been targeted by an organization of Native American activists, the National Coalition Against Racism in Sports and the Media. This group has singled out the Chief, contending that he constitutes a negative portrayal of Native Americans, and all such portrayals are indefensible. But the ad asserts that the Chief is not a racist mascot. It quotes two definitions of *racism* from *Webster's Dictionary*: "a belief that race is the primary determinant of human traits and capacities and that racial differences produce an inherent superiority" and "racial prejudice or discrimination." Under the first definition, the ad claims, the Chief is racist only to the extent "that a Native American is perceived as a higher quality of human than others." In this case, Native Americans should be honored, because the university is honoring them through the Chief. Under the second definition, the ad says, the university's elevation of the Native American does not "show a prejudice against him nor discrimination."

The ad also argues that the presence of the Chief does not create a racist environment at the university, citing an increase in the number of minority students and faculty members on the campus. The ad also cites a 1995 report by the U.S. Department of Education that concluded there was insufficient evidence to show a racially hostile environment on the campus. The ad does not cite the 2000 accreditation report by the North Central Association of Colleges and Schools, which said, "There are inconsistencies between exemplary diversity policies and practices and the University's policies regarding the Chief."

Citing Trustee Plummer's report (see Chapter 11), the ad agrees that no compromise is possible, but it then presents a somewhat different reading of Plummer's text. The ad states that if the Chief is retired, the Board of Trustees will be perceived as responding to special interests and transitory pressures. The university will lose its tangible symbol, and hence the values associated with the Chief will be lost. Keeping the Chief will benefit Native Americans and other underserved populations by taking advantage of the challenges faced by these groups. By retiring the Chief, the Board will revoke his value for all future generations, thereby tarnishing the university's image.

Under this semiotic scenario, the "Honor the Chief" group presents itself as one of the university's biggest supporters. The Chief and the university mutually reinforce one another. They interact on the same symbolic plane. To attack one of them is to attack both of them.

An Anti-Red Pedagogy

This full page ad for the Chief presents and defends an anti-red pedagogy. It articulates a form of white racism that reads race biologically (human traits, capacities). It does so from within an essentializing framework. It accepts the notion of inferior and superior races. It treats race as a performance (the Chief's halftime dance), but this is a performance that is done to entertain whites. No manner of amateur anthropological exaggeration can read the Chief's halftime performances as an indigenous dance form that has spiritual meaning for Native Americans.

The Chief addressed by the ad's text is a white male person. As Crue (2002) observes, this is a form of black- or redface minstrelsy. A white male in a racialized costume acts in a way that represents an imaginary version of the dark-skinned other. This is not pure blackface minstrelsy, but it is close (Crue 2002). In this performance, the white male in redface entertains the white audience. He gives them an imaginary version of a Native American authentic dance. Of course, all of the signifiers of Native Americanness are manipulated by the white male performer. To invoke Spike Lee for a moment, who is being bamboozled here?

In creating a performance connected to the Illini tribe, which has all but disappeared, the supporters of the Chief keep alive the idea of the vanishing American Indian. The Chief, this imaginary figure, allows whites to maintain a set of racist myths about their own past. Such performances must be challenged (Spindel 2000; Prochaska 2001; Springwood and King 2001:332; Crue 2002).

Under the cover of local Boy Scout troops, the Chief visits class-rooms in the area, where he dances and lets little boys and girls touch his costume. The Boy Scouts of America is an organization that denies membership to gay men. At one level, the Chief's performance history is folded into this organization and its antigay politics.

The text of the Chief supporters' ad reads history selectively, ignor-ing those official documents that in fact connect the Chief to a racist environment on campus. The text politicizes the anti-Chief forces, asso-ciating them with a secret campaign. If successful, this campaign would sacrifice the Chief to an unjust, "politically correct" cause, and this would be a grave injustice. In order to justify this reading, the text has to marginalize the anti-Chief forces, and this it does. It must also create its own version of racism, which excludes the pro-Chief group's celebration of the Chief. Perversely, the ad then applies this definition to the Chief's critics, claiming that the critics are acting with racial prej-udice and discrimination when they seek to remove the Chief from public display.

This is quintessential contemporary neoliberal racial politics. The postcolonial, racist imagination imposes its morality and will on racial-ized others and their defenders. Invoking the tarnished specter of polit-ical correctness, it belittles those who would defend the other in the name of progressive racial justice.

Of course, the anti-Chief forces also accuse Chief supporters of racism. In their mutual accusations, both groups ignore what might be called the "Foucault effect" (Foucault 1980b:131). Foucault suggests that scholars should look at the effects of discourses on social practices, including other discourses. This strategy avoids entanglements and arguments over intentions, purposes, and beliefs. The Foucault effect focuses attention on the consequences of actions, on their effects. If the effect, or consequence, of a discourse is to create a hostile racial environment, then it matters little whether the proponents of the discourse are racist. The discourse is racist. Name-calling can end.

But those who are belittled, and those who are treated as racial caricatures, will soon have their day. W. E. B. Du Bois saw this nearly a century ago. Denouncing the lynching of black men by white mobs as a great white American pastime, he shouted off the pages of his newspaper, *The Crisis:*

> Once more a howling mob of the best citizens in a foremost State of the Union has vindicated the self-evident superiority of the white race.... Let the eagle scream!... But let every black American gird up his loins. The great day is coming. We have crawled and pleaded for justice, and we have been cheerfully spit upon and murdered and burned. We will not endure it forever. If we must die, in God's name lets us perish like men and not bales of hay. (Quoted in Lewis 2002:29; Lewis quotes Dray 2002:182)

Let the eagle scream!

Notes

1. Representative works regarding this performance turn include the works of McCall (2000), Mienczakowski (2001), Conquergood (1998), Schechner (1988, 1993, 1998), Pelias (1999), Phelan and Lane (1998), and Dailey (1998b).

2. Yvonna Lincoln and I have defined the seven moments of inquiry, all of which operate in the present, as follows: the traditional (1900–1950), the modernist (1950–70), blurred genres (1970–86), the crisis of representation (1986–90), postmodern or experimental (1990–95), postexperimental (1995–2000), and the future (2000 and onward) (Denzin and Lincoln 2000:2–3). For criticisms and discussions of this model, see Atkinson, Coffey, and Delamont (1999, 2001); Delamont, Coffey, and Atkinson (2000); Coffey and Atkinson (1996); and Atkinson, Coffey, Delamont, Lofland, and Lofland (2001).

3. Throughout, I will connect *reflexive ethnography* with *autoethnography,* using both terms to reference the most recent developments in performance ethnography. In this book, I build on and extend my arguments in *Interpretive Ethnography* (Denzin 1997:90–125), moving those arguments into the spaces of autoethnography—the production of first-person, multilayered ethnographic texts that move outward from the writers' lives (see Ellis and Bochner 2000:739). Thus understood, performance becomes performance autoethnography. The researcher becomes the research subject. This is the topic of reflexive performance autoethnography. In autoethnography, researchers conduct, write, and perform ethnographies of their own experience.

4. Put another way: Being's presence in the world is always processual, a process of doing, of acting.

5. An earlier version of this chapter appears in Denzin (2002a). I thank Kathy Charmaz and her editorial staff, as well as Laurel Richardson, Andy Fontana, and Art Frank, for their comments and suggestions for revisions. A performative cultural studies enacts a critical cultural pedagogy. It does so by using dialogue, performative writing, and the staging and performance of texts involving audience members (see Schutz 2001:146).

6. For Kincheloe and McLaren (2000) *cultural pedagogy* refers to the ways that cultural production functions "as a form of education, as it generates knowledge, shapes values, and constructs identity"; it refers to "the ways

264   PERFORMANCE ETHNOGRAPHY

particular cultural agents produce particular hegemonic ways of seeing" (p. 285). Critical pedagogy (see McLaren 1998:441) attempts to disrupt and deconstruct these cultural practices performatively, in the name of a "more just, democratic, and egalitarian society" (Kincheloe and McLaren 2000:285; but see Lather 1998).

7.   Although this text is a call to performance, it is not an example of performance writing per se (see Bochner and Ellis 2002; Madison 1999; Phelan 1998, 1993). I do not intend this chapter to be a deconstruction of the classic academic style, but I do want to privilege texts that are meant to be performed.

8.   For Du Bois, race and racism were social constructions, performances, minstrelsy, blackface, powerful devices that produced and reproduced the color line. Du Bois believed that African Americans need performance spaces where they can control how race is constructed. Consequently, as Elam (2001:5–6) observes, African American theater and performance have been central sites for the interrogation of race and the color line (see also Elam and Krasner 2001). As Elam (2001) notes, "The inherent 'constructedness' of performance and the malleability of the devices of the theatre serve to reinforce the theory that blackness . . . and race . . . are hybrid, fluid concepts" (pp. 4–5). Stuart Hall (1996:473) is correct in his observation that persons of color have never been successful in escaping the politics and theaters of (racial) representation.

9.   McChesney's (1999) definition of democracy is as good as any: In a democracy, "the many should and do make the core political decisions" (p. 4). This definition authorizes democracy in the participatory but not the representational mode. A viable participatory democracy takes the word away from those neoliberal discourses that have reduced democracy to a system that suits the needs of capitalism and the attendant corporate colonization of public life in the United States today (Giroux 2001b:122).

10.   I first wrote these words on September 14, 2001, three days after the terrorist attacks on the World Trade Center in New York City and the Pentagon in Washington, D.C.

11.   Cultural studies, in a generic sense, represents a body of work concerned with culture and power, with politicizing theory and theorizing politics, with the political nature of knowledge production, an orientation to the texts and contexts of the object of cultural analysis, a commitment to a theory of articulation and to the belief that theory offers a necessary explanatory framework for the object of inquiry (Sterne 1999:260–64). A fundamental problem involves how to construct the object of study in terms of a theory of articulation that asserts that all correspondences between objects have to be made (Sterne 1999:263). Ideally, as Sterne (1999:262) observes, cultural studies is antisexist, anticapitalist, antiracist, antiheteronormative, and anticolonial in its politics and interventionist in its politics. That is, scholars of cultural studies have a desire to shape the political considerations of policy makers (p. 267). In turn, the present performative, interpretive interactionist version of cultural

studies focuses on four interrelated issues: (a) the study of personal troubles, epiphanies, and turning point moments in the lives of interacting individuals; (b) the connection of these moments to the liminal, ritual structures of daily life; (c) the intersection and articulation of race-, class-, and sex-based oppressions with turning-point experiences; and (d) the production of critical pedagogical performance texts that critique these structures of oppression while presenting a politics of possibility that imagines how things could be different (see also Denzin 1992:80–81).

12.   In Austin's theory, according to Conquergood (1998), "the term performative designated the kind of utterance that actually does something in the world, e.g. promising, forgiving . . . as opposed to 'constative' utterances that merely report on a state of affairs independent of the act of enunciation" (p. 32; for criticisms, see Garoian 1999:4; Austin 1962:5, 14–15, 108; Perinbanayagam 1991:113). Pollock (1998b) notes that Derrida "reworks Austin's performativity as citationality . . . dissolving constative into performative speech" (p. 39).

13.   Schechner (1998) observes that this is the "performative Austin introduced and Butler and queer theorists discuss" (p. 362).

14.   I take the title of this section from Conquergood (1998).

15.   Performance writing shows, rather than tells. It is writing that speaks performatively, enacting what it describes. Performance writing is evocative, reflexive, multivocal, citational, and always incomplete (Pollock 1998a:80–95; Phelan 1998:13).

16.   Sharon Irish has helped clarify my understanding of the definitions of these terms. She suggests that community or public art usually occurs outside museums and galleries, thereby emphasizing the hoped-for connection between artist and audience (see also Garoian 1999:27). Garoian (1999:42) treats postmodern performance art as a new genre of public art that invites citizens to participate in the production and the collective ownership of performances that intervene in public spaces. Arts-based inquiry, based on cultural performance art pedagogy, is also part of this movement (see Finley forthcoming; Mullins forthcoming).

17.   In countless public works Lacy has focused attention on rape, women's rights, immigration, racism, aging, and domestic violence,

18.   For example, in *The Electronic Disturbance*, the Critical Art Ensemble, an anarchist group, models a form of local and global resistance in cyberspace.

19.   A "mystory" is simultaneously a personal mythology, a public story, and a performance that critiques (Denzin 1997:116; Ulmer 1989:210). The mystory is a montage text, cinematic and multimedia in shape, filled with sounds, music, and images taken from the writer's personal history. This personal text (script) is grafted onto discourses from popular culture and locates itself against the specialized knowledges that circulate in the larger society.

20.   In this chapter, I build on and extend my work in *Interpretive Ethnography* (Denzin 1997, chap. 4).

21.   A performance conception of oral literature (and folklore), with an emphasis on the performance event (the telling of a story or myth), is also an important part of this tradition (see Bauman 1986:3; Tedlock 1983:3–6). Later in this chapter, I conflate performance text and performance event, using performance to describe the interpretive event that performatively enacts an evocative (performance) text.

22.   Historical performance ethnography exists along another borderline, the site where embodied and gendered history is first recovered from archival sources and then performed by the researcher (see Latham 1997:172).

23.   In writing this history, I rely heavily on virtually every essay in Dailey's edited volume *The Future of Performance Studies* (1998b), including Dailey (1998a, 1998c), Strine (1998), Pelias (1998), Miller (1998), Bell (1998), Gilbert (1998), Gentile (1998), Doyle (1998), Rosen (1998), Robertson (1998), Pineau (1998), Worley (1998), Hill (1998), Girton (1998), Kendig (1998), Alexander (1998), Langellier (1998), Hantzis (1998), Lockford (1998), Carlin (1998), Smith (1998), Corey (1998), Spry (1998), Jenkins (1998), Madison (1998), Hartnett (1998), Gingrich-Philbrook (1998), Chesebro (1998), and Gray (1998).

24.   In a coperformance, traditional audience members participate in the performance event. This form of critical performance autoethnography has taken shape over the course of the past decade at the University of Illinois in collaborative work involving graduate students in kinesiology, education, communications, social work, advertising, and anthropology. My treatment of this genre draws from this body of work, thus I do not address the full range of performance practices that circulate in this field (for such a review, see Denzin 1997:92–102).

25.   As Turner (1986b:34–35) describes them, liminal experiences are always part of larger, processually structured social dramas (see discussion below). A liminal experience is bracketed by public action on both sides, beginning with a breach of an everyday code of conduct and moving to a crisis (where the liminal experience occurs), with people taking sides, applying redressive or remedial pressures on the person, culminating in the social reintegration or exclusion of the person from the social group. There are four main types of epiphanies: major, cumulative, minor, and relived (see Denzin 2001b:37; on the connection between personal narratives and liminal moments of experience, see Stern and Henderson 1993:45–46).

26.   The mystory is a site for the intersection of multiple forms of writing performance, including personal experience narratives, conversations, short stories, poetry, layered texts, testimonios, and memoirs.

27.   For Nietzsche, theory is performative and literary, and hence all claims to truth are based on language, appearances, and fictions (see Crawford 1995).

28.   In the educational context, McLaren (1999) changes this conclusion, showing how schooling is a dramaturgical, ritual performance. Teaching is organized around three types of ritual performances: the teacher-as-liminal-servant,

the teacher-as-entertainer-servant, and the teacher-as-hegemonic-overlord. In the roles of entertainers and overlords, teachers perform the narratives of the dominant culture. In the role of the liminal servant, teachers subvert this traditional pedagogy.

29.   Stern and Henderson (1993:382–83, 546) define performance art as a hybrid, improvisatory, antiestablishment, multimedia, interventionist, open-ended form of performance that is opposed to the commodification of art. Performance art uses the principles of juxtaposition, incongruence, simultaneity, collage, and assemblage, "drawing for its materials not only upon the live bodies of the performers but upon media images, television monitors, projected images, visual images, film, poetry, autobiographical material, narrative, dance, architecture, and music" (pp. 382–83). In the early 1990s, a number of performance artists (Holly Hughes, Karen Finley, Tim Miller, John Fleck) came into conflict with the chairman of the National Endowment for the Arts, who judged their work (as well as that of Robert Mapplethorpe and Andres Serrano) to be offensive to the public taste—"read *homoerotic*" (Stern and Henderson 1993:433).

30.   As I have argued in Chapter 1, the rise of performance art corresponds to the politicization of art and culture associated with the Vietnam War and the Watergate scandal, as well as with the women's movement (Sayre 1990:98). It was co-opted in the 1980s by the New Wave movement (see Birringer 1993:173).

31.   Elsewhere, I have criticized this movement, in its 1990s form, for its emphasis on a postpositivist epistemology and its refusal to engage the politics of culture seriously (Denzin 1997:108–14).

32.   Recall from the discussion of cultural and critical pedagogy in note 6, above, that critical pedagogy disrupts those cultural practices that instill hegemonic ways of seeing and being. A critical performative pedagogy enacts these disruptions.

33.   I borrow these distinctions from McLaren's (2001:121) discussion of the differences between teaching, pedagogy, critical pedagogy, and revolutionary pedagogy.

34.   I draw here from Denzin (2001b:38–39).

35.   Benjamin (1968b) contends that Brecht's epic theater is didactic and participatory because it "facilitates . . . interchange between audience and actors . . . and every spectator is enabled to become a participant" (p. 154).

36.   Broadhurst (1999:20–23) contrasts purely aesthetic performance theories (e.g., Kant's sublime) with theories that stress the politics of performance (e.g., Brecht's demand that theater have an immediate political effect on audiences). Political theater, of course, can be staged within a presentational, representational, or commonsense frame. Broadhurst adds a fourth frame, or type: liminal theater, a hybridized theater that mixes political and traditional aesthetic techniques within an experimental reflexive frame (p. 14). Liminal

theater might manipulate the many variations (absurd, German epic, cruelty) on the traditional (Elizabethan, Stuart, Restoration, realist, neoclassical, romanticist, comedy, chamber, story, reader's, people's) theater model (see Turner 1986a:27–31).

37.   Through the techniques of Method acting, actors produce faithful renderings of everyday interactions and conversations. The audience does not see performers (persons) playing characters; they see only the characters.

38.   In this style of theater, there is no attempt to dissolve the performer into the role. The emphasis is on stylization, not on realism.

39.   A confusion in such response, often termed the *affective fallacy* (Bacon 1979:196), occurs when an individual is taken in by a performance and neglects to critique the text on which the performance is based. Of course, this relationship is always dialectical (see Tedlock 1983:236).

40.   Improvisational and critical ethnodramas often draw on interviews and conversations, use composite characters, offer multiple tellings of the same events, and shift concern away from verisimilitude toward dramatic reinterpretation and cultural critique (see Mienczakowski 2001:473–74). Audience members may be coperformers in these productions. When the postproduction method of forum theater (Boal [1979] 1985, 1995) is used, audience members and performers discuss each performance after it is concluded, and scripts and future performances are modified on the basis of these conversations.

41.   In this section I rework my earlier discussion in Denzin (1997:115–20).

42.   Although this narrative could be divided into speaking parts, when he first performed it, LaRaviere delivered it as a dramatic monologue.

43.   Bai, LaRaviere, and Campuzano all performed their narratives for a graduate seminar held in fall 2001 at the Institute of Communications Research, University of Illinois, Urbana. On the day Bai performed her story, four other students also performed stories about their grandmothers.

44.   See Denzin (2002b) for an earlier version of this chapter. I thank Jay Gubrium and Jim Holstein for their comments.

45.   The underlying logic of the sports interview is mocked in the following dialogue from Ron Shelton's 1988 film *Bull Durham*. Kevin Costner, who plays an aging pitcher named Crash Davis, says to his protégé, played by Tim Robbins, "Now you are going to the Big Show. You have to learn how to talk to interviewers. When they ask you how it feels to be pitching in Yankee Stadium, you say, 'I just thank the good Lord for all his gifts. I owe it all to him. I just take it one game, one pitch at a time.'"

46.   These interview formats blur with the three types of relationships between interviewer and interviewee that Mishler (1986) identifies: informant and reporter, collaborators, and advocates.

47.   Although prejudice crosses color lines in this film, racial intolerance is connected to the psychology of the speaker (e.g., Vito). It is "rendered as the *how* of personal bigotry" (Guerrero 1993:154). The economic and political

features of institutional racism are not taken up. That is, in Lee's film, "the *why* of racism is left unexplored" (Guerrero 1993:154).

48. I have drawn portions of this chapter from Denzin (2001c, 2002b).

49. At one level, the reflexive interview implements Gubrium and Holstein's (1998:165) concept of *analytic bracketing*, which is the attempt to deal with the multiple levels of meaning in the interview context, including how the story is told, the context of the story, its audience, and so on. Heyl (2001) notes that reflexive interviewing allows individuals to connect in mutually empowering ways.

50. See note 2, above, for a review of the seven moments of inquiry (see also Denzin and Lincoln 2000:2-3). Some define the postmodern as "contemporary modernist" (Dillard 1982:20).

51. Of course, the transcribed interview is a problematic production (see Poland 2002).

52. I want to avoid the debate about whether it is "really possible, even in theory, to divide utterances between the performative and the constative" (Sedgwick 1998:106–7), to distinguish utterances that merely say from those that do. Words have material effects on people. Subjects, as gendered selves, are constituted in and through their performative acts—that is, acts that both do and say something (e.g., "With these words I thee wed"; see Sedgwick 1998:107; see also Butler 1993a:24, 1997:97, 1999:11). There is "no abiding, gendered subject" (Butler 1990:140) who precedes a performance (see also Butler 1990:25, 141).

53. A performance is an interpretive event. A performance, such as an interview, is a bounded, theatrical social act, a dialogic production (on the interview as a social act, see also Kuhn 1962:196–97).

54. Recall the discussion of interview formats and types in Chapter 3. Each type is produced by the apparatuses connected to the machinery of the interview apparatus.

55. I borrow the term *postmodern interview* from Fontana and Frey (1994:368, 2000).

56. A film version (filmed performance) of *Twilight*, directed by Marc Levin, was released in September 2000; in the film, Smith portrays an assortment of characters from the 1992 text.

57. The dramaturges for *Twilight* were Dorrine Kondo, a Japanese American anthropologist; Hector Tobar, a Guatemalan American journalist who had covered the L.A. riots for the *Los Angeles Times;* and Elizabeth Alexander, an African American poet.

58. For example, John Dos Passos's 1937 trilogy *U.S.A.* contains sections labeled "Newsreel" and "Camera Eye." In Dos Passos's text, real lives intersect with fictional lives; that is, fictional characters interact with real-world political personalities. In *The Souls of Black Folk* (1903), Du Bois uses musical notation and words from poems and songs to mark transitions between passages.

59. I conducted this interview in collaboration with my colleagues Belden Fields, Walter Feinberg, and Nicole Roberts.

60. Again, regarding the seven moments of inquiry, see note 2, above.

61. These narratives enact Turner's (1986a) fourfold processual model of breach, crisis, redress, and reintegration or schism.

62. Scholars take three basic positions on the issue of evaluative criteria. *Foundationalists* apply the same positivist criteria to qualitative research as are employed in quantitative inquiry, contending that is there is nothing special about qualitative research that demands a special set of evaluative criteria. *Quasi-foundationalists* contend that a set of criteria unique to qualitative research must be developed (see Smith and Deemer 2000). *Nonfoundationalists* reject in advance all epistemological criteria.

63. Some definitions are in order here. *Aesthetics* refers to theories of beauty; *ethics* refers to theories of ought, of right; and *epistemology* refers to theories of knowing. An *anti-aesthetic* denies a privileged aesthetic realm. I seek a radical anti-aesthetic that operates as political critique, challenging at every turn the aestheticization of everyday life and modernist ethical models (Eagleton 1990:119; Featherstone 1991:67; Jameson 1981:299). (In this section I draw from Denzin 2001d:326–27.)

64. I thank Clifford Christians for clarifying these principles.

65. These characteristics parallel Du Bois's (1926:134) four criteria for real black theater; such theater, he said, should be about us, by us, for us, near us.

66. In this section I draw from Denzin (1997:282–83).

67. In formulating the rules in this paragraph, I plagiarize Raymond Chandler's "Twelve Notes on the Mystery Story" (1995).

68. In this section I draw from Denzin (2002d:182–83; see also Denzin 2000a).

69. A parallel movement is occurring in the world of cinema, where Chicana/o and black filmmakers are using voice-overs, first-person and off-screen narration, mise-en-scène, and montage as ways of disturbing traditional gendered images of the racial subject (for a review, see Denzin 2002d:183–84).

70. See also Botkin (1980); Martin and Barasch (1984); Kittredge (1987); Taylor (1987); Martin (1992); Clow and Snow (1994); Newby and Hunger (1996); Hasselstrom, Collier, and Curtis (1997, 2001); Glasrud and Champion (2000); Jones and Wetmore (2000); Farr and Bevis (2001); Welch (1979, 2000, 2001).

71. For the past decade, at the annual meetings of the Midwest Sociological Society and the Society for the Study of Symbolic Interaction I have participated in cultural studies (and postmodernism) sessions with an expanding and contracting group that has always seemed to include Patricia Clough and Michal McCall, and often Laurel Richardson and Anahid Kassabian. The topic has frequently been postmodern mothers; the method has been autoethnographic and the format performance-based. In related sessions, other regular participants have included James Carey, David Altheide, John Johnson, Andy Fontana, David Dickens, Carolyn Ellis, Art Bochner, Allen Shelton, and Andrew Herman. These presentations have usually been published in *Studies in Symbolic Interaction, Cultural Studies: A Research Annual,*

or *Cultural Studies* ↔ *Critical Methodologies* (for one response to these sessions, see Olesen 2001; see also Richardson 1997:80).

72.   In seeking to move beyond straight ethnographic voyeurism, I turned to ethnographies of the postmodern visual cinematic culture (Denzin 1995a:208–11) and then to autoethnographic, performance-based cultural critique (see Denzin 1997, 2001b).

73.   See Denzin (1999b) for an earlier version of this chapter.

74.   See Denzin (1999a) for an earlier version of this chapter. I thank Katherine E. Ryan, Laurel Richardson, Rosanna Hertz, and Barry Glassner for their comments on earlier drafts.

75.   There are various stories about how the town got its name. The generally accepted theory is that the "Crow Indians who inhabited the area colored their lodges with red clay" (Graetz 1997:23).

76.   The town has a Web site. Using any Internet search engine, you can simply type "Red Lodge, Montana," and within seconds you can be looking at a map of downtown Red Lodge.

77.   For more about the Red Lodge Rendezvous, see the Rendezvous Committee's Web site at http://members.tripod.

78.   *The Big Sky*, a 1952 film directed by Howard Hawks and based on A. B. Guthrie, Jr.'s 1947 novel of the same name, offers Hollywood's and Guthrie's version of what a mountain man should look like (see D'Arc 2001:73–80; see also Welch 2001).

79.   Chase (1986:12) explains that the beavers' dams slowed the spring runoff of mountain streams, and so discouraged erosion and siltation. This kept the water clear for trout. In addition, beaver ponds raised the water table, thereby adding moisture that promoted vegetation (willow, aspen, berries, grass) and habitat for waterfowl, minks, and otters.

80.   See Denzin (2000c) for an earlier version of this chapter. I would like to thank Kathy Charmaz, Carla Boyce-Surber, Christopher Schmitt, Katherine Ryan, Laurel Richardson, Andrea Fontana, Richard Harvey Brown, Patricia Clough, Carolyn Ellis, Jack Bratich, Shawn Miklaucic, Michael Elavsky, and Nathan Summers for their helpful comments on earlier drafts. This mixed-genre chapter (see Richardson, 2000b, 2002a), which builds on Chapter 8, draws on multiple writing forms and traditions, including autoethnography, narratives of the self, traditional ethnography, the ethnographic story, nature writing, literary nonfiction, the personal memoir, and cultural criticism.

81.   As I have in Chapter 8, in this chapter I attempt to implement the arguments I have presented in Part I of this volume, forging the foundations of a minimalist, performance-based sociology, an anthropology of performance and experience that studies how people enact and construct meaning in their daily lives. This performative sociology (Butler 1990) presumes that "there is no performer prior to the performed, that the performance is performative" (Butler 1993b:645). It seeks a form of first-person writing that stays close to the performance itself. It understands that it is not possible to write an objective,

neutral account of performing Montana. There is no original against which any given performance can be assessed. Montana performances are constantly changing. Every account of a performance is personal and locally situated.

82.   These stories, or narratives of the self, represent a form of evocative writing that is highly personalized. Richardson (1994) describes how the writer of such a narrative tells a story about lived experience: "Using dramatic recall, strong metaphors, images, characters, unusual phrasings, puns, subtexts, and allusions, the writer constructs a sequence of events, a 'plot,' holding back on interpretation, asking the reader to 'relive' the events emotionally with the writer. Narratives of the self do not read like traditional ethnography because they use the writing techniques of fiction. They are specific stories of particular events. Accuracy is not the issue; rather, narratives of the self seek to meet literary criteria of coherence, verisimilitude, and interest" (p. 521). Stegner (1990) puts it this way: "Accuracy means less to me than suggestiveness" (p. ix). Richardson reminds us that these narratives of the self are staged as imaginative renderings, thereby allowing the writer to exaggerate and entertain, to make points "without tedious documentation" (p. 521).

83.   Thus do I attempt to insert my work into the stream of work that has come before, to make it intertextual with the writings of Ehrlich, Blount, Williams, Silko, Shange, Abbey, Stegner, Kittredge, Senior, Schullery, Rawlings, and others.

84.   My grandfather was Waldo William Townsley. Schullery (1994:213, 1997:160) notes that a man named John Townsley was a midcentury Yellowstone Park superintendent (see also Everhart 1998:164–65).

85.   When I was 10 years old we did get as far as Des Moines, Iowa, for the last day of the Iowa State Fair. It rained on our tent, but Grandpa made pancakes for breakfast, and that made the trip special.

86.   In the late 1970s, the Sun Dance ski lodge operated on the mountain above the six cabins; it was named for the way sunlight dances off of newly fallen snow. The Sun Dance estate owners took the name from the now-defunct ski lodge.

87.   All of the names in this story are pseudonyms.

88.   See Denzin (2002c) for an earlier version of this chapter. I thank Katherine E. Ryan, Kathy Charmaz, Patrick Jorgensen, and Laurel Richardson for their helpful comments on earlier drafts. I present this chapter as a layered text (on this form, see Ronai 1998, 1999; see also Richardson 1999); I intend it as a montage that moves back and forth between and among memories, events, history, and interpretations.

89.   See Chapter 8 for a discussion of the background of this 50-year-old annual community event celebrating ethnic history in Red Lodge (see also Lampi 1998:79, 170–74; Olp 2000).

90.   This song was written in honor of the 74 miners killed in the Smith Mine Disaster of 1943 (Zupan and Owens 2000:135–36). The Smith Mine was located in Washoe, 5 miles outside of Red Lodge.

91.   An entire wall in the Carbon County Peaks to Plains Museum is devoted to the rodeo-riding members of the Greenough family (Turk, Alice, Bill, Marge, and Deb; see Zupan and Owens 2000:208–12).

92.   There are hints of a Greek drama present in this spectacle. The chief is not incurring the wrath or anger of the gods, but he is performing before a nearly all-white audience and refusing to defer to them.

93.   Alexie's viewpoint is captured in his screenplay for the movie *Smoke Signals* (1998), directed by Chris Eyre. The film is based in part on stories from Alexie's book *The Lone Ranger and Tonto Fistfight in Heaven* (1993). Alexie seems to be saying that Indians are trapped in a mythic western past that relives the racist ideologies that sustain the cowboy/Indian dichotomy. As long as Indians replay this past, they will be trapped in the present (Alexie 1993:22).

94.   Paul Revere and the Raiders was a rock and roll band that had some success in the 1970s. I thank Michael Elavsky and Robert Sloane for bringing these lines to my attention.

95.   I thank Kathy Charmaz and Laurel Richardson for their help in shaping my remarks in this section.

96.   I have witnessed far too many doctoral dissertation defenses where committee members have refused to consider autoethnographic performance texts on the texts' own grounds, thereby sending the candidates back to the writing table to write the kinds of dissertations the committee members, not the candidates, wanted written.

97.   Chief Illiniwek (also known simply as the Chief) is an imaginary Native American named after the Native nations of Illinois and the long-disappeared Peoria tribe. His costume, made by Oglala Indians, reenacts imperialist nostalgic imagery associated with the 19th- and early-20th-century Wild West shows of George Catlin and William Cody (see White 1997; Reddin 1999; King and Springwood 2001:51–52; see also Welch 2000). There never was an Illiniwek tribe (see King and Springwood 2001:46). Of course, Chief Heywood Big Day stepped into a part of this Wild West tradition on Montana Night in Red Lodge when he greeted Bill Greenough and smiled at Miss Montana.

98.   As in Chapter 10, I present these materials as a layered text, a montage that moves among original sources and documents, newspaper clippings, memories, events, history, and interpretations (on this form see Ronai 1998, 1999; see also Richardson 1999). Many of the lines that are spoken are quoted directly from published sources. I have imposed a narrative order upon them and, in some cases, have put into poetic form material that was originally published as prose.

99.   According to Bogle (1994:140–41), the "Huck Finn fixation" aligns a good white man who is an outcast with a trusty black sidekick who is also an outcast. The white man grows in stature through his association with the black man, who seems "to possess the soul the white man searches for" (p. 140). The myth of cowboys and Indians lingers as a vital part of the heritage of the New West. Magazines such as *Cowboys and Indians, True West,* and *Wild West* make available

stories about Indian art, the violent Apaches, the Blackfoot and Cree Wars, and articles with titles such as "Tommy Lee Jones, Part Cowboy, Part Indian."

100. The Crow Indians, now confined to a reservation in eastern Montana, originally inhabited all of Carbon, Stillwater, and Yellowstone Counties, from the Beartooth Mountains on the west to the Yellowstone River and North and South Dakota to the east, and from the Clark's Fork of the Yellowstone south to Wyoming (see Zupan and Owens 2000:4–6).

101. I never intended to turn Red Lodge and its residents, a town and a community I love deeply, into a site of research. But the events discussed in this chapter require comment. It seemed as if these issues followed me from Champaign to Red Lodge.

102. Over the course of his writing career, Wallace Stegner (1909–93) wrote 12 novels and 7 nonfiction works. He won numerous prestigious awards for his work, including the Pulitzer Prize in 1971. Stegner was also a national figure in the environmental movement and a major historian of the American West (see Benson 1997). I agree with Cook-Lynn's (1996) refusal to accept Stegner's view that history for the northern Plains Indians "sort of stopped at 1890" (pp. 29–30; see Stegner 1962:66). To read Stegner, she contends, is to endorse his view that Native Americans occupy a marginal place at best in the history of the American West. She explicitly criticizes Stegner's views of Native Americans as he reveals them in *Wolf Willow* (1962), his autoethnographic account of his childhood in Cypress Hills, in southern Saskatchewan, where his family homesteaded from 1914 to 1920. In *Wolf Willow,* Stegner speaks of the Plains Indians destroying "the world that nourished them" (p. 66). He describes the homestead setting of his childhood as a semicivilized world (p. 57), as being on the "disappearing edge of nowhere" (p. 24); he describes "growing up as a sensuous little savage" (p. 25) in a new country that had no history (p. 28). Cook-Lynn's point, of course, is that the Plains Indian world was drenched in history, culture, and tradition, a history that fourth-generation European immigrants, including Stegner's family, could not see, but helped destroy.

I take the title of this chapter, in part, from Schullery (1997). I thank Kathy Charmaz, Patricia Clough, Andy Fontana, Laurel Richardson, Christopher Schmitt, Rebecca Small, and Walt Harrington for their comments on earlier versions of this text.

103. The grandfather I discuss in this chapter is my mother's father.

104. To repeat, my grandfather was Waldo William Townsley. John Townsley was a Yellowstone Park superintendent in the mid-20th century (Schullery 1994:213; 1997:160; see also Everhart 1998:164–65). John Townsley had a son named Forrest. When I was 10 years old, Grandma Townsley invited an Uncle Forrest and Aunt Elizabeth Townsley to visit the farm where we lived. They came from Milwaukee. Aunt Elizabeth was an interior decorator. She decorated Grandma's living room. The Victorian walnut love seat she picked out for Grandma's house in 1950 sits on the balcony in my home today. In searching for Yellowstone, I claim my place in this version of Townsley family history.

105. I define fascism as a conservative, extreme right-wing political, economic, and sociolegal state formation characterized by authoritarian forms of government, extreme nationalism, manufactured consent at key levels of public opinion, racism, a large military-industrial complex, foreign aggressiveness, anticommunism, state-supported corporate capitalism, state-sponsored violence, extreme restrictions on individual freedom, and tendencies toward an "Orwellian condition of perpetual war . . . [and] a national security state in which intelligence agencies and the military replace publicly elected officials in deciding national priorities" (Rorty 2002:13).

106. Here there are obvious political connections to Guy Debord's (1970) situationist project.

107. Smith (1999:99) presents 10 performative ways to be colonized, 10 ways in which science, technology, and Western institutions place indigenous peoples—indeed, any group of human beings—their languages, cultures, and environments, at risk. These ways include the Human Genome Diversity Project as well as scientific efforts to reconstruct previously extinct indigenous peoples and projects that deny global citizenship to indigenous peoples while commodifying, patenting, and selling indigenous cultural traditions and rituals.

108. The testimonio has a central place in Smith's list of projects. She begins her discussion of the testimonio with these lines from Menchú (1984): "My name is Rigoberta Menchú, I am twenty-three years old, and this is my testimony" (p. 1). The testimonio presents oral evidence to an audience, often in the form of a monologue. As Smith (1999) describes it, the indigenous testimonio is "a way of talking about an extremely painful event or series of events." The testimonio can be constructed as "a monologue and as a public performance" (p. 144).

109. Other projects involve a focus on testimonies, new forms of storytelling, and returning to, as well as reframing and regendering, key cultural debates.

110. Federal protection of human subjects has been in effect in the United States since 1974, now codified in Title 45, Part 46, of the U.S. Code of Federal Regulations. Part 46 was last revised November 13, 2001, effective December 13, 2001. IRBs review all federally funded research involving human subjects to ensure the ethical protection of those subjects.

111. As early as 1969, Vine Deloria, Jr., proposed that an anthropologist wanting to study a Native American culture should be required to apply to a tribal council for permission to do the research, and that the council should give permission only if the researcher "raised as a contribution to the tribal budget an amount of money equal to the amount he proposed to spend in his study" (p. 95).

112. The Family Education Rights and Privacy Act, the Protection of Pupil Rights Amendment, and the Parental Freedom of Information Amendment extend additional privacy rights to children (see Shavelson and Towne 2002:152–53).

113.   Researchers are exempted from the Common Rule if they can show that their research involves (a) normal educational practice; (b) the use of educational tests, interviews, survey procedures, or the observation of public behavior, *unless* confidentiality cannot be maintained or disclosure of partici-pation would place subjects at risk of criminal or civil liability (Puglisi 2001:34); and (c) collecting or studying existing data, documents or records if they are publicly available, and they can maintain confidentiality (that is, private infor-mation must not be linked to individual subjects). An IRB review may be expe-dited if the research involves (a) materials previously collected for nonresearch purposes; (b) collection of data from voice, video, digital, or image recordings for research purposes; or (c) research on language, communication, cultural beliefs, or cultural practices that presents no more than minimal risk to subjects. An IRB may waive the requirement of informed consent when four conditions are met: (a) the research presents no more than minimal risk to the subjects, (b) the waiver does not adversely affect the rights and welfare of the subjects, (c) the research cannot be carried out without the waiver, and (d) where appropriate, the subjects are provided with additional pertinent information after participation (Puglisi 2001:34).

114.   Supporters of the Chief, who use the slogan "Honor the Chief and the Tradition for Which He Stands," assumed that the university's Board of Trustees would vote the following Thursday, November 15, on eliminating the Chief as the university's mascot/symbol. The Board did not take up the Chief issue, and their meeting was disrupted by anti-Chief protesters.

References

Abbey, Edward. 1984. "The Author's Preface to His Own Book." Pp. ix–xv in *Edward Abbey, The Best of Edward Abbey.* San Francisco: Sierra Club Books.

———. 1994. "Something About Mac, Cows, Poker, Ranchers, Cowboys, Sex, and Power . . . and Almost Nothing About American Lit." Pp. 137–58 in *Northern Lights: A Selection of New Writing From the American West,* edited by Deborah Clow and Donald Snow. New York: Vintage.

Abram, David. 1996. *The Spell of the Sensuous.* New York: Vintage.

Alexander, Bryant Keith. 1998. "Performing Culture in the Classroom: Excerpts From an Instructional Diary." Pp. 170–80 in *The Future of Performance Studies: Visions and Revisions,* edited by Sheron J. Dailey. Washington, DC: National Communication Association.

———. 1999. "Performing Culture in the Classroom: An Instructional (Auto)Ethnography." *Text and Performance Quarterly* 19:307–31.

———. 2000. "Skin Flint (or, The Garbage Man's Kid): A Generative Autobiographical Performance Based on Tami Spry's *Tattoo Stories.*" *Text and Performance Quarterly* 20:97–114.

———. Forthcoming. "Bu(o)ying Condoms: A Prophylactic Performance of Sexuality (or Performance as Cultural Prophylactic Agency)." *Cultural Studies↔Critical Methodologies.*

Alexie, Sherman, 1993. *The Lone Ranger and Tonto Fistfight in Heaven.* New York: HarperCollins.

Altheide, David L. 1995. *An Ecology of Communication.* New York: Aldine de Gruyter.

Altheide, David L. and Robert P. Snow. 1991. *Media Worlds in the Postjournalism Era.* New York: Aldine de Gruyter.

American Association of University Professors. 1981. "Regulations Governing Research on Human Subjects: Academic Freedom and the Institutional Review Board." *Academe* 67:358–70.

———. 2001. "Protecting Human Beings: Institutional Review Boards and Social Science Research." *Academe* 87(3):55–67.

———. (2002). "Should All Disciplines Be Subject to the Common Rule? Human Subjects of Social Science Research." *Academe* 88(1):1–15.

Aronowitz, Stanley. 1998. "Introduction." Pp. 1–19 in Paulo Freire, *Pedagogy of Freedom: Ethics, Democracy, and Civic Courage.* Boulder, CO: Rowman & Littlefield.

Atkinson, Paul, Amanda Coffey, and Sara Delamont. 1999. "Ethnography: Post, Past, Present." *Journal of Contemporary Ethnography* 28:460–71.

———. 2001. "Editorial: A Debate About Our Canon." *Qualitative Research* 1:5–21.

Atkinson, Paul, Amanda Coffey, Sara Delamont, John Lofland, and Lyn Lofland. 2001. "Editorial Introduction." Pp. 1–7 in *Handbook of Ethnography,* edited by Paul Atkinson, Amanda Coffey, Sara Delamont, John Lofland, and Lyn Lofland. London: Sage.

Atkinson, Paul and Martyn Hammersley. 1994. "Ethnography and Participant Observation." Pp. 248–61 in *Handbook of Qualitative Research,* edited by Norman K. Denzin and Yvonna S. Lincoln. Thousand Oaks, CA: Sage.

Atkinson, Paul and David Silverman. 1997. "Kundera's *Immortality:* The Interview Society and the Invention of the Self. " *Qualitative Inquiry* 3:304–25.

Austin, J. L. 1962. *How to Do Things With Words.* Cambridge, MA: Harvard University Press.

Bacon, Wallace A. 1979. *The Art of Interpretation,* 3d ed. New York: Holt, Rinehart & Winston.

Bai, Ruoyun. 2001. "Grandma's Stories." Unpublished manuscript, Institute of Communications Research, University of Illinois at Urbana-Champaign.

Baker, Houston, Jr. 1997. "The Black Arts Movement." Pp. 1791–1806 in *The Norton Anthology of African American Literature,* edited by Henry Louis Gates, Jr., and Nellie Y. McKay. New York: W. W. Norton.

Bakhtin, Mikhail. 1986. *Speech Genres and Other Late Essays.* Austin: University of Texas Press.

Baraka, Amiri [LeRoi Jones]. 1979. "The Revolutionary Theatre." Pp. 131–36 in Amiri Baraka, *Selected Plays and Prose of Amiri Baraka/LeRoi Jones.* New York: William Morrow.

———. 1997. *The Autobiography of LeRoi Jones.* Chicago: Lawrence Hill.

———. [1969] 1998. "Black Art." Pp. 1501–2 in *Call and Response: The Riverside Anthology of the African American Literary Tradition,* edited by Patricia Liggins Hill. Boston: Houghton Mifflin.

Bass, Rick. 1996. *The Book of Yaak.* Boston: Houghton Mifflin.

Bauman, Richard. 1986. *Story, Performance, Event: Contextual Studies of Oral Narratives.* Cambridge: Cambridge University Press.

Bauman, Zygmunt. 1999. *In Search of Politics.* Stanford, CA: Stanford University Press.

Beaumont, Shelley. 1997. "'Redskin' Mascot Up for a Vote." *Carbon County News,* October 8, 1A–2A.

Becker, Howard S. 1967. "Whose Side Are We On?" *Social Problems* 14:239–47.

Behar, Ruth. 1996. *The Vulnerable Observer: Anthropology That Breaks Your Heart.* Boston: Beacon.

Bell, Elizabeth. 1998. "Accessing the Power to Signify: Learning to Read in Performance Studies." Pp. 57–59 in *The Future of Performance Studies: Visions and Revisions*, edited by Sheron J. Dailey. Washington, DC: National Communication Association.

Benjamin, Walter. 1968a. "The Storyteller." Pp. 83–110 in Walter Benjamin, *Illuminations*, edited by Hannah Arendt; translated by Harry Zohn. New York: Harcourt, Brace & World.

———. 1968b. "What Is Epic Theater?" Pp. 149–56 in Walter Benjamin, *Illuminations*, edited by Hannah Arendt; translated by Harry Zohn. New York: Harcourt, Brace & World.

Benson, Jackson J. 1996. *Wallace Stegner: His Life and Work*. New York: Penguin.

Berry, Wendell. 1981. *Recollected Essays: 1965–1980*. New York: Farrar, Straus & Giroux.

———. 1998. "The Peace of Wild Things." P. 30 in Wendell Berry, *The Selected Poems of Wendell Berry*. Washington, DC: Counterpoint.

Beverley, John. 2000. "Testimonio, Subalternity, and Narrative Authority." Pp. 555–65 in *Handbook of Qualitative Research*, 2d ed., edited by Norman K. Denzin and Yvonna S. Lincoln. Thousand Oaks, CA: Sage.

Birringer, Johannes. 1993. *Theatre, Theory, Postmodernism*. Bloomington: Indiana University Press.

Bishop, Russell. 1998. "Freeing Ourselves From Neo-colonial Domination in Research: A Maori Approach to Creating Knowledge." *International Journal of Qualitative Studies in Education* 11:199–219.

Blew, Mary Clearman. 1977. *Lambing Out and Other Stories*. Norman: Oklahoma University Press.

———. 1990. *Runaway: A Collection of Stories*. Lewiston, ID: Confluence.

———. 1991. *All but the Waltz: A Memoir of Five Generations in the Life of a Montana Family*. New York: Penguin.

———. 1994. *Balsamroot*. New York: Penguin.

———. 1999. *Bone Deep in Landscape: Writing, Reading and Place*. Norman: University of Oklahoma Press.

———. 2000. *Sister Coyote: Montana Stories*. New York: Lyons.

Blumer, Herbert. 1933. *Movies and Conduct*. New York: Macmillan.

Blunt, Judy. 1994. "Breaking Clean." Pp. 297–303 in *Northern Lights: A Selection of New Writing From the American West*, edited by Deborah Clow and Donald Snow. New York: Vintage.

Boal, Augusto. [1979] 1985. *Theatre of the Oppressed*. New York: Theatre Communications Group.

———. 1995. *The Rainbow of Desire: The Boal Method of Theatre and Therapy*, translated by Adrian Jackson. New York: Routledge.

Bochner, Arthur P. 2000. "Criteria Against Ourselves." *Qualitative Inquiry* 6:266–72.

Bochner, Arthur P. and Carolyn Ellis. 1996a. "Introduction: Talking Over Ethnography." Pp. 13–45 in *Composing Ethnography: Alternative Forms of*

Qualitative Writing, edited by Carolyn Ellis and Arthur P. Bochner. Walnut Creek, CA: AltaMira.

———. 1996b. "Taking Ethnography Into the Twenty-First Century." *Journal of Contemporary Ethnography* 25:3–5.

———. 2002. "How Does a Conference Begin?" Pp. 1–10 in *Ethnographically Speaking: Autoethnography, Literature, and Aesthetics*, edited by Arthur P. Bochner and Carolyn Ellis. Walnut Creek, CA: AltaMira.

Bogle, Donald. 1994. *Toms, Coons, Mulattoes, Mammies, and Bucks: An Interpretive History of Blacks in American Films*, 3d ed. New York: Continuum.

Botkin, B. A., ed. 1980. *A Treasury of Western Folklore*. New York: Bonanza.

Bourdieu, Pierre. 1996. "Understanding." *Theory, Culture & Society* 13:17–37.

———. 1999. *Acts of Resistance*. New York: New Press.

Bourdieu, Pierre and Loïc Wacquant. 1992. *An Invitation to Reflexive Sociology*. Chicago: University of Chicago Press.

Bracci, Sharon L. and Clifford G. Christians. 2002. "Editors' Introduction." Pp. 1–15 in *Moral Engagement in Public Life: Theorists for Contemporary Ethics*, edited by Sharon L. Bracci and Clifford G. Christians. New York: Peter Lang.

Branaman, Ann. 1997. "Goffman's Social Theory." Pp. xlv–lxxxii in *The Goffman Reader*, edited by Charles Lemert and Ann Branaman. Malden, MA: Blackwell.

Brayboy, Bryan McKinley. 2000. "The Indian and the Researcher: Tales From the Field." *International Journal of Qualitative Studies in Education* 13:415–26.

Brissett, Dennis and Charles Edgley, eds. 1990. *Life as Theater: A Dramaturgical Sourcebook*, 2d ed. New York: Aldine de Gruyter.

Broadhurst, Susan. 1999. *Liminal Acts: A Critical Overview of Contemporary Performance and Theory*. New York: Cassell.

Bruner, Edward M. 1986. "Experience and Its Expressions." Pp. 3–30 in *The Anthropology of Experience*, edited by Victor W. Turner and Edward M. Bruner. Urbana: University of Illinois Press.

———. 1989. "Tourism, Creativity, and Authenticity." *Studies in Symbolic Interaction* 10:109–14.

———. 1996. "Abraham Lincoln as Authentic Reproduction: A Critique of Postmodernism." *American Anthropologist* 96:397–415.

Burawoy, Michael. 1998. "The Extended Case Method." *Sociological Theory* 16:4–33.

———. 2000. "Introduction: Reaching for the Global." Pp. 1–40 in Michael Burawoy, Joseph A. Blum, Sheba George, Zsuzsa Gille, Teresa Gowan, Lynne Haney, et al., *Global Ethnography: Forces, Connections, and Imaginations in a Postmodern World*. Berkeley: University of California Press.

Burke, Kenneth. 1969. *Rhetoric of Motives*. Berkeley: University of California Press.

Butler, Judith. 1990. *Gender Trouble: Feminism and the Subversion of Identity*. New York: Routledge.

————. 1993a. *Bodies That Matter: On the Discursive Limits of "Sex."* New York: Routledge.

————. 1993b. "Imitation and Gender Insubordination" [excerpt]. Pp. 637–48 in *Social Theory: The Multicultural and Classic Readings,* edited by Charles Lemert. Boulder, CO: Westview.

————. 1997. *Excitable Speech: A Politics of the Performative.* New York: Routledge.

————. 1999. "Revisiting Bodies and Pleasures." *Theory, Culture & Society* 16:11–20.

Campuzano, Hugo. 2001. "In the Name of Tradition." Unpublished manuscript, Institute of Communications Research, University of Illinois at Urbana-Champaign.

Capo, Kay Ellen. 1983. "Performance of Literature as Social Dialect" *Literature in Performance* 4:31–36.

Carlin, Phyllis Scott. 1998. "'I Have to Tell You . . .': The Unfolding of Personal Stories in Life Performance." Pp. 226–31 in *The Future of Performance Studies: Visions and Revisions,* edited by Sheron J. Dailey. Washington, DC: National Communication Association.

Carspecken, Phil Francis. 1996. *Critical Ethnography in Educational Research.* New York: Routledge.

————. 1999. *Four Scenes for Posing the Question of Meaning and Other Essays in Critical Philosophy and Critical Methodology.* New York: Peter Lang.

Chandler, Raymond. 1995. "Twelve Notes on the Mystery Story." Pp. 1004–11 in Raymond Chandler, *Later Novels and Other Writings.* New York: Penguin.

Chase, Alston. 1986. *Playing God in Yellowstone.* New York: Atlantic Monthly Press.

Chesebro, James W. 1998. "Performance Studies as Paradox, Culture, and Manifesto: A Future Orientation." Pp. 310–19 in *The Future of Performance Studies: Visions and Revisions,* edited by Sheron J. Dailey. Washington, DC: National Communication Association.

Chomsky, Noam. 1996. *Class Warfare: Interviews With David Barasamian.* Monroe, ME: Common Courage.

Christian, Barbara T. 1997. "Literature Since 1970." Pp. 2011–20 in *The Norton Anthology of African American Literature,* edited by Henry Louis Gates, Jr., and Nellie Y. McKay. New York: W. W. Norton.

Christians, Clifford G. 1986. "Reporting and the Oppressed." Pp. 109–30 in *Responsible Journalism,* edited by Deni Elliott. Beverly Hills, CA: Sage.

————. 1995. "The Naturalistic Fallacy in Contemporary Interactionist-Interpretive Research." *Studies in Symbolic Interaction* 19:125–30.

————. 1997. "The Ethics of Being in a Communications Context." Pp. 3–23 in *Communication Ethics and Universal Values,* edited by Clifford G. Christians and Michael Traber. Thousand Oaks, CA: Sage.

————. 1998. "The Sacredness of Life." *Media Development* 2:3–7.

———. 2000. "Ethics and Politics in Qualitative Research." Pp. 133–55 in *Handbook of Qualitative Research*, 2d ed., edited by Norman K. Denzin and Yvonna S. Lincoln. Thousand Oaks, CA: Sage.

———. 2002. "Introduction." In "Ethical Issues and Qualitative Research" [Special issue]. *Qualitative Inquiry* 8:407–10.

Christians, Clifford G., John P. Ferre, and P. Mark Fackler. 1993. *Good News: Social Ethics and the Press*. New York: Oxford.

Clifford, James and George E. Marcus, eds. 1986. *Writing Culture: The Poetics and Politics of Ethnography*. Berkeley: University of California Press.

Clough, Patricia Ticineto. 1994. *Feminist Thought: Desire, Power and Academic Discourse*. Cambridge, MA: Blackwell.

———. 1998. *The End(s) of Ethnography: From Realism to Social Criticism*, 2d ed. New York: Peter Lang.

———. 2000a. "Comments on Setting Criteria for Experimental Writing." *Qualitative Inquiry* 6:278–91.

———. 2000b. "Judith Butler." Pp. 754–73 in *The Blackwell Companion to Major Social Theorists*, edited by George Ritzer. Malden, MA: Blackwell.

Clow, Deborah and Donald Snow, eds. 1994. *Northern Lights: A Selection of New Writing From the American West*. New York: Vintage.

Coffey, Amanda. 1999. *The Ethnographic Self: Fieldwork and the Representation of Identity*. London: Sage.

Coffey, Amanda and Paul Atkinson. 1996. *Making Sense of Qualitative Data: Complementary Research Strategies*. Thousand Oaks, CA: Sage.

Cohn, Ruby. 1988. "Realism." P. 815 in *The Cambridge Guide to Theatre*, edited by Martin Banham. Cambridge: Cambridge University Press.

Collins, Patricia Hill. 1990. *Black Feminist Thought: Knowledge, Consciousness, and the Politics of Empowerment*. New York: Routledge, Chapman & Hall.

———. 1998. *Fighting Words: Black Women and the Search for Justice*. Minneapolis: University of Minnesota Press.

Comaroff, Jean and John L. Comaroff. 2001. "Millennial Capitalism: First Thoughts on a Second Coming." Pp. 1–56 in *Millennial Capitalism and the Culture of Neoliberalism*, edited by Jean Comaroff and John L. Comaroff. Durham, NC: Duke University Press.

Comolli, Jean-Louis and Jean Narboni. [1969] 1971. "Cinema/Ideology/ Criticism, Part I." *Screen* 12:27–36.

Conquergood, Dwight. 1985. "Performing as a Moral Act: Ethical Dimensions of the Ethnography of Performance." *Literature in Performance* 5:1–13.

———. 1986. "Performing Cultures: Ethnography, Epistemology, and Ethics." In *Miteinander sprechen and handeln: Festschrift fur Hellmut Geissner*, edited by Edith Slembek. Frankfurt: Scriptor.

———. 1991. "Rethinking Ethnography: Towards a Critical Cultural Politics." *Communication Monographs* 58:179–94.

———. 1992. "Ethnography, Rhetoric and Performance." *Quarterly Journal of Speech* 78:80–97.

———. 1998. "Beyond the Text: Toward a Performative Cultural Politics." Pp. 25–36 in *The Future of Performance Studies: Visions and Revisions,* edited by Sheron J. Dailey. Washington, DC: National Communication Association.

Cook-Lynn, Elizabeth. 1996. *Why I Can't Read Wallace Stegner and Other Essays.* Madison: University of Wisconsin Press.

Corey, Frederick C. 1998. "The Personal: Against the Master Narrative." Pp. 249–53 in *The Future of Performance Studies: Visions and Revisions,* edited by Sheron J. Dailey. Washington, DC: National Communication Association.

Crawford, Claudia. 1995. *To Nietzsche: Dionysus, I Love You! Ariadne.* Albany: State University of New York Press.

Crue, Cyd A. 2002. "White Racism/Redface Minstrels: Regimes of Power in Representation." Ph.D. dissertation, Department of Sociology, University of Illinois at Urbana-Champaign.

Dailey, Sheron J. 1998a. "Editor's Note." Pp. ix–xii in *The Future of Performance Studies: Visions and Revisions,* edited by Sheron J. Dailey. Washington, DC: National Communication Association.

———, ed. 1998b. *The Future of Performance Studies: Visions and Revisions.* Washington, DC: National Communication Association.

———. 1998c. "Personal Narratives: Problems and Possibilities." Pp. 199–202 in *The Future of Performance Studies: Visions and Revisions,* edited by Sheron J. Dailey. Washington, DC: National Communication Association.

D'Arc, James V. 2001. "A. B. Guthrie, Jr., in Hollywood: Variations on the Writing Experience." Pp. 73–103 in *Fifty Years After* The Big Sky: *New Perspectives on the Fiction and Films of A. B. Guthrie, Jr.,* edited by William E. Farr and William W. Bevis. Helena: Montana Historical Society Press.

Davis, Angela Y. 1998. *Blues Legacies and Black Feminism: Gertrude "Ma" Rainey, Bessie Smith, and Billie Holiday.* New York: Pantheon.

Dawson, Patrick. 1996. "Not Another Fish Story From Occupied Montana." Pp. 10–23 in *Writing Montana: Literature Under the Big Sky,* edited by Rick Newby and Suzanne Hunger. Helena: Montana Center for the Book.

Debord, Guy. 1970. *Society of the Spectacle.* Detroit: Black & Red.

Delamont, Sara, Amanda Coffey, and Paul Atkinson. 2000. "The Twilight Years?" *International Journal of Qualitative Studies in Education* 13:223–38.

Deloria, Vine, Jr. 1969. *Custer Died for Your Sins: An Indian Manifesto.* New York: Macmillan.

Denzin, Norman K. 1984. *On Understanding Emotion.* San Francisco: Jossey-Bass.

———. 1991. *Images of Postmodern Society: Social Theory and Contemporary Cinema.* London: Sage.

———. 1992. *Symbolic Interactionism and Cultural Studies: The Politics of Interpretation.* Cambridge: Blackwell.

———. 1995a. *The Cinematic Society: The Voyeur's Gaze.* Thousand Oaks, CA: Sage.

——. 1995b. "Information Technologies, Communicative Acts, and the Audience: Couch's Legacy to Communication Research." *Symbolic Interaction* 18:247–68.

——. 1997. *Interpretive Ethnography: Ethnographic Practices for the 21st Century.* Thousand Oaks, CA: Sage.

——. 1999a. "Performing Montana." Pp. 147–58 in *Qualitative Sociology as Everyday Life,* edited by Barry Glassner and Rosanna Hertz. Thousand Oaks, CA: Sage.

——. 1999b. "Two-Stepping in the '90s." *Qualitative Inquiry* 5:568–72.

——. 2000a. "Aesthetics and the Practices of Qualitative Inquiry." *Qualitative Inquiry* 6:256–65.

——. 2000b. "The Practices and Politics of Interpretation." Pp. 897–922 in *Handbook of Qualitative Research,* 2d ed., edited by Norman K. Denzin and Yvonna S. Lincoln. Thousand Oaks, CA: Sage.

——. 2000c. "Rock Creek History." *Symbolic Interaction* 23:71–81.

——. 2001a. "Confronting Ethnography's Crisis of Representation." *Journal of Contemporary Ethnography* 31:482–507.

——. 2001b. *Interpretive Interactionism,* 2d ed. Thousand Oaks, CA: Sage.

——. 2001c. "The Reflexive Interview and a Performative Social Science." *Qualitative Research* 1:23–46.

——. 2001d. "The Seventh Moment: Qualitative Inquiry and the Practices of a More Radical Consumer Research." *Journal of Consumer Research* 28:324–30.

——. 2001e. "Symbolic Interactionism, Poststructuralism and the Racial Subject." *Symbolic Interaction* 24:243–49.

——. 2002a. "The Call to Performance." *Symbolic Interaction* 25:327–46.

——. 2002b. "The Cinematic Society and the Reflexive Interview." Pp. 833–48 in *Handbook of Interview Research: Context and Method,* edited by Jaber F. Gubrium and James A. Holstein. Thousand Oaks, CA: Sage.

——. 2002c. "Cowboys and Indians." *Symbolic Interaction* 25:251–61.

——. 2002d. *Reading Race: Hollywood and the Cinema of Racial Violence.* London: Sage.

——. 2002e. "Week Four." *Qualitative Inquiry* 8:199-202.

——. 2003. "Searching for Yellowstone." *Symbolic Interaction* 26:181–93.

——. Forthcoming a. "Reading and Writing Performance." *Qualitative Research.*

——. Forthcoming b. "Redskins Everywhere." *Cultural Studies* ↔ *Critical Methodologies.*

Denzin, Norman K., A. Belden Fields, Walter Feinberg, and Nicole Roberts. 1997. "Remembering and Forgetting Recent Racial Politics." *Taboo: Journal of Culture and Education* 2:191–208.

Denzin, Norman K. and Yvonna S. Lincoln. 2000. "Introduction: The Discipline and Practice of Qualitative Research." Pp. 1–28 in *Handbook of Qualitative Research,* 2d ed., edited by Norman K. Denzin and Yvonna S. Lincoln. Thousand Oaks, CA: Sage.

Derrida, Jacques. 1973. *Speech and Phenomena.* Evanston, IL: Northwestern University Press.

———. 1988. *Limited, Inc.* Evanston, IL: Northwestern University Press.

DeVault, Marjorie L. 1999. *Liberating Method: Feminism and Social Research.* Philadelphia: Temple University Press.

Dewey, John. [1922] 1930. *Human Nature and Conduct.* New York: Modern Library.

Diamond, Elin. 1996. "Introduction." Pp. 1–12 in *Performances and Cultural Politics,* edited by Elin Diamond. New York: Routledge.

Diawara, Mantha. 1996. "Black Studies, Cultural Studies: Performative Acts." Pp. 300–306 in *What Is Cultural Studies? A Reader,* edited by John Storey. London: Arnold.

Dillard, Annie. 1974. *Pilgrim at Tinker Creek.* New York: Harper & Row.

———. 1982. *Living by Fiction.* New York: Harper & Row.

Dimitriadis, Greg. 2001. *Performing Identity/Performing Culture: Hip Hop as Text, Pedagogy, and Lived Practice.* New York: Peter Lang.

Dimitriadis, Greg and Cameron McCarthy. 2001. *Reading and Teaching the Postcolonial: From Baldwin to Basquiat and Beyond.* New York: Teachers College Press.

Doig, Ivan. 1978. *This House of Sky.* New York: Harcourt Brace.

Donmoyer, Robert and June Yennie-Donmoyer. 1995. "Data as Drama: Reflections on the Use of Readers Theatre as an Artistic Mode of Data Display." *Qualitative Inquiry* 1:402–28.

Dorst, John D. 1999. *Looking West.* Philadelphia: University of Pennsylvania Press.

Dos Passos, John. 1937. *U.S.A.* New York: Modern Library.

Dowd, Maureen. 2002. "Texas on the Tigris." *New York Times,* October 13, sec. 4, p. 13.

Doyle, Mary Agnes Draland. 1998. "End-Game Poetics and the Performative." Pp. 76–80 in *The Future of Performance Studies: Visions and Revisions,* edited by Sheron J. Dailey. Washington, DC: National Communication Association.

Dray, Philip. 2002. *At the Hands of Persons Unknown: The Lynching of Black America.* New York: Random House.

Du Bois, W. E. B. 1903. *The Souls of Black Folk.* New York: Fawcett.

———. 1926. "Krigwa Players Little Negro Theatre: The Story of a Little Theatre Movement." *Crisis,* July, 134–36.

———. [1901] 1978. "The Problem of the Twentieth Century Is the Problem of the Color Line." Pp. 281–89 in W. E. B. Du Bois, *On Sociology and the Black Community,* edited by Dan S. Green and Edward Driver. Chicago: University of Chicago Press (originally published, 1901).

Dunn, Robert G. 1998. *Identity Crises: A Social Critique of Postmodernity.* Minneapolis: University of Minnesota Press.

Eagleton, Terry. 1990. *The Ideology of the Aesthetic*. Oxford: Blackwell.

Eason, David. 1984. "The New Journalism and the Image-World: Two Modes of Organizing Experience." *Critical Studies in Mass Communication* 1:51–65.

———. 1986. "On Journalistic Authority: The Janet Cooke Scandal." *Critical Studies in Mass Communication* 3:429–47.

Ebert, Roger. 2001a. "New Thoughts on the Chief." *Daily Illini* (University of Illinois at Urbana-Champaign), March 20, 8.

———. 2001b. "Noble Spirit More Than Just a Mascot." *Daily Illini* (University of Illinois at Urbana-Champaign), March 7, 10.

Ehrlich, Gretel. 1985. *The Solace of Open Spaces*. New York: Penguin.

———. 1988. "River History." Pp. 69–72 in *Montana Spaces: Essays and Photographs in Celebration of Montana*, edited by William Kittredge. New York: Lyons & Burford.

Elam, Harry J., Jr. 2001. "The Device of Race." Pp. 3–16 in *African American Performance and Theater History: A Critical Reader*, edited by Harry J. Elam, Jr., and David Krasner. New York: Oxford University Press.

Elam, Harry J., Jr., and David Krasner, eds. 2001. *African American Performance and Theater History: A Critical Reader*. New York: Oxford University Press.

Ellis, Carolyn. 2000. "Creating Criteria: An Ethnographic Short Story." *Qualitative Inquiry* 6:273–77.

Ellis, Carolyn and Arthur P. Bochner. 1996. "Introduction: Talking Over Ethnography." Pp. 13–45 in *Composing Ethnography: Alternative Forms of Qualitative Writing*, edited by Carolyn Ellis and Arthur P. Bochner. Walnut Creek, CA: AltaMira.

———. 2000. "Autoethnography, Personal Narrative, Reflexivity: Researcher as Subject." Pp. 733–68 in *Handbook of Qualitative Research*, 2d ed., edited by Norman K. Denzin and Yvonna S. Lincoln. Thousand Oaks, CA: Sage.

Etherton, Michael. 1988. "Third World Popular Theatre." Pp. 991–92 in *The Cambridge Guide to Theatre*, edited by Martin Banham. Cambridge: Cambridge University Press.

Everhart, Bill. 1998. *Take Down the Flag and Feed the Horses*. Urbana: University of Illinois Press.

Farnell, Brenda. 1998. "Retire the Chief." *Anthropology Newsletter* 39(4):1, 4.

Farr, William E. and William W. Bevis. eds. 2001. *Fifty Years After* The Big Sky: *New Perspectives on the Fiction and Films of A. B. Guthrie, Jr.* Helena: Montana Historical Society Press.

Featherstone, Mike. 1991. *Consumer Culture and Postmodernism*. London: Sage.

Fiedler, Leslie. [1949] 1971a. "Montana; or The End of Jean-Jacques Rousseau." Pp. 133–41 in Leslie Fiedler, *The Collected Essays of Leslie Fiedler*, vol. 1. New York: Stein & Day.

———. 1971b. "Montana: P.S." Pp. 331–36 in Leslie Fiedler, *The Collected Essays of Leslie Fiedler*, vol. 2. New York: Stein & Day.

———. 1971c. "Montana: P.P.S." Pp. 337–42 in Leslie Fiedler, *The Collected Essays of Leslie Fiedler*, vol. 2. New York: Stein & Day.

———. 1988. "The Montana Face." Pp. 744–52 in *The Last Best Place: A Montana Anthology*, edited by William Kittredge and Annick Smith. Seattle: University of Washington Press.

Fine, Gary Alan. 1998. *Morel Tales: The Culture of Mushrooming*. Cambridge, MA: Harvard University Press.

Fine, Michelle. 2002. "The Mourning After." *Qualitative Inquiry* 8:137–45.

Fine, Michelle, Rosemarie Roberts, Maria Torre, Debora Upegui, Iris Bowen, Kathy Boudin, et al. 2003. "Participatory Action Research: From Within and Beyond Prison Bars." Pp. 173–98 in *Qualitative Research in Psychology: Expanding Perspectives in Methodology and Design*, edited by Paul M. Camic, Jean E. Rhodes, and Lucy Yardley. Washington, DC: American Psychological Association.

Finley, Susan. 2000. "'Dream Child': The Role of Poetic Dialogue in Homeless Research." *Qualitative Inquiry* 6:432–34.

———. Forthcoming. "Arts-Based Inquiry in QI: Seven Years From Crisis to Guerrilla Warfare." *Qualitative Inquiry.*

Foley, Doug. 2002. "Critical Ethnography: The Reflexive Turn." *International Journal of Qualitative Studies in Education* 15:469–90.

Fontana, Andrea and James H. Frey. 1994. "Interviewing: The Art of Science." Pp. 361–76 in *Handbook of Qualitative Research*, edited by Norman K. Denzin and Yvonna S. Lincoln. Thousand Oaks, CA: Sage.

———. 2000. "The Interview: From Structured Questions to Negotiated Text." Pp. 645–72 in *Handbook of Qualitative Research*, 2d ed., edited by Norman K. Denzin and Yvonna S. Lincoln. Thousand Oaks, CA: Sage.

Ford, Nick Aaron. [1950] 1998. "A Blueprint for Negro Authors." Pp. 1112–14 in *Call and Response: The Riverside Anthology of the African American Literary Tradition*, edited by Patricia Liggins Hill. New York: Houghton Mifflin.

Foster, Hal. 1983. "Postmodernism: A Preface." Pp. ix–xvi in *The Anti-aesthetic: Essays on Postmodern Culture*, edited by Hal Foster. Port Townsend, WA: Bay.

Foucault, Michel. 1980a. *The History of Sexuality*, vol. 1, *An Introduction*, translated by Robert Hurley. New York: Pantheon.

———. 1980b. *Power/Knowledge: Selected Interviews and Other Writings, 1972-1977*, edited by C. Gordon; translated by L. Marshall, J. Mepham, and K. Soper. New York: Pantheon.

Franklin, Adrian. 2001. "Performing Live: An Interview With Barbara Kirshenblatt-Gimblett." *Tourist Studies* 1:211–32.

Fraser, Nancy. 1993. "Clintonism, Welfare, and the Antisocial Wage: The Emergence of a Neoliberal Imaginary." *Rethinking Marxism* 6:9–23.

Fregoso, Rosa Linda. 1993. *The Bronze Screen: Chicana and Chicano Film Culture*. Minneapolis: University of Minnesota Press.

Freire, Paulo. 1998. *Pedagogy of Freedom: Ethics, Democracy, and Civic Courage*, translated by Patrick Clarke. Boulder, CO: Rowman & Littlefield.

———. [1992] 1999. *Pedagogy of Hope: Reliving Pedagogy of the Oppressed*. New York: Continuum.

————. 2001. *Pedagogy of the Oppressed*, 30th anniversary ed. New York: Continuum.

Garfinkel, Harold. 1996. "Ethnomethodology's Program." *Social Psychology Quarterly* 59:5–21.

Garoian, Charles R. 1999. *Performing Pedagogy: Toward an Art of Politics*. Albany: State University of New York Press.

Gayle, Addison, Jr. [1971] 1997. "The Black Aesthetic." Pp. 1870-77 in *The Norton Anthology of African American Literature*, edited by Henry Louis Gates, Jr., and Nellie Y. McKay. New York: W. W. Norton.

Geertz, Clifford. 1973. *The Interpretation of Cultures: Selected Essays*. New York: Basic Books.

Gentile, John S. 1998. "Bringing Literature in Performance to the Table." Pp. 72–75 in *The Future of Performance Studies: Visions and Revisions*, edited by Sheron J. Dailey. Washington, DC: National Communication Association.

Gilbert, Joanne R. 1998. "Our Texts, Ourselves: Performing Literature in the Undergraduate Classroom." Pp. 60–62 in *The Future of Performance Studies: Visions and Revisions*, edited by Sheron J. Dailey. Washington, DC: National Communication Association.

Gingrich-Philbrook, Craig. 1998. "What I 'Know' About the Story (for Those About to Tell Personal Stories on Stage)." Pp. 298–300 in *The Future of Performance Studies: Visions and Revisions*, edited by Sheron J. Dailey. Washington, DC: National Communication Association.

————. 2000. "The Personal and Political Solo Performance: Editor's Introduction." *Text and Performance Quarterly* 20:vii–x.

Giroux, Henry A. 1992. *Border Crossings: Culture Workers and the Politics of Education*. New York: Routledge.

————. 1994. *Disturbing Pleasures: Learning Popular Culture*. New York: Routledge.

————. 2000a. *Impure Acts: The Practical Politics of Cultural Studies*. New York: Routledge.

————. 2000b. *Stealing Innocence: Corporate Culture's War on Children*. New York: Palgrave Macmillan.

————. 2001a. "Cultural Studies as Performative Politics." *Cultural Studies* ↔ *Critical Methodologies* 1:5–23.

————. 2001b. *Public Spaces, Private Lives: Beyond the Culture of Cynicism*. Boulder, CO: Rowman & Littlefield.

————. 2003. *The Abandoned Generation: Democracy Beyond the Culture of Fear*. New York: Palgrave Macmillan.

Giroux, Henry A. and Peter McLaren. 1989. "Introduction." Pp. xi–xxxv in *Critical Pedagogy, the State, and Cultural Struggle*, edited by Henry A. Giroux and Peter McLaren. Albany: State University of New York Press.

Girton, Bethany. 1998. "The Future of Performance Studies in the High School Classroom." Pp. 156–57 in *The Future of Performance Studies: Visions and*

Revisions, edited by Sheron J. Dailey. Washington, DC: National Communication Association.

Glasrud, Bruce A. and Laurie Champion. 2000. "African Americans in the West: A Short Story Tradition." Pp. 1–14 in *The African American West: A Century of Short Stories,* edited by Bruce A. Glasrud and Laurie Champion. Boulder: University of Colorado Press.

Glass, Ronald David. 2001. "On Paulo Freire's Philosophy of Praxis and the Foundations of Liberation Education." *Educational Researcher* 30:15–25.

Glassner, Barry and Rosanna Hertz, eds. 1999. *Qualitative Sociology as Everyday Life.* Thousand Oaks, CA: Sage.

Goffman, Erving. 1959. *The Presentation of Self in Everyday Life.* New York: Doubleday.

Gonzalez, Francisca E. 1998. "Formations of *Mexicana*ness: *Trenzas de Identidades Multiples*—Growing Up *Mexicana:* Braids of Multiple Identities." *International Journal of Qualitative Studies in Education* 11:81–102.

Gottschalk, S. 2000. "Escape From Insanity: 'Mental Disorder' in the Postmodern Moment." Pp. 18–48 in *Pathology and the Postmodern: Mental Illness as Discourse and Experience,* edited by Dwight Fee. Thousand Oaks, CA: Sage.

Graetz, Rick. 1997. "Sojourn to the Sky: The Beartooth Highway." *Montana Magazine,* July/August, 18–26.

Grande, Sandy. 2000. "American Indian Identity and Intellectualism: The Quest for a New Red Pedagogy." *International Journal of Qualitative Studies in Education* 13:343–60.

Graveline, Fyre Jean. 2000. "Circle as Methodology: Enacting an Aboriginal Paradigm." *International Journal of Qualitative Studies in Education* 13:361–70.

Gray, Paul H. 1998. "Cast Down Your Bucket Where You Are." Pp. 320–24 in *The Future of Performance Studies: Visions and Revisions,* edited by Sheron J. Dailey. Washington, DC: National Communication Association

Grossberg, Lawrence. 2001. "Why Does Neo-liberalism Hate Kids? The War on Youth and the Culture of Politics." *Review of Education, Pedagogy and Cultural Studies* 23:111–36.

Gubrium, Jaber F. and James A. Holstein. 1997. *The New Language of Qualitative Method.* New York: Oxford University Press.

———. 1998. "Narrative Practice and the Coherence of Personal Stories." *Sociological Quarterly* 39:163–87.

Guerrero, Ed. 1993. *Framing Blackness: The African American Image in Film.* Philadelphia: Temple University Press.

Gunsalus, C. K. 2002. "Point of View: Rethinking Protections for Human Subjects." *Chronicle of Higher Education,* November 15, B24.

Guthrie, A. B., Jr. 1947. *The Big Sky.* New York: William Sloane.

Haines, Aubrey L. 1996a. *The Yellowstone Story: A History of Our First National Park,* vol. 1, rev. ed. Niwot: University Press of Colorado.

————. 1996b. *The Yellowstone Story: A History of Our First National Park*, vol. 2, rev. ed. Niwot: University Press of Colorado.

Hall, Stuart. 1996. "What Is This 'Black' in Black Popular Culture?" Pp. 465–75 in *Stuart Hall: Critical Dialogues in Cultural Studies*, edited by David Morley and Kuan-Hsing Chen. London: Routledge.

Hammersley, Martyn. 2001. "Which Side Was Becker On? Questioning Political and Epistemological Radicalism." *Qualitative Research* 1:91–110.

Hantzis, Darlene M. 1998. "Reflections on 'A Dialogue With Friends: "Performing" the "Other"/Self' OJA 1995." Pp. 203–6 in *The Future of Performance Studies: Visions and Revisions*, edited by Sheron J. Dailey. Washington, DC: National Communication Association.

Haraway, Donna J. 1985. "A Manifesto for Cyborgs: Science, Technology and Socialist Feminism in the 1980s." *Socialist Review* 80:65–107.

————. 1991. *Simians, Cyborgs, and Women: The Reinvention of Nature*. New York: Routledge.

Hardt, Michael and Antonio Negri. 2000. *Empire*. Cambridge, MA: Harvard University Press.

Harms, John and Douglas Kellner 1991. "Critical Theory and Advertising." *Current Perspectives in Social Theory* 11:41–67.

Harrington, Walt. 1999. *Crossings: A White Man's Journey Into Black America*. Columbia: University of Missouri Press.

————. 2002. *The Everlasting Stream*. New York: Atlantic Monthly Press.

Harris, William J. 1998. "Crossroads Blues: African American History and Culture, 1960 to the Present." Pp. 1343–85 in *Call and Response: The Riverside Anthology of the African American Literary Tradition*, edited by Patricia Liggins Hill. Boston: Houghton Mifflin.

Hartnett, Stephen John. 1998. "'Democracy Is Difficult': Poetry, Prison, and Performative Citizenship." Pp. 287–97 in *The Future of Performance Studies: Visions and Revisions*, edited by Sheron J. Dailey. Washington, DC: National Communication Association.

————. 2001. "Visiting Mario." *Broken Chains*, summer, 25–40.

Hasselstrom, Linda, Gaydell Collier, and Nancy Curtis. 1997a. "Introduction: Grass Widows and Wrinklebelly Women." Pp. xiii–xxi in *Leaning Into the Wind: Women Write From the Heart of the West*, edited by Linda Hasselstrom, Gaydell Collier, and Nancy Curtis. Boston: Houghton Mifflin.

————, eds. 1997b. *Leaning Into the Wind: Women Write From the Heart of the West*. Boston: Houghton Mifflin.

————, eds. 2001. *Woven on the Wind: Women Write About Friendship in the Sagebrush West*. Boston: Houghton Mifflin.

Hassen, Leona Lampi. 2000. "Ethnic Groups and Culture." Pp. 169–75 in *Red Lodge: Saga of a Western Area Revisited*, edited by Shirley Zupan and Harry J. Owens. Red Lodge, MT: Carbon County Historical Society.

Heshusius, Lous. 1994. "Freeing Ourselves From Objectivity: Managing Subjectivity or Turning Toward a Participatory Mode of Consciousness?" *Educational Researcher* 23(3):15–22.

Heyl, Barbara Sherman. 2001. "Ethnographic Interviewing." Pp. 369–83 in *Handbook of Ethnography*, edited by Paul Atkinson, Amanda Coffey, Sara Delamont, John Lofland, and Lyn Lofland. London: Sage.

Hill, Randall T. G. 1997. "Performance and the 'Political Anatomy' of Pioneer Colorado." *Text and Performance Quarterly* 17:236–55.

———. 1998. "Performance Pedagogy Across the Curriculum." Pp. 141–44 in *The Future of Performance Studies: Visions and Revisions*, edited by Sheron J. Dailey. Washington, DC: National Communication Association.

Holstein, James A. and Jaber F. Gubrium. 1995. *The Active Interview*. Thousand Oaks, CA: Sage.

———. 2000. *The Self We Live By: Narrative Identity in a Postmodern World*. New York: Oxford University Press.

hooks, bell. 1990. *Yearning: Race, Gender, and Cultural Politics*. Boston: South End.

———. 1996. *Reel to Real: Race, Sex, and Class at the Movies*. New York: Routledge:

Irving, Washington. [1837] 1986. *The Adventures of Captain Bonneville, U.S.A., in the Rocky Mountains and the Far West*, edited by Edgeley W. Todd. Norman: University of Oklahoma Press.

Jackson, Michael. 1998. *Minimia Ethnographica*. Chicago: University of Chicago Press.

Jackson, Shannon. 1993. "Ethnography and the Audition: Performance as Ideological Critique." *Text and Performance Quarterly* 13:21–43.

James, Allison, Jennifer Hockey, and Andrew Dawson, eds. 1997. *After Writing Culture: Epistemology and Praxis in Contemporary Anthropology*. London: Routledge.

Jameson, Fredric, 1981. *The Political Unconscious: Narrative as a Socially Symbolic Act*. Ithaca, NY: Cornell University Press.

———. 1990. *Signatures of the Visible*. New York: Routledge.

Jenkins, Mercilee M. 1998. "Personal Narratives Changed My Life: Can They Foretell the Future?" Pp. 264–71 in *The Future of Performance Studies: Visions and Revisions*, edited by Sheron J. Dailey. Washington, DC: National Communication Association.

Jones, Allen and Jeff Wetmore, eds. 2000. *The Big Sky Reader*. New York: St. Martin's.

Jones, Joni L. 1997. "Performing Osun Without Bodies: Documenting the Osun Festival in Print." *Text and Performance Quarterly* 17:69–93.

Jones, Stacy Holman. 2002. "The Way We Were, Are, and Might Be: Torch Singing as Autoethnography." Pp. 44–56 in *Ethnographically Speaking: Autoethnography, Literature, and Aesthetics*, edited by Arthur P. Bochner and Carolyn Ellis. Walnut Creek, CA: AltaMira.

Jordan, June. 1998. *Affirmative Acts*. New York: Anchor.

Joyce, Joyce Ann. 1987. "The Black Canon: Reconstructing Black American Literary Criticism." *New Literary History* 18:335–44.

Karenga, Maulana. [1972] 1997. "Black Art: Mute Matter Given Force and Function." Pp. 1973-77 in *The Norton Anthology of African American Literature*, edited by Henry Louis Gates, Jr., and Nellie Y. McKay. New York: W. W. Norton.

Kellner, Douglas. 1997. "Aesthetics, Ethics, and Politics in the Films of Spike Lee." Pp. 73–106 in *Spike Lee's* Do the Right Thing, edited by Mark A. Reid. New York: Cambridge University Press.

Kemmis, Stephen and Robin McTaggart. 2000. "Participatory Action Research." Pp. 567–605 in *Handbook of Qualitative Research*, 2d ed., edited by Norman K. Denzin and Yvonna S. Lincoln. Thousand Oaks, CA: Sage.

Kendig, Daun. 1998. "How to Survive in Hog Heaven: Thoughts for the Next Millennium." Pp. 158–61 in *The Future of Performance Studies: Visions and Revisions*, edited by Sheron J. Dailey. Washington, DC: National Communication Association.

Kincheloe, Joe L. 2001. "Describing the Bricolage: Conceptualizing a New Rigor in Qualitative Research." *Qualitative Inquiry* 7:679-92.

Kincheloe, Joe L. and Peter McLaren. 2000. "Rethinking Critical Theory and Qualitative Research." Pp. 279–313 in *Handbook of Qualitative Research*, 2d ed., edited by Norman K. Denzin and Yvonna S. Lincoln. Thousand Oaks, CA: Sage.

King, C. Richard and Charles Fruehling Springwood. 2001. *Beyond the Cheers: Race as Spectacle in College Sport*. Albany: State University of New York Press.

Kirshenblatt-Gimblett, Barbara. 1998. *Destination Culture: Tourism, Museums, and Heritage*. Berkeley: University of California Press.

Kittredge, William. 1987. *Owning It All*. San Francisco: Murray House.

———. 1992. *Hole in the Sky: A Memoir*. New York: Vintage.

———. 1996. *Who Owns the West?* San Francisco: Murray House.

Kittredge, William and Annick Smith, eds. 1988. *The Last Best Place: A Montana Anthology*. Seattle: University of Washington Press.

Krieger, Susan. 1996. *The Family Silver: Essays on Relationships Among Women*. Berkeley: University of California Press.

Kuhn, Manford H. 1962. "The Interview and the Professional Relationship." Pp. 193–206 in *Human Behavior and Social Processes*, edited by Arnold M. Rose. Boston: Houghton Mifflin.

Laclau, Ernesto. 1990. *New Reflections on the Revolution of Our Time*. London: Verso.

Lacy, Suzanne. 1995. "Cultural Pilgrimages and Metaphoric Journeys." Pp. 1–20 in *Mapping the Terrain: New Genre Public Art*, edited by Suzanne Lacy. Seattle: Bay.

Ladson-Billings, Gloria. 2000. "Racialized Discourses and Ethnic Epistemologies." Pp. 257–77 in *Handbook of Qualitative Research*, 2d ed., edited by Norman K. Denzin and Yvonna S. Lincoln. Thousand Oaks, CA: Sage.

Laermans, Rudi. 1993. "Bringing the Consumer Back In." *Theory, Culture & Society* 10:153–61.

Lampi, Leona. 1998. *At the Foot of the Beartooth Mountains*. Coeur d'Alene, ID: Bookage.

Langellier, Kristin M. 1998. "Voiceless Bodies, Bodiless Voices: The Future of Personal Narrative Performance." Pp. 207–13 in *The Future of Performance*

Studies: Visions and Revisions, edited by Sheron J. Dailey. Washington, DC: National Communication Association.

———. 1999. "Personal Narrative, Performance, Performativity: Two or Three Things I Know for Sure." *Text and Performance Quarterly* 19:125–44.

LaRaviere, Troy Anthony. 2001. "Remembering Me." Forthcoming. *Studies in Symbolic Interaction* 26.

Latham, Angela J. 1997. "Performance, Ethnography, and History: An Analysis of Displays of Female Bathers in the 1920s." *Text and Performance Quarterly* 17:170–81.

Lather, Patti. 1993. "Fertile Obsession: Validity After Poststructuralism." *Sociological Quarterly* 34:673–94.

———. 1998. "Critical Pedagogy and Its Complicities: A Praxis of Stuck Places." *Educational Theory* 48:487–97.

———. 2001. "Postmodernism, Post-structuralism and Post (Critical) Ethnography: Of Ruins, Aporias and Angels." Pp. 477–92 in *Handbook of Ethnography,* edited by Paul Atkinson, Amanda Coffey, Sara Delamont, John Lofland, and Lyn Lofland. London: Sage.

Lemert, Charles. 1997. "Goffman." Pp. ix–xliii in *The Goffman Reader,* edited by Charles Lemert and Ann Branaman. Malden, MA: Blackwell.

Leopold, Aldo. 1949. *A Sand County Almanac.* New York: Oxford University Press.

Lewis, David Levering. 2002. "An American Pastime: Review of P. Dray, *At the Hands of Persons Unknown: The Lynching of Black America,* and J. Madison, *A Lynching in the Heartland: Race and Memory in America. New York Review of Books,* November 21, 27–29.

Limerick, Patricia Nelson. 2000. *Something in the Soil: Legacies and Reckonings in the New West.* New York: W. W. Norton.

Lincoln, Yvonna S. 1995. "Emerging Criteria for Quality in Qualitative and Interpretive Inquiry." *Qualitative Inquiry* 1:275–89.

———. 2002. "Grief in an Appalachian Register." *Qualitative Inquiry* 8:146-49.

Lincoln, Yvonna S. and Gaile Cannella. 2002. "Qualitative Research and the Radical Right: Cats and Dogs and Other Natural Enemies." Paper presented at the annual meeting of the American Education Research Association, New Orleans, April.

Lincoln, Yvonna S. and William G. Tierney. 2002. "'What We Have Here Is a Failure to Communicate . . .': Qualitative Research and Institutional Review Boards (IRBs)." Paper presented at the annual meeting of the American Education Research Association, New Orleans, April.

Lockford, Lesa. 1998. "Emergent Issues in the Performance of a Border-Transgressive Narrative." Pp. 214–20 in *The Future of Performance Studies: Visions and Revisions,* edited by Sheron J. Dailey. Washington, DC: National Communication Association.

Lopez, Ana M. 1991. "Are All Latins From Manhattan? Hollywood, Ethnography, and Cultural Colonialism." Pp. 404–24 in *Unspeakable*

Images: Ethnicity and the American Cinema, edited by Lester D. Friedman. Urbana: University of Illinois Press.

Lopez, Gerardo R. 1998. "Reflections on Epistemology and Standpoint Theories: A Response to 'A Maori Approach to Creating Knowledge.'" *International Journal of Qualitative Studies in Education* 11:225–31.

Lyman, Stanford M. 1990. *Civilization: Contents, Discontents, Malcontents and Other Essays in Social Theory.* Fayetteville: University of Arkansas Press.

Lyman, Stanford M. and Arthur J. Vidich. 1988. *Social Order and the Public Philosophy: An Analysis and Interpretation of the Work of Herbert Blumer.* Fayetteville: University of Arkansas Press.

Maclean, Norman. 1976. *A River Runs Through It and Other Stories.* Chicago: University of Chicago Press.

Macnaghten, Phil and John Urry. 1998. *Contested Natures.* London: Sage.

Madison, D. Soyini. 1993. "'That Was My Occupation': Oral Narrative, Performance, and Black Feminist Thought." *Text and Performance Quarterly* 13:213–32.

———. 1998. "Performances, Personal Narratives, and the Politics of Possibility." Pp. 276–86 in *The Future of Performance Studies: Visions and Revisions,* edited by Sheron J. Dailey. Washington, DC: National Communication Association.

———. 1999. "Performing Theory/Embodied Writing." *Text and Performance Quarterly* 19:107–24.

Mamet, David. 1997. *True and False: Heresy and Common Sense for the Actor.* New York: Pantheon.

Marcus, George E. 1998. *Ethnography Through Thick and Thin.* Princeton, NJ: University of Princeton Press.

Martin, Russell, ed. 1992. *New Writers of the Purple Sage.* New York: Penguin.

Martin, Russell and Marc Barasch, eds. 1984. *Writers of the Purple Sage.* New York: Penguin.

Marx, Karl. [1888] 1983. "Theses on Feuerbach." Pp. 155–58 in *The Portable Karl Marx,* edited by Eugene Kamenka. New York: Penguin.

McCall, Michal M. 2000. "Performance Ethnography: A Brief History and Some Advice." Pp. 421–33 in *Handbook of Qualitative Research,* 2d ed., edited by Norman K. Denzin and Yvonna S. Lincoln. Thousand Oaks, CA: Sage.

———. 2001. "Three Stories of Loss and Return." *Cultural Studies↔Critical Methodologies* 1:50–61.

McCall, Michal M. and Howard S. Becker. 1990. "Performance Science." *Social Problems* 32:117–32.

McChesney, Robert W. 1999. *Rich Media, Poor Democracy: Communication Politics in Dubious Times.* Urbana: University of Illinois Press.

McLaren, Peter. 1997a. "The Ethnographer as Postmodern Flaneur: Critical Reflexivity and Posthybridity as Narrative Engagement." Pp. 143–77 in *Representation and the Text: Re-framing the Narrative Voice,* edited by William G. Tierney and Yvonna S. Lincoln. Albany: State University of New York Press.

——. 1997b. *Revolutionary Multiculturalism: Pedagogies of Dissent for the New Millennium.* Boulder, CO: Westview.

——. 1998a. "Revolutionary Pedagogy in Post-revolutionary Times: Rethinking the Political Economy of Critical Education." *Educational Theory* 48:431–62.

——. 1998b. "Whiteness Is . . . : The Struggle for Postcolonial Hybridity." Pp. 63–75 in *White Reign: Deploying Whiteness in America,* edited by Joe L. Kincheloe, Shirley R. Steinberg, Nelson M. Rodriguez, and Ronald E. Chennault. New York: St. Martin's.

——. 1999. *Schooling as a Ritual Performance: Toward a Political Economy of Educational Symbols and Gestures,* 3d ed. Boulder, CO: Rowman & Littlefield.

——. 2001. "Che Guevara, Paulo Freire, and the Politics of Hope: Reclaiming Critical Pedagogy." *Cultural Studies ↔ Critical Methodologies* 1:108–31.

Mead, George Herbert. 1938. *The Philosophy of the Act.* Chicago: University of Chicago Press.

Menchú, Rigoberta. 1984. *I, Rigoberta Menchú: An Indian Woman in Guatemala,* edited by Elizabeth Burgos-Debray; translated by Ann Wright. London: Verso.

Merleau-Ponty, Maurice. 1962. *Phenomenology of Perception.* London: Routledge.

Mienczakowski, Jim. 1992. *Synching Out Loud: A Journey Into Illness.* Brisbane: Griffith University, Reprographics.

——. 1994. "Reading and Writing Research." *NADIE Journal, International Research Issue* 18:45–54.

——. 1995. "The Theatre of Ethnography: The Reconstruction of Ethnography Into Theatre With Emancipatory Potential." *Qualitative Inquiry* 1:360–75.

——. 2001. "Ethnodrama: Performed Research—Limitations and Potential." Pp. 468–76 in *Handbook of Ethnography,* Paul Atkinson, Amanda Coffey, Sara Delamont, John Lofland, and Lyn Lofland. London: Sage.

Mienczakowski, Jim and Stephen Morgan. 1993. *Busting: The Challenge of the Drought Spirit.* Brisbane: Griffith University, Reprographics.

——. 2001. "Ethnodrama: Constructing Participatory, Experiential, and Compelling Action Research Through Performance." Pp. 219–27 in *Handbook of Action Research: Participative Inquiry and Practice,* edited by Peter Reason and Hilary Bradbury. Thousand Oaks, CA: Sage.

Miles, Malcolm. 1997. *Art State and the City: Public Art and Urban Futures.* New York: Routledge.

Miller, Lynn C. 1998. "The Study of Literature in Performance: A Future?" Pp. 51–55 in *The Future of Performance Studies: Visions and Revisions,* edited by Sheron J. Dailey. Washington, DC: National Communication Association.

Mills, C. Wright. 1959. *The Sociological Imagination.* New York: Oxford University Press.

Mishler, Elliott, G. 1986. *Research Interviewing: Context and Narrative.* Cambridge, MA: Harvard University Press.

Morrison, Toni. 1994. "Rootedness: The Ancestor as Foundation." Pp. 490–97 in *The Woman That I Am: The Literature and Culture of Contemporary Women of Color,* edited by D. Soyini Madison. New York: St. Martin's.

Mullins, C. A. Forthcoming. "Guest Editor's Introduction: A Self-Fashioned Gallery of Aesthetic Practice." *Qualitative Inquiry.*

Nagel, Joanne. 2001. "Racial, Ethnic, and National Boundaries: Sexual Intersections and Symbolic Interactions." *Symbolic Interaction* 24:123–39.

Naylor, Gloria. 1998. "Excerpt from *Mamma Day.*" Pp. 1838–42 in *Call and Response: The Riverside Anthology of the African American Literary Tradition,* edited by Patricia Liggins Hill. Boston: Houghton Mifflin.

Nelson, Cary and Dilip Parameshwar Gaonkar. 1996. "Cultural Studies and the Politics of Disciplinarity." Pp. 1–22 in *Disciplinarity and Dissent in Cultural Studies,* edited by Cary Nelson and Dilip Parameshwar Gaonkar. New York: Routledge.

Nelson, Richard. 1983. *Make Prayers to the Raven: A Koyukon View of the Northern Forest.* Chicago: University of Chicago Press.

Nero, Charles L. 1998. "Toward a Gay Black Aesthetic: Signifying in Contemporary Black Gay Literature." Pp. 1973–87 in *Call and Response: The Riverside Anthology of the African American Literary Tradition,* edited by Patricia Liggins Hill. Boston: Houghton Mifflin.

Newby, Rich and Suzanne Hunger, eds. 1996. *Writing Montana: Literature Under the Big Sky.* Helena: Montana Center for the Book.

Noriega, Chon A. 1992. "Between a Weapon and a Formula: Chicano Cinema and Its Contexts." Pp. 141–67 in *Chicanos and Film: Representation and Resistance,* edited by Chon A. Noriega. Minneapolis: University of Minnesota Press.

Oakley, Anne. 1981. "Interviewing Women: A Contradiction in Terms?" Pp. 30–61 in *Doing Feminist Research,* edited by Helen Roberts. London: Routledge & Kegan Paul.

Olesen, Virginia L. 2000. "Feminisms and Qualitative Research At and Into the Millennium." Pp. 215–55 in *Handbook of Qualitative Research,* 2d ed., edited by Norman K. Denzin and Yvonna S. Lincoln. Thousand Oaks, CA: Sage.

——. 2001. "'Do Whatever You Want': Audience(s) Created, Creating, Recreating." *Qualitative Inquiry* 7:267–73.

Olp, Susan. 2000. "Montana Day Joins the 50th Festival of Nations." *Billings Gazette,* August 8, 2A–2B.

Oudes, Bruce. 1989. *From the President: President Nixon's Secret Files.* New York: Harper & Row.

Paget, Marianne A. 1990a. "Life Mirrors Work Mirrors Text Mirrors Life . . . ." *Social Problems* 37:137–48.

——. 1990b. "Performing the Text." *Journal of Contemporary Ethnography* 19:136–55.

——. 1993. *A Complex Sorrow,* edited by Marjorie L. DeVault. Philadelphia: Temple University Press.

Park, R. E. 1950. "An Autobiographical Note." Pp. v–ix in R. E. Park, *Race and Culture: Essays in the Sociology of Contemporary Man*. New York: Free Press.

Parker, Laurence. 1998. "Race Is . . . Race Ain't: An Exploration of the Utility of Critical Race Theory in Qualitative Research in Education." *International Journal of Qualitative Studies in Education* 11:43–55.

Parker, Laurence, Donna Deyhle, Sofia Villenas, and Kristin Crosland Nebeker. 1998. "Guest Editors' Introduction: Critical Race Theory and Qualitative Studies in Education." *International Journal of Qualitative Studies in Education* 11:5–6.

Pelias, Ronald J. 1998. "Meditations and Mediations." Pp. 14–22 in *The Future of Performance Studies: Visions and Revisions*, edited by Sheron J. Dailey. Washington, DC: National Communication Association.

———. 1999. *Writing Performance: Poeticizing the Researcher's Body*. Carbondale: Southern Illinois University Press.

Perinbanayagam, R. S. 1985. *Signifying Acts*. Carbondale: Southern Illinois University Press.

———. 1991. *Discursive Acts*. New York: Aldine de Gruyter.

———. 2000. *The Presence of Self*. Boulder, CO: Rowman & Littlefield.

Peterson, Eric E. and Kristin Langellier. 1997. "The Politics of Personal Narrative Methodology." *Text and Performance Quarterly* 17:135–52.

Phelan, Peggy. 1993. *Unmarked: The Politics of Performance*. New York: Routledge.

———. 1998. "Introduction: The Ends of Performance." Pp. 1–19 in *The Ends of Performance*, edited by Peggy Phelan and Jill Lane. New York: New York University Press.

Phelan, Peggy and Jill Lane, eds. 1998. *The Ends of Performance*. New York: New York University Press.

Pinar, William F. 1994. *Autobiography, Politics and Sexuality: Essays in Curriculum Theory 1972–1992*. New York: Peter Lang.

Pineau, Elyse Lamm. 1998. "Performance Studies Across the Curriculum: Problems, Possibilities and Projections." Pp. 128–35 in *The Future of Performance Studies: Visions and Revisions*, edited by Sheron J. Dailey. Washington, DC: National Communication Association.

Pitzl-Waters, Jason and Jacqueline Enstrom-Waters. 2002. "Holy Names and Master Races, the Art of Richard Prairie Posner." *Octopus*, February 22–28, 6–7.

Pizarro, Marc. 1998. "'Chicana/o Power': Epistemology and Methodology for Social Justice and Empowerment in Chicana/o Communities." *International Journal of Qualitative Studies in Education* 11:57–79.

Poland, Blake D. 2002. "Transcription Quality." Pp. 629–49 in *Handbook of Interview Research: Context and Method*, edited by Jaber F. Gubrium and James A. Holstein. Thousand Oaks, CA: Sage.

Pollock, Della. 1998a. "Performing Writing." Pp. 73–103 in *The Ends of Performance*, edited by Peggy Phelan and Jill Lane. New York: New York University Press.

————. 1998b. "A Response to Dwight Conquergood's Essay 'Beyond the Text: Towards a Performative Cultural Politics.'" Pp. 37–46 in *The Future of Performance Studies: Visions and Revisions*, edited by Sheron J. Dailey. Washington, DC: National Communication Association.

————. 1999. *Telling Bodies Performing Birth: Everyday Narratives of Childbirth.* New York: Columbia University Press.

Pomeroy, Earl. 1957. *In Search of the Golden West: The Tourist in Western America.* Lincoln: University of Nebraska Press.

Porter, Eileen J. 2000. "Setting Aside the Identity-Furor: Staying Her Story-Course of Same-ness." *Qualitative Inquiry* 6:238–50.

Prattis, J. Iain. 1985. "Dialectics and Experience in Fieldwork: The Poetic Dimension." Pp. 266–83 in *Reflections: The Anthropological Muse*, edited by J. Iain Prattis. Washington, DC: American Anthropological Association.

Pritchard, Ivor A. 2002. "Travelers and Trolls: Practitioner Research and Institutional Review Boards." *Educational Researcher* 31:3–13.

Prochaska, David. 2001. "At Home in Illinois: Presence of Chief Illiniwek." Pp. 157–88 in *Team Spirits: The Native American Mascots Controversy*, edited by C. Richard King and Charles Fruehling Springwood. Lincoln: University of Nebraska Press.

Puglisi, Tom. 2001. "IRB Review: It Helps to Know the Regulatory Framework." *APS Observer*, May/June, 1, 34–35.

Raban, Jonathan. 1981. *Old Glory: A Voyage Down the Mississippi.* New York: Random House.

Radford-Hill, Sheila. 2000. *Further to Fly: Black Women and the Politics of Empowerment.* Minneapolis: University of Minnesota Press.

Rains, Frances V., Jo Ann Archibald, and Donna Deyhle. 2000. "Introduction: Through Our Eyes and in Our Own Words—the Voices of Indigenous Scholars." *International Journal of Qualitative Studies in Education* 13:337–42.

Rawlins, C. L. 1994. "The Meadow at the Corner of Your Eye." Pp. 389–95 in *Northern Lights: A Selection of New Writing From the American West*, edited by Deborah Clow and Donald Snow. New York: Vintage.

Reason, Peter, ed. 1994. *Participation in Human Inquiry.* London: Sage.

Red Lodge Chamber of Commerce. 1982. *Festival of Nations, Red Lodge, Montana* [brochure]. Red Lodge, MT: Author.

Reddin, Paul. 1999. *Wild West Shows.* Urbana: University of Illinois Press.

Reinharz, Shulamit. 1992. *Feminist Methods in Social Research.* New York: Oxford University Press.

Reynolds, Larry T. 2000. "General Introduction: Sociology in Its Time and Place." Pp. 1–15 in *Self-Analytical Sociology: Essays and Explorations in the Reflective Mode*, edited by Larry T. Reynolds. Rockport, TX: Magner.

Rice, Rebecca. 1990. "Losing Faith (or Gaining Perspective)." Pp. 205–13 in *Remaking America: The Art of Social Change*, edited by Mark O'Brien and Craig Little. Santa Cruz, CA: New Society.

Richardson, Laurel. 1994. "Writing: A Method of Inquiry." Pp. 516–29 in *Handbook of Qualitative Research,* edited by Norman K. Denzin and Yvonna S. Lincoln. Thousand Oaks, CA: Sage.

———. 1997. *Fields of Play: Constructing an Academic Life.* New Brunswick, NJ: Rutgers University Press.

———. 1999. "Paradigms Lost." *Symbolic Interaction* 22:79–91.

———. 2000a. "Evaluating Ethnography." *Qualitative Inquiry* 6:253–55.

———. 2000b. "Writing: A Method of Inquiry." Pp. 923–48 in *Handbook of Qualitative Research,* 2d ed., edited by Norman K. Denzin and Yvonna S. Lincoln. Thousand Oaks, CA: Sage.

———. 2002a. "Poetic Representation of Interviews." Pp. 877–91 in *Handbook of Interview Research: Context and Method,* edited by Jaber F. Gubrium and James A. Holstein. Thousand Oaks, CA: Sage.

———. 2002b. "Small World." *Cultural Studies ↔ Critical Methodologies* 2:23–25.

Robertson, Catherine. 1998. "Performativity v. Textuality: Some Second Thoughts." Pp. 86–89 in *The Future of Performance Studies: Visions and Revisions,* edited by Sheron J. Dailey. Washington, DC: National Communication Association.

Roediger, David. 2002. *Colored White: Transcending the Racial Past.* Berkeley: University of California Press.

Ronai, Carol Rambo. 1998. "Sketching With Derrida: An Ethnography of a Researcher/Erotic Dancer." *Qualitative Inquiry* 4:405–20.

———. 1999. "The Next Night *Sous Rature:* Wrestling With Derrida's Mimesis." *Qualitative Inquiry* 5:114–29.

Rorty, Richard. 1980. *Philosophy and the Mirror of Nature.* Princeton, NJ: University of Princeton Press.

———. 2002. "Fighting Terrorism With Democracy." *The Nation,* October 21, 11–14.

Rosaldo, Renato. 1989. *Culture and the Truth.* Boston: Beacon.

Rosen, Eric. 1998. "Professional Theatre and Performance Studies: Reflections on a New Direction." Pp. 81–85 in *The Future of Performance Studies: Visions and Revisions,* edited by Sheron J. Dailey. Washington, DC: National Communication Association.

Rothman, Hal K. 1998. *Devil's Bargain: Tourism in the Twentieth-Century American West.* Lawrence: University Press of Kansas.

Ryan, Katherine, Jennifer Greene, Yvonna S. Lincoln, Sandra Mathison, and Donna M. Mertens. 1998. "Advantages and Challenges of Using Inclusive Evaluation Approaches in Evaluation Practice." *American Journal of Evaluation* 19:101–22.

Saldana, Johnny. 2002. "A Play, 'Finding My Place: The Brad Trilogy.'" Pp. 167–210 in Harry F. Wolcott, *Sneaky Kid and Its Aftermath: Ethics and Intimacy in Fieldwork.* Walnut Creek, CA: AltaMira.

Sartre, Jean-Paul. 1981. *The Family Idiot: Gustave Flaubert,* vol. 1, *1821–1857.* Chicago: University of Chicago Press.

Saussure, Ferdinand de. 1966. *Course in General Linguistics*. New York: McGraw-Hill.

Sayre, Henry. 1990. "Performance." Pp. 91–104 in *Critical Terms for Literary Study*, edited by Frank Lentricchia and Thomas McLaughlin. Chicago: University of Chicago Press.

Scarce, Ric. 1990. *Eco-warriors: Understanding the Radical Environmental Movement*. Chicago: Noble.

Schechner, Richard. 1985. *Between Theatre and Anthropology*. Philadelphia: University of Philadelphia Press.

———. 1988. *Performance Theory* (rev. ed.). New York: Routledge.

———. 1993. *The Future of Ritual: Writings on Culture and Performance*. New York: Routledge.

———. 1998. "What Is Performance Studies Anyway?" Pp. 357–62 in *The Ends of Performance*, edited by Peggy Phelan and Jill Lane. New York: New York University Press.

Scheurich, J. J. 1995. "A Postmodernist Critique of Research Interviewing." *International Journal of Qualitative Studies in Education* 8:239–52.

Schullery, Paul. 1994. *Mountain Time: A Yellowstone Memoir*. Boulder, CO: Roberts Rinehart.

———. 1997. *Searching for Yellowstone: Ecology and Wonder in the Last Wilderness*. Boston: Houghton Mifflin.

Schutz, Aaron. 2001. "Theory as Performative Pedagogy: Three Masks of Hannah Arendt." *Educational Theory* 51:127–50.

Scott, Joan W. 1993. "The Evidence of Experience." Pp. 397–415 in *The Lesbian and Gay Studies Reader*, edited by Henry Abelove, Michele Aina Barale, and David M. Halperin. New York: Routledge.

Sedgwick, Eve Kosofsky. 1998. "Teaching 'Experimental Critical Writing.'" Pp. 104–15 in *The Ends of Performance*, edited by Peggy Phelan and Jill Lane. New York: New York University Press.

Senior, Dawn. 1997. "Never Alone." Pp. 335–36 in *Leaning Into the Wind: Women Write From the Heart of the West*, edited by Linda Hasselstrom, Gaydell Collier, and Nancy Curtis. Boston: Houghton Mifflin.

Shaffer, Marguerite S. 2001. *See America First: Tourism and National Identity, 1880–1940*. Washington, DC: Smithsonian Institution Press.

Shavelson, Richard J. and Lisa Towne, eds. 2002. *Scientific Research in Education: Committee on Scientific Principles for Education Research*. Washington, DC: National Academy Press.

Shoemaker, Nancy. 1997. "How Indians Got to Be Red." *American Historical Review* 102:625–44.

Slovic, Scott. 1999. "William Kittredge: A Portrait." Pp. 81–99 in William Kittredge, *Taking Care: Thoughts on Storytelling and Belief*. Minneapolis: Milkwood.

Smith, Anna Deavere. 1993. *Fires in the Mirror: Crown Heights, Brooklyn, and Other Identities*. New York: Doubleday.

———. 1994. *Twilight: Los Angeles, 1992.* New York: Doubleday.

———. 2000. *Talk to Me: Listening Between the Lines.* New York: Random House.

Smith, Dorothy E. 1989. "Sociological Theory: Methods of Writing Patriarchy." Pp. 34–64 in *Feminism and Sociological Theory,* edited by Ruth A. Wallace. Newbury Park, CA: Sage.

———. 1990a. *The Conceptual Practices of Power: A Feminist Sociology of Knowledge.* Boston: Northeastern University Press.

———. 1990b. *Texts, Facts, and Femininity: Exploring the Relations of Ruling.* New York: Routledge.

Smith, John K. and Deborah K. Deemer. 2000. "The Problem of Criteria in the Age of Relativism." Pp. 877–96 in *Handbook of Qualitative Research,* 2d ed., edited by Norman K. Denzin and Yvonna S. Lincoln. Thousand Oaks, CA: Sage.

Smith, Linda Tuhiwai. 1999. *Decolonizing Methodologies: Research and Indigenous Peoples.* Dunedin, New Zealand: University of Otago Press.

Smith, Robert E. 1998. "A Personal Look at Personal Narratives." Pp. 237–39 in *The Future of Performance Studies: Visions and Revisions,* edited by Sheron J. Dailey. Washington, DC: National Communication Association.

Spencer, Jonathan. 2001. "Ethnography After Postmodernism." Pp. 443–52 in *Handbook of Ethnography,* edited by Paul Atkinson, Amanda Coffey, Sara Delamont, John Lofland, and Lyn Lofland. London: Sage.

Spender, Stephen. [1947] 1984. "Introduction." Pp. vii–xxiii in Malcolm Lowry, *Under the Volcano.* New York: New American Library.

Spindel, Carol. 2000. *Dancing at Halftime: Sports and the Controversy Over American Indian Mascots.* New York: New York University Press.

Springwood, Charles Fruehling and C. Richard King. 2001. "Epilogue: Closing Arguments: Opening Dialogues." Pp. 328–36 in *Team Spirits: The Native American Mascots Controversy,* edited by C. Richard King and Charles Fruehling Springwood. Lincoln: University of Nebraska Press.

Spry, Tami. 1998. "Performative Autobiography: Presence and Privacy." Pp. 254–63 in *The Future of Performance Studies: Visions and Revisions,* edited by Sheron J. Dailey. Washington, DC: National Communication Association.

Stegner, Wallace. 1943. *The Big Rock Candy Mountain.* New York: Doubleday.

———. 1962. *Wolf Willow: A History, a Story, and a Memory of the Last Plains Frontier.* New York: Viking.

———. 1979. *Recapitulation.* New York: Doubleday.

———. 1980a. "Coda: Wilderness Letter." Pp. 145–53 in Wallace Stegner, *The Sound of Mountain Water: The Changing American West.* New York: Doubleday.

———. 1980b. *The Sound of Mountain Water: The Changing American West.* New York: Doubleday.

———. 1990. "Foreword." Pp. iv–xi in Wallace Stegner, *Collected Stories of Wallace Stegner.* New York: Penguin.

————. [1989] 1992a. "Letter, Much Too Late." Pp. 22–33 in Wallace Stegner, *Where the Bluebird Sings to the Lemonade Springs: Living and Writing in the West*. New York: Random House.

————. 1992b. *Where the Bluebird Sings to the Lemonade Springs: Living and Writing in the West*. New York: Random House.

Stern, Carol Simpson and Bruce Henderson. 1993. *Performance Texts and Contexts*. New York: Longman.

Sterne, Jonathan. 1999. "Thinking the Internet: Cultural Studies Versus the Millennium." Pp. 257–87 in *Doing Internet Research: Critical Issues and Methods for Examining the Net*, edited by Steve Jones. Thousand Oaks, CA: Sage.

Strine, Mary S. 1998. "Mapping the 'Cultural Turn' in Performance Studies." Pp. 3–9 in *The Future of Performance Studies: Visions and Revisions*, edited by Sheron J. Dailey. Washington, DC: National Communication Association.

Stringer, Ernest T. 1999. *Action Research*, 2d ed. Thousand Oaks, CA: Sage.

Strong, William E. 1876. *A Trip to the Yellowstone National Park in July, August, and September, 1875*, edited by Richard Bartlett. Norman: University of Oklahoma Press.

Stucky, Nathan. 1993. "Toward an Aesthetics of Natural Performance." *Text and Performance Quarterly* 13:168–80.

Stuebner, Stephen. 1999. "Jon Marvel vs. the Marlboro Man: Idaho Architect Gets Nasty in Hopes of Healing Public Lands." *High Country News*, August 2, 1, 8–9.

Taussig, Michael. 1993. *Mimesis and Alterity: A Particular History of the Senses*. New York: Routledge.

Taylor, J. Golden, ed. 1987. *A Literary History of the American West*. Fort Worth: Texas Christian University Press.

Tedlock, Barbara. 2000. "Ethnography and Ethnographic Representation." Pp. 455–86 in *Handbook of Qualitative Research*, 2d ed., edited by Norman K. Denzin and Yvonna S. Lincoln. Thousand Oaks, CA: Sage.

Tedlock, Dennis. 1983. *The Spoken Word and the Word of Interpretation*. Philadelphia: University of Pennsylvania Press.

Tillman, Linda C. 1998. "Culturally Specific Research Practices: A Response to Bishop." *International Journal of Qualitative Studies in Education* 11:221–24.

Trinh T. Minh-ha. 1989a. *Surname Viet Given Name Nam* [film]. New York: Women Make Movies, Museum of Modern Art, Cinenova, Idera, Image Forum.

————. 1989b. *Woman, Native, Other: Writing Postcoloniality and Feminism*. Bloomington: Indiana University Press.

————. 1991. *When the Moon Waxes Red: Representation, Gender and Cultural Politics*. New York: Routledge.

————. 1992. *Framer Framed*. New York: Routledge.

Turner, Frederick Jackson. 1894. "The Significance of the Frontier in American History." Pp. 199–227 in *American Historical Association Annual Report for the Year 1893*. Washington, DC: American Historical Association.

Turner, Victor W. (with Edie Turner). 1982. "Performing Ethnography." *Drama Review* 26:33–50.

———. 1986a. *The Anthropology of Performance.* New York: Performing Arts Journal Publications.

———. 1986b. "Dewey, Dilthey, and Drama: An Essay in the Anthropology of Experience." Pp. 33–44 in *The Anthropology of Experience,* edited by Victor W. Turner and Edward M. Bruner. Urbana: University of Illinois Press.

Tyler, Stephen. 1986. "Post-modern Ethnography: From Document of the Occult to Occult Document." Pp. 122–40 in *Writing Culture: The Poetics and Politics of Ethnography,* edited by James Clifford and George E. Marcus. Berkeley: University of California Press.

Ulmer, Gregory L. 1989. *Teletheory.* New York: Routledge.

Utley, Robert M. 1997. *A Life Wild and Perilous: Mountain Men and the Paths to the Pacific.* New York: Henry Holt.

Vecsey, G. 2000. "Kurt Warner Gives Hope to Others." *New York Times,* February 1, C29.

Vidich, Arthur J. and Stanford M. Lyman. 1994. "Qualitative Methods: Their History in Sociology and Anthropology." Pp. 23–59 in *Handbook of Qualitative Research,* edited by Norman K. Denzin and Yvonna S. Lincoln. Thousand Oaks, CA: Sage.

Visweswaran, Kamala. 1994. *Fictions of Feminist Ethnography.* Minneapolis: University of Minnesota Press.

Weems, Mary. 2002. *I Speak from the Wound That Is My Mouth.* New York: Peter Lang.

Weiss, P. 1988. "Party Time in Atlanta." *Columbia Journalism Review,* September/October, 27–34.

Welch, James. 1979. *The Death of James Loney.* New York: Penguin.

———. 2000. *The Heartsong of Charging Elk.* New York: Doubleday.

———. 2001. "The West From Two Perspectives." Pp. 175–86 in *Fifty Years After The Big Sky: New Perspectives on the Fiction and Films of A. B. Guthrie, Jr.,* edited by William E. Farr and William W. Bevis. Helena: Montana Historical Society Press.

Wellin, Christopher. 1996. "'Life at Lake Home': An Ethnographic Performance in Six Voices; An Essay on Method, in Two." *Qualitative Sociology* 19:497–515.

West, Cornel. 1993a. "Foreword." Pp. xvii–xxii in Anna Deavere Smith, *Fires in the Mirror: Crown Heights, Brooklyn, and Other Identities.* New York: Doubleday.

———. 1993b. *Keeping the Faith: Philosophy and Race in America.* New York: Routledge.

———. 1994. *Race Matters.* New York: Vantage.

White, Richard. 1997. "When Frederick Jackson Turner and Buffalo Bill Cody Both Played Chicago in 1893." Pp. 201–12 in *Frontier and Region: Essays in Honor of Martin Ridge,* edited by Robert C. Ritchie and Paul Andrew Hutton. Albuquerque: University of New Mexico Press.

Williams, Terry Tempest. 2000. *Leap*. New York: Vantage.

Willis, Paul. 1990. *Common Culture: Symbolic Work at Play in the Everyday Culture of the Young*. Milton Keynes, UK: Open University Press.

———. 2000. *The Ethnographic Imagination*. Cambridge: Polity.

Willis, Paul and Mat Trondman. 2000. "Manifesto for Ethnography." *Ethnography* 1:5–16.

Wilson, August. 1996. "The Ground on Which I Stand." *American Theatre*, September 11.

Wittgenstein, Ludwig. 1961. *Tractatus Logico-Philosophicus*. London: Routledge.

Wolcott, Harry F. 2002. *Sneaky Kid and Its Aftermath: Ethics and Intimacy in Fieldwork*. Walnut Creek, CA: AltaMira.

Wood, Paul. 2001. "Chief Furor Leaves Boy Ostracized." *News-Gazette* (Urbana-Champaign, IL), March 11, A1, B6.

Worley, David W. 1998. "Is Critical Performative Pedagogy Practical?" Pp. 136–40 in *The Future of Performance Studies: Visions and Revisions*, edited by Sheron J. Dailey. Washington, DC: National Communication Association.

Zupan, Shirley and Harry J. Owens, eds. 2000. *Red Lodge: Saga of a Western Area Revisited*. Red Lodge, MT: Carbon County Historical Society.

Index

About the Author

Norman K. Denzin is Distinguished Professor of Communications, College of Communications Scholar, and Research Professor of Communications, Sociology and Humanities at the University of Illinois, Urbana-Champaign. He is the author of numerous books, including *Interpretive Ethnography: Ethnographic Practices for the 21st Century*, *The Cinematic Society: The Voyeur's Gaze*, *Images of Postmodern Society*, *The Research Act: A Theoretical Introduction to Sociological Methods*, *Interpretive Interactionism*, *Hollywood Shot by Shot*, *The Recovering Alcoholic*, and *The Alcoholic Self*, which won the Charles Cooley Award from the Society for the Study of Symbolic Interaction in 1988. In 1997 he was awarded the George Herbert Award from the Society for the Study of Symbolic Interaction. He is the past editor of *Sociological Quarterly*, coeditor of *Qualitative Inquiry*, coeditor of the *Handbook of Qualitative Research*, editor of the book series *Studies in Symbolic Interaction*, and founding editor of the journal *Cultural Studies ↔ Critical Methodologies*.

CPSIA information can be obtained at www.ICGtesting.com
Printed in the USA
BVOW08s2300091213

338627BV00001B/16/A

9 780761 910398